How We Think

About the Author

Dr Marius Ostrowski FRHistS FRSA is a social scientist, political theorist, and historian focusing on how ideas and ideologies emerge and gain influence among the general population. He has authored books including *Ideology* (2022) and *A Radical Bargain for Europe* (2024), and he is Editor-in-Chief of the *Journal of Political Ideologies*. He has held Fellowships at All Souls College and the Blavatnik School of Government, University of Oxford, and at the Robert Schuman Centre for Advanced Studies at the European University Institute, Florence. Ostrowski is also an Honorary Professor at the Centre for Research into Ideas and the Study of Political Ideologies, University of Nottingham. Born in Frankfurt, he speaks fluent German, French, Italian, Russian, and English.

How We Think

Ten Thinker-Types to Understand Ourselves and Those Around Us

MARIUS OSTROWSKI

hodder press

First published in Great Britain in 2026 by Hodder Press
An imprint of Hodder & Stoughton Limited
An Hachette UK company

The authorised representative in the EEA is Hachette Ireland, 8 Castlecourt Centre, Dublin 15, D15 XTP3, Ireland (email: info@hbgi.ie)

1

Copyright © Marius Ostrowski 2026

The right of Marius Ostrowski to be identified as the Author of the Work has been asserted by him in accordance with the Copyright, Designs and Patents Act 1988.

All rights reserved. No part of this publication may be reproduced, stored in a retrieval system, or transmitted, in any form or by any means without the prior written permission of the publisher, nor be otherwise circulated in any form of binding or cover other than that in which it is published and without a similar condition being imposed on the subsequent purchaser.

'The wheel of thinker-types' © Marius Ostrowski

A CIP catalogue record for this title is available from the British Library

Hardback ISBN 9781529366303
Trade Paperback ISBN 9781529366310
ebook ISBN 9781529366327

Typeset in Bembo MT by Hewer Text UK Ltd, Edinburgh
Printed and bound in Great Britain by Clays Ltd, Elcograf S.p.A.

Hodder & Stoughton policy is to use papers that are natural, renewable and recyclable products and made from wood grown in sustainable forests. The logging and manufacturing processes are expected to conform to the environmental regulations of the country of origin.

Hodder & Stoughton Limited
Carmelite House
50 Victoria Embankment
London EC4Y 0DZ

www.hodderpress.co.uk

To the memory of my mother,
and the ways she shaped my mind.

Contents

Introduction	1
1. Happy Camper	25
2. Jokester	46
3. Gloomster	66
4. Agoniser	88
5. Hothead	109
6. Cool Cat	131
7. Keen Bean	153
8. Worrywart	173
9. Quibbler	195
10. Reveller	217

Conclusion	239
Epilogue	243
Acknowledgements	263
Notes	267
Index	301

Introduction

We are surrounded by people who think differently from us. It is a difference we encounter every day: with family and friends, in class and at work, among familiar faces or perfect strangers. We can find this a source of great comfort and insight or confusion and misunderstanding – a helpful asset or an awkward hurdle as we go about our lives. Why does one colleague want to bounce their ideas off us, while another prefers to go it alone? Among our fellow students, why does this one tend to go in feelings first, while that one opts for the cerebral approach? When we make plans, why does one friend seem to say yes to all of our suggestions, and another keep picking holes in them? Why is one child so thin-skinned and impressionable, and the other so boisterous and independent-minded? Why is this public figure so blunt and up-front, and that one so vague and evasive? Why do they think their way? Why do we think ours? And why does how *they* think and how *we* think so often not align?

The chances are that we have already tried to come up with our own informal answers to these questions. To answer them completely, we would need to transport ourselves directly into other people's minds. Instead, imagine if, every time we encounter someone who thinks differently from us, we had a way of showing us what it is like to experience the world the way they do. What it means to go through the process of thinking *their* way rather than ours. At the same time, imagine if we could shed light on the factors that shape how they think, and determine exactly what part they played in making them the thinkers they are today. In other words, imagine if we could take ourselves out of our embedded, familiar ways of thinking and put ourselves in the position of thinking like the people around us. And, as well as helping us understand them, imagine if we could turn the same lens onto ourselves. Dig deep into the semi-conscious and unconscious recesses of our minds to uncover their workings, to trace the moving parts that go into how we think too.

That is where this book comes in. It is here to give us a new set of tools to better understand *how we think* and *why we do so*, to help us navigate the ways we all think differently. To do this, I draw together findings from throughout my career as a social researcher. In one form or another, the question this book sets out to answer has preoccupied me since I was a graduate student. Back then, I was grappling with complex problems such as where government gets its legitimacy from, whether democracy needs people to agree on a set of shared values, and how we should measure what the public has to say about the issues in the news. After all, this was the era of debt crises and fiscal austerity, student protests and urban riots, workers' strikes and secessionist referendums. A time of people talking past each other politically, economically, in our faiths, in our communities and our private lives. In essay after paper after conversation, as I watched all this unfold from my university town at the scraggly western end of the Eurasian landmass, I found myself circling back to the question of how and why we think the way we do.

The journey this question has taken me on has ranged far afield, as I cast my net wider and wider in search of clues. It has carried me across countries, and several decades back in time – including stops in 1920s Germany, 1950s America, and 1980s France, with many more besides. Along the way, it has introduced me to an army of commentators, all probing how we think and why from a wide array of different angles. Political scientists who ask why we disagree – often radically – and what we can do about it. Philosophers who study how we experience and understand the world, and how we reflect on what we know about it. Psychologists who carry out experiments to find the key ingredients of how our minds work. Sociologists who examine how our interactions with those around us influence our thoughts and behaviour. Historians who look at how our ideas change over time, and from place to place. And supporting them, anthropologists and behavioural economists, cultural theorists and linguists, neuroscientists and opinion pollsters. Centuries of intellectual labour, sediments of carefully accumulated insights, across a dizzying array of disciplines and areas of enquiry. (To give you a sense of the research on offer, I have included an epilogue at the end of the book for you to delve into at your leisure.)

Everything I have learned throughout this process over the best part of the last two decades, I have distilled into this book. As journeys go, it has been less a speed run and more a scenic wander, with plenty of side quests and scouring hidden caverns for bits of arcane treasure. By corralling these strands of knowledge, and joining up the dots between them, I have attacked the question of how we think and why from every angle I could find. Wrangling it on countless walks and hikes, perched in a succession of European flats and offices, hammering away at the keys of my laptop (and my piano). Building models, compiling endless spreadsheets, sketching gargantuan diagrams on faculty whiteboards. Poring over demographic breakdowns in social attitudes data, and sifting through dusty interwar archives. The more I kept looking, I began to see common threads emerge. Complex alignments and convergences, where different researchers' descriptions of how we behave as 'thinkers' started to pull together. Distinct characters took shape and faded into focus. Initially as unkempt ghosts, then fleshed out in increasingly vivid detail. Glimpses of people I half knew – from my reading or real life. A flash of memory transporting me all the way back to physics class. An old boss blundering unbidden into my consciousness. My close friends staring back at me from the page.

After unearthing and refining all these resemblances, and working through their similarities and differences, I came to a clear and unmistakeable conclusion: when we think, every one of us exhibits a set of identifiable tendencies in the way we do so, which give us our particular kind of thinking. These tendencies are shaped and brought out in our minds by social experiences we have over the course of our lives – through our childhood, our schooling, the jobs we do, where we grow up, the places we call home, the friends and families we gather around us, and the lifestyles we choose. Some of the people around us share similar tendencies and social experiences to us, and think in more or less the same way. Others have their own, separate tendencies and experiences, and think very differently. I call these various tendencies *thinker-types*, and my research suggests that there are ten of them we can reliably find scattered about in our everyday lives.

Let me sketch them out for you.

- **Happy Camper**: That friend who has just lost their job and has no clue what their next move will be, but is entirely optimistic that things will turn out all right. Joy-filled, warm, pootling placidly through life.

INTRODUCTION

- **Jokester**: The one who throws the best parties, cracks the sharpest jokes, always pulls you into another round of games – as long as they get to win. Gleeful, irreverent, with a flair for provocative fun.
- **Gloomster**: The older sibling carrying the can for their tearaway junior, upending their own life to reckon with their misadventures. Subdued, sluggish, liable to earnest brooding.
- **Agoniser**: The activist mobilising for better welfare, negotiating with the authorities, running for council, taking all kinds of pushback on the chin. Plaintive, outraged, urgently looking to fix things.
- **Hothead**: The friend who just has to be right and do things their way – where to meet, what to eat, which opinions to share, brooking no argument. Excitable, irascible, consumed by the problems of the moment.
- **Cool Cat**: The one who will always put you up in a pinch, sit patiently and listen, go along with pretty much anything, but generally hangs back and lets you sort yourself out. Quiet, resolute, benevolent but a little remote.
- **Keen Bean**: The creative who is constantly on the move, meeting people, building grand palaces of the imagination – and plastering them all over the internet. Zesty, precocious, always probing for new discoveries.
- **Worrywart**: The friend who overthinks a moment of disagreement, stewing long after it has passed, convinced they have said the wrong thing. Nervy, brittle, prone to long, painstaking deliberation.
- **Quibbler**: The colleague who picks apart your work, disputing this, correcting that, giving endless feedback, insisting that you fix the problem. Cagey, sceptical, lingering reluctantly over what repels them.

- **Reveller**: The friend who sweeps you up, makes you the centre of their plans, gives you their undivided attention, and deluges you with thoughtful gifts. Dreamy, magnetic, overflowing with more to give.

All of us find ourselves drawn strongly towards at least one – and sometimes several – of these thinker-types. Some of them may be familiar to us already. We may recognise them from our day-to-day experiences. The highly strung overachiever in our dance class. Our strange and curmudgeonly upstairs neighbour. Closer to home, the lackadaisical dreamer we share a house with – who also happens to be our child, our parent, or our partner. And closest of all, we may be getting the sense with some of the thinker-types that we are looking ever so slightly in the mirror. If so, then I want you to hold onto these initial impressions and see how far you change or confirm them as you keep reading.

My contention is that we can all describe how we think in terms of these ten thinker-types, either singly or in some combination, and use them to explain why we might find ourselves gravitating towards certain ways of thinking more than others. This book explains how these thinker-types work and where they come from. How we can spot them, quickly and insightfully. How our social experiences leave traces that shape which thinker-types we tend towards. And how far we are all entrenched in how we think – and what we can do to change it.

What is a thinker-type?

A thinker-type is a specific style of thinking. When we think, we rely on several 'elements of thinking' that work together to create our thoughts. There are five of these:

INTRODUCTION

1. Our underlying *personality*;
2. The *emotions* we feel;
3. The *information* we gather;
4. The *predispositions* we judge by;
5. Our *reasoning* intellect.

How we use each of these elements, and how we fit them together, exhibits certain patterns. If we combine these patterns, we find that they coalesce into a number of distinctive overarching mindsets. The thinker-types I listed above are labels that reflect the kind of thinking that characterises each mindset, and a way to represent our array of separate 'thinking parts' as a united 'thinking whole'. Both in how we present our thinking to the world around us, and how we experience the thinking that other people present to us.

Our *personality* and *emotions* together give us our mental outlook. This is our 'starting position', the broad-brush reaction that colours everything else we do in our minds. The rest of how we think follows on from them. Our mental outlooks – especially our emotions – are key to determining our thinker-types, as they are our first 'line of contact' whenever we experience anything.

In turn, our *information* and *predispositions* marry together to create our mental picture of our surroundings. This is our interpretation of what is going on, informed by the broad-brush reaction our mental outlook gives us. It is this interpretation that we are thinking about when we apply our *reasoning* to formulate thoughts, develop arguments, and draw our conclusions about the world. Every thinker-type has its own unique mental outlook, mental picture, and way of formulating thoughts. That is why each of them thinks differently from all the others.

To see how the ten thinker-types take shape, we first need to break down each of these elements that make up how we think into its own series of subsidiary components. We can think of these components as the fundamental building blocks of our thinking. Each one represents an unconscious choice we make between two possible directions in which our thinking can go, which lie at opposite ends of a continuous spectrum of possibility. Every one of us falls at some point along each of these spectrums, either around the middle or more towards the extremes.

To start with, our personality takes the form of several personality traits, which we exhibit to varying degrees of intensity:

- Are we more *open* or more *closed to experience*? By way of illustrating the difference: When you saw this book, did you maybe stop in your tracks to grab it off the shelf, or are you instead reading it after someone you trust recommended it to you? Or something else entirely, which might fall somewhere on the spectrum in between these two?
- *Conscientious* or *careless*? Have you been reading every word on every page, or idly riffling through it?
- *Emotional* or *emotionally stable*? Are you gripped by concern about what thinker-type you might be, or more casually intrigued?
- *Extroverted* or *introverted*? Are you already thinking about sharing this with your book club or on social media, or do you just want to curl up with it in a quiet corner?
- *Agreeable* or *disagreeable*? Did you take the thinker-types pretty much as read, or are you itching to pick a quarrel about them?
- '*Honest–humble*' or '*biased–superior*'? This composite trait captures how fair or sincere we tend to be in dealing with others, how liable to bend the rules for personal gain, and

INTRODUCTION

how fixated we are on our own special status. So, for instance, are you thinking about how this book might help you understand and improve yourself, or how it allows you to judge and get ahead of other people?

Then the same goes for our emotions, which we can define broadly to encapsulate all our positive and negative moods, temperaments, and other 'affective' states — short-term and long-lasting, specific and diffuse:

- *Happy* or *sad*? Is this cheering you up or bringing you down? Are you entertained or daunted? Perhaps a bit of both to some extent?
- *Angry* or *calm*? Is your mind crowded by annoyances, or are you feeling blissfully detached?
- *Fearful and anxious*, or *eager and seeking*? Does what you might learn about how you think worry you or fill you with excitement?
- *Disgusted* or *desiring*? Think of this as aversion, disinterest, or sickened rejection, in contrast to craving, longing, or urgent yearning. Is your head already full of queries and criticisms, or are you appreciatively hungry for more?

When we move onto our next two elements, information and predispositions, the options get even more complex:

- *New*, *previous*, or *long-unused*? We may have acquired the facts that underpin our views at very different points in time: right this instant, fairly recently, or dredged up from our distant memories. Are you focusing on what you are reading here, or is your mind wandering onto other books you have read, lately or a while back?

- *Positive* or *negative* facts about the world? 'Good news' or 'bad news', in our subjective assessment. Are you picking out the highlights, or lingering over what bothers you?
- *Pro* or *con* in how we judge them? Whether we are favourably or unfavourably disposed in our response. At first instinct, do you like or dislike what you are reading?
- Do we go for *high and diverse* amounts of information, or *low and limited*? Are you absorbing every last detail or only a few big things? And is this one of several books you are reading, or the only one?
- Do we process information *fast* or *slow*, are we *selective* or *indiscriminate*? Are you devouring it in a matter of seconds, or settling in for the long haul? Are you reading in a certain order, or flicking back and forth at random?
- Do we *revise and revisit* what we believe, or *defend and maintain* it? Are you changing your mind about how you think, or entrenching behind your battlements?
- Are our values more *conservative and reactionary*, or *progressive and radical*? Are you fretting about how this is challenging what you know, or sussing out what new thing it brings to the table?
- Are we *compliant* or *defiant* towards what others believe? Our values can be more or less aligned or at odds, consistent or inconsistent, with those of the people around us. Are you inclined to agree with what you are reading here, or poised to reject it?
- And are our mental pictures more *personality-*, *emotion-*, or *reasoning-congruent*? How we see the world can align more with our gut instincts, our affective states in the moment, or our fuller reflections. Are you focusing on what resonates with who you think you are deep down, how you are

feeling right now, or are you waiting to mull on it some more?

Finally, when we deploy our reasoning, are our arguments:

- *Rational* or *irrational*? As you make up your mind, are you coming up with rigorous arguments, or a jumbled collection of scattered thoughts? Or something like a heady mixture of the two?
- *Reasonable* or *unreasonable* in how far we take others' views on board? Are you having no trouble factoring in what I am telling you, or struggling to carve out room for my perspective?
- Based on *heuristic* 'rules of thumb' or *non-heuristic* long-form thinking? We may rely on mental shortcuts when we formulate our thoughts, including 'anchoring' associations, assumptions, and stereotypes that foreground our own perspectives. Are you looking for key clues and signals to help you fast-track your way to a view on this book, or trying to come to a completely fresh conclusion about it?

We can illustrate all of these components of how we think as a series of adjustable 'sliders' (see fig. 0.1). That way, we can mark how far any of us leans towards any one of them as part of our overall mindset. Maybe you already have an idea about where on each of these spectrums you fall. Hovering near the middle between extroverted and introverted. A balanced mix of happy and sad. Picking up equal amounts of negative and positive information. Or instead, way out at the extremes. Ridiculously radical. Intensely disgusted. Always reasonable. Hold onto these first impressions as you go on.

So how do we get from these elements of thinking and their components to the ten thinker-types? With so many options to choose from, there is a potentially overwhelming number of mindsets that combine our personality traits, emotions, and the rest in various ways. Maybe not an infinite number, but certainly a lot more than ten. A galaxy of constellations that have not made the grade for our zodiac. Nevertheless, as my research went on, I was struck by just how far these options actually cluster together in practice. Certain personality traits and emotions correlate with each other, which narrows down the kinds of mental outlook we can exhibit. Neither personality traits nor emotions map neatly or exclusively onto any single one of the ten thinker-types. But which traits and emotions we are prone to undoubtedly steers us towards some thinker-types more than others. And the traits we have and the emotions we experience most often also lead us to specific ways of getting information, predispositions, and methods of reasoning rather than others. That narrows down what mental pictures we are likely to form about the world, as well as how we reflect on them. (Again, for those of you who want to know more, take a look in the epilogue.) The result of all this narrowing-down is that there are a lot fewer overarching mindsets than we might initially suspect. But why?

The reason is that how we think works as a series of layers, where the five elements that go into how we think build on each other to create our finished thoughts. When we think, we move from the foundational layers of personality and emotions (our mental outlook), through the middle layers of information and predispositions (our mental picture), to the reasoned reflection that sits at the summit of our mindset. All the elements of our thinking are causally linked, precisely and elaborately. But some of them are more fundamental to how we think than others.

Specifically, our mental outlook strongly rules in particular mental pictures and ways of formulating thoughts, and just as firmly rules others out. We can think of it as moving through a series of rooms in a house, each of which has several doors with more rooms behind them. All of them eventually lead us out into the garden. But *which* door we choose in each room affects what we have to choose from in the rooms beyond it, and the overall route we take to the outside. Or we can see it as a filter we impose on a photo, with its settings for brightness, contrast, definition, saturation, sharpness, and so on. Any filter lets some version of the image shine through. But depending on which filter we apply, its settings combine to crisp up some edges and dull others, deepen certain colours while fading others into grey, highlight some details and sift out others entirely.

When we think, we do all this unconsciously. We are generally not aware that we are piling on successive layers to construct our thinking – what we 'notice' is the final outcome we are left with once all these layers have come together. But all of us trace a path up and through these five layers to get to the overall mindsets that determine how we react to our experiences. And the options for precisely which paths we can take are laid out for us by these ten thinker-types and their distinctive mindsets.

We will see how each thinker-type works over the course of this book. That will start to give us a sense of which ones might have had a particular hand in carving out the path we ourselves follow in how we think. Yet we must not forget that when we think, we are not just displaying a disaggregated set of 'thinking characteristics'. Instead, with each thinker-type, all these points fit together in a specific way. No doubt, it is valuable to examine the constituent parts that make up each thinker-type, so we can really get under the skin of how each of them thinks. But what makes thinker-types as a whole more than just the sum of their parts – what makes them thinker-types at all – is the unique 'thinking dynamic' that emerges when all these parts fit together.

Fig. 0.1: The elements and component spectrums of how we think		
Personality traits		
Open to experience	▭▭▭▭▭▭▭▭▭▭	Closed to experience
Conscientious	▭▭▭▭▭▭▭▭▭▭	Careless
Emotional	▭▭▭▭▭▭▭▭▭▭	Emotionally stable
Extroverted	▭▭▭▭▭▭▭▭▭▭	Introverted
Agreeable	▭▭▭▭▭▭▭▭▭▭	Disagreeable
Honest–humble	▭▭▭▭▭▭▭▭▭▭	Biased–superior
Emotions		
Happy (joyful)	▭▭▭▭▭▭▭▭▭▭	Sad
Angry	▭▭▭▭▭▭▭▭▭▭	Calm
Fearful (anxious)	▭▭▭▭▭▭▭▭▭▭	Eager (seeking)
Disgusted	▭▭▭▭▭▭▭▭▭▭	Desiring

MENTAL OUTLOOK

INTRODUCTION

	Information	
	New ▊▊▊ Previous ▊▊▊ Long-unused	
Mental Picture	Positive ▊▊▊▊▊▊▊▊ Negative	
	Personality-congruent ▊▊▊▊▊▊▊▊ Emotion-congruent	
	High ▊▊▊▊▊▊▊▊ Low	
	Diverse ▊▊▊▊▊▊▊▊ Limited	
	Fast ▊▊▊▊▊▊▊▊ Slow	
	Selective ▊▊▊▊▊▊▊▊ Indiscriminate	
	Predispositions	
	New ▊▊▊▊▊▊▊▊ Previous	
	Revise/revisit ▊▊▊▊▊▊▊▊ Defend/maintain	
	Pro ▊▊▊▊▊▊▊▊ Con	
	Conservative/reactionary ▊▊▊▊▊▊▊▊ Progressive/radical	
	Compliant ▊▊▊▊▊▊▊▊ Defiant	
	Emotion-congruent ▊▊▊▊▊▊▊▊ Reasoning-congruent	
Formulating Thoughts	Reasoning	
	Rational ▊▊▊▊▊▊▊▊ Irrational	
	Reasonable ▊▊▊▊▊▊▊▊ Unreasonable	
	Heuristic ▊▊▊▊▊▊▊▊ Non-heuristic	

What shapes our minds?

Once the ten thinker-types crystallised in my mind, I began to see them pop up in all sorts of places. The various antics of politicians in the news made a lot more sense once I read them in thinker-type terms. That one, grinning with a pint and a thumbs up, is pretty much a stereotypical Jokester. Another, earnestly droning on about growth and values and the rule of law, is actually a Cool Cat. That one carping from the backbenches – a dyed-in-the-wool Quibbler. The same too for characters in books and films, plays and TV series. Before long, applying what we know about the ten thinker-types becomes a game of spotting the clues that will let us work out precisely whom we are dealing with. And when we have enough to make an educated guess, this deepens and enriches our understanding of what is going on in their minds – especially where it stands in contrast to our own.

But dividing the world into thinker-types is only the first part of understanding how we think and why. As much as they might tell us about what we are all like as thinkers, we have to do a bit more digging to understand what makes us the particular kind of thinkers that we are. First off, how do we know which thinker-type we are? Have we always been the same one? Or did we 'grow into' it over time? If so, at what point in our lives do we become our thinker-type? As toddlers, at school, or sometime later? What were we before that? An 'emerging' version of that thinker-type, a different thinker-type, or none at all? And how come we ended up as *this* thinker-type specifically? Did we have the choice of a different one? Are thinker-types something we can even choose? And once we have 'reached' one thinker-type, can we change to a different one?

To answer this, we can treat the elements that make up our thinker-types as thinking *tools*. Like physical tools, we have them at our disposal. But we do not necessarily use all of them, or use them equally, every time we think. All of us have personalities, feel emotions, collect information, hold predispositions, and are able to reason. And we all have inside us embryonic versions of the different components that make up each element. This gives us the capacity to display *all* these traits, experience *all* these emotions, and so on – at least occasionally, or to a limited degree. But how strongly each of them comes out in how we think is still up for grabs. Like a painter reaching for the pencils rather than charcoals, watercolours instead of oils, brushes over spatulas, we are dextrous enough that the baseline skill to use *any* of them is there. But we are more practised and less rusty with some than others. And there are some we clearly favour and rely on much more readily for our signature style. That is what our thinker-types are: our signature thinking style. Not just what we have to think with, but how we use it.

That distinction lies at the heart of how different corners of social research try to riddle through how we think and why. Some look at where we get our thinking tools from in the first place. Others want to know how we end up wielding some tools more than others. The range of identified causes and culprits is almost as wide-ranging as the number of perspectives on offer. Some locate the origins of how we think deep in the physical, biological make-up of our brains and bodies. They see our personality traits, emotions, and so on, as a 'natural' part of who we are. Coded into our genes, implanted from birth, predetermined by our anatomy and neurology. That perspective is broadly shared by neuroscience, physiology, and psychiatry. Others lay more weight on the way we acquire and develop how we think through our contexts and lived experiences. They see the way we use our personality, emotions, and the rest as something we 'socially' learn (and can unlearn). Behaviour we get accustomed to, which we can reinforce or revise, practise or neglect. That view lies more on the side of anthropology, cultural analysis, philosophy, social psychology, and sociology. (Once again, see the epilogue for more details.) To fully understand why we think the way we do, we need to bring all these different perspectives into conversation with each other in a common ground of enquiry.

We can capture why we think how we think as a process of cumulative, iterative overlays, each of which adds to — but also overrides — however we used to think *before*. How we think is not there, fully developed, right from the get-go. Instead, how we think now is the result of a long journey of learning that started when we were born. Our genes give us the baseline thinking tools we need. They put in place the nascent personality tendencies, emotional capabilities, reasoning capacities, and all the rest, that enable us to think at all. Then, step by step, we gain the use of our tools; we develop our elements of thinking. Whether, how, and how far our tendencies, capacities, and so on, actually manifest when we think is down to how they are brought out by the situations in which we find ourselves. Everything we go through either reinforces or challenges how we have been thinking up to now. It shapes our overall mindsets by either shoring up or switching out which traits, emotions, styles of reasoning, and so on, are dominant in how we think. It either reaffirms or 'reruns' our previous unconscious choices — from the foundational layers of our mental outlook all the way up to the summit of our reflections.

The layers of how we think meet the overlays of how our social experiences shape our minds to give us the mindset we have at any given moment. As thinkers, we are works in progress. We are never truly 'complete' Agonisers, Hotheads, Keen Beans, and so on. We are only ever 'resting' there as a temporary centre of our mental gravity. At any point, something in our day-to-day lives may rattle the components of how we think. The potential for change is always there. Either gradually, like an AI busily engaged in machine learning, or as an almighty jolt, like St Paul's conversion on the road to Damascus. If thinking is like moving through rooms in a house, then that house is always ready for some fixer-upper renovations. We can put the doors in different places. Change them from Rococo to Art Nouveau. Block them off or knock them through. Renovate enough, and eventually the whole layout will change for good. If it is a photo filter, then we can always fiddle with the effect on the image underneath. Play with the contrast or saturation. Remove this filter or that one, replace it with another one entirely. Or simply add endless new filters on top of each other, burying the image deep below.

We are constantly learning (and relearning) what thinker-type we are over the course of our entire lives. When we start out in our infancy with our rudimentary elements of thinking, we have no way to gauge what is going on or how we should think about it. We work out how to use what we have to form our earliest thoughts based on cues from other people, starting with our parents and families, the neighbourhoods where we grow up, and our early schooling. Our thinker-type emerges and evolves through the interplay between us and society. We grow into thinking like a Gloomster, a Happy Camper, or a Reveller because of what we experience in our upbringing, then our studies, then our job training – all the 'teachable moments' where we get social cues about how we should be. Every new role we take on, every new situation we face presents us with a new set of influences telling us to think this way or that. Well into adulthood, our minds remain malleable and plastic enough to absorb these influences and integrate them into our mindsets. Influence layers upon influence. We sit in between all these different pulls as they back each other up or cancel each other out. That is who we are as thinkers – the net product of all the different thinking versions of us we have been encouraged to be.

We are also not necessarily confined just to one thinker-type – and we may well feel an affinity to several. The ten thinker-types are 'ideal types' – 'pure' combinations of the five elements of how we think. Since we all have the basic forms of these elements in common, the relationship between thinker-types is not a hard black-and-white divide, but more like a succession of points on a continuum, or a set of spokes around a wheel (see fig. 0.2). Some of them even overlap or bleed into each other at the margins. Our different social roles and situations may ask us to strive for wholly separate thinker-types, or unite several at once. We are called to think one way at work, and another entirely at home, among friends, or at the ballot box. As we move from one social setting to another, how we think is pulled this way and that. It is not impossible to find people who fit just one thinker-type and none of the others – but it is pretty rare. It is far more likely that we are divided, even torn, between at least two or three main ones, with a couple more hinted at on the side.

The more we recognise the journeys that have led us to how we think now – the thinker-type or types we currently most strongly identify with – the more easily we can change our minds when necessary, and transform how we think in future. The key point here is that thinker-types are not absolute, immutable descriptions of how we think, but tendencies we can conform to at different times and to varying degrees. They influence our mindsets, but they are not prisons for our minds: we wield a lot of power to channel how we think in the direction we choose. If our social roles or situations 'ask' us to think like an Agoniser or a Keen Bean, we can lean into one or the other, or both. We can push ourselves to step outside our comfort zone and reach for a different thinker-type – maybe deliberately turn 180 degrees to

INTRODUCTION

Fig. 0.2: The wheel of thinker-types

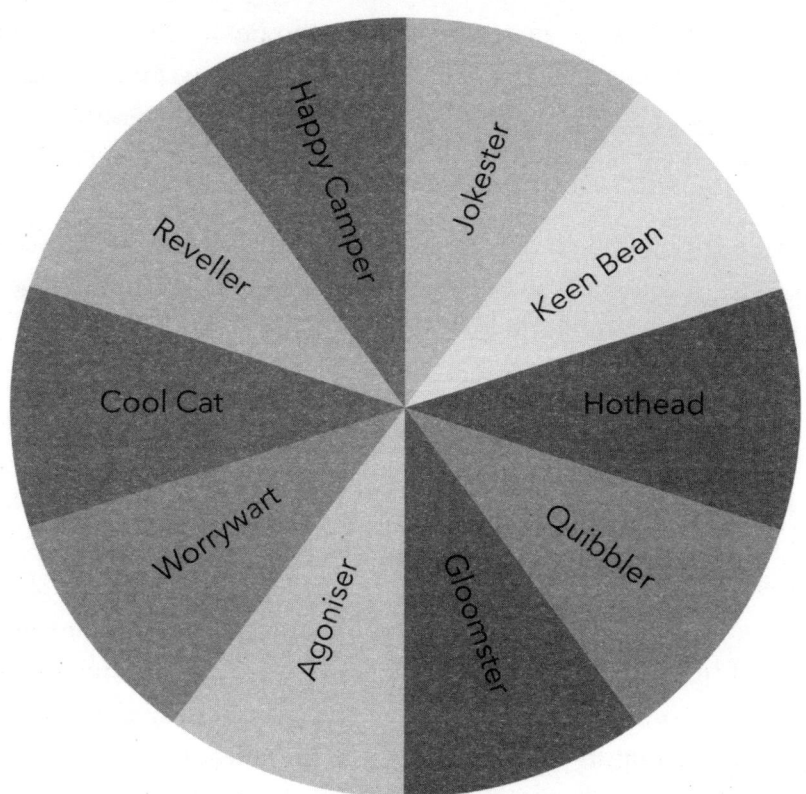

the Jokester or the Worrywart. We can try to ride out the tensions between the thinker-types, and switch to (e.g.) the Quibbler or Cool Cat depending on the context, although that gets harder to sustain the more these thinker-types clash. Or we can find where they align and reconcile them into a semi-stable hybrid of our own creation. Our minds are porous and mutable enough for all these ways of cross-fertilising our thinking styles to be viable.

The way we find ourselves thinking now, our default internal approach to the world, may feel deeply ingrained in our minds and completely entwined with who we are – but that does not mean it is fixed forever. We can rethink if we want to. Maybe we decide to stick with the tried-and-tested thinking tools we are accustomed to using. And maybe we are perfectly willing to go along with the signature thinking style our life experiences seem to be steering us towards. But equally, we may find ourselves at odds with parts of the mindset we have inherited from our own past selves. Looking to work on ourselves, to improve. To down tools and pick up new ones, to try out a new direction. To stand out from how everyone else who happens to share our situation thinks. To think about how we want to think, in line with the person we want to be.

A user's guide to thinking

Ten thinker-types, ten mindsets. Ten mental outlooks onto what is going on around us; ten mental pictures we create to capture it; ten ways to formulate our thoughts. A model that helps us shed light on how and why our world is filled with people who think differently to us. Who look at the world through different eyes, conjure distinct images of it in their minds, and sometimes argue with each other about what they see. As we start to understand better the exact ways in which we think and why, we can use this model to bridge the gaps between how *we ourselves* think and how *those around us* think. It gives us the opportunity to look in detail at how each thinker-type thinks, and the tools to start seeing things from their perspective – which lets us put ourselves in the same 'headspace' as them.

For my part, I have found developing these thinker-types and exploring how we come to fit into them highly illuminating. It has opened a window into why the people I deal with day after day may be thinking the way they do. It has certainly helped explain things that partly eluded me before. Casual chats and blazing rows. Total impasses and effortless harmony. Moments of seamless agreement, of talking at cross-purposes, of being lost for words. All of these interactions now make much more sense if I reframe them in terms of which thinker-types are involved. It gets appreciably easier to grasp where they are all coming from. Perhaps more importantly, I know better how to respond to them in terms that they know what to do with.

All in all, understanding how we think and why we do so leaves us with a much better sense of what it takes to be a fluid, responsive, and responsible thinker in a constantly changing world. We can all take encouragement for how we want to think in future from how we see other people think now. So as you move through the book, consider what it is telling you about how you think and why. How you think now. How you used to think previously. And how you might reframe your thinking and to what end. Not the end of the road, but the start of a new journey ripe with possibility.

While you do, just remember three things:

1. We can relate to all the thinker-types, even just a little bit, because we carry a little kernel of them all inside us. Sure, we may spend most of our lives inhabiting some of them and their mindsets a lot more than the rest. But the other thinker-types are never completely alien to us – we just have to find the right way in.
2. We always have an opportunity to explore thinking in new ways, because we are ultimately in charge of how we use the thinking tools available to us. We can choose to regulate ourselves, to 'be more X', 'dial down Y', 'find a better balance between P and Q'. Do we like the sound of one thinker-type more than the one we think we are? Then we can treat this book as an introductory 'taster' for how to bring out that mindset more in our everyday thinking. Give it a whirl, take it for a spin, see where it takes us.

3. There are no 'good' and 'bad' thinker-types, only thinker-types that lend themselves to various needs and situations. All ten have unique advantages to offer. We can harness them, learn from them, make them our own. And all ten have tendencies that can easily flip into liabilities if we let them get out of hand. So use them carefully and keep them in check – for our own sake and others' too.

Understanding our own thinker-types should help us forgive ourselves for our own foibles, while allowing us to exult in our strengths, and foster those parts of our mindsets that will enhance our lives. And understanding the thinker-types of those around us should help us see things more clearly through their eyes, what is there and what is missing, what looms large and what shrinks away. If 'good' thinking is about anything, it is about letting our mindsets do what we want them to do for us. Letting them work for us rather than against us. This task attaches itself to each of us in its own special way. But it is a task we all share.

CHAPTER 1

Happy Camper

Some people just seem to see life from its sunniest side. A while ago, I was sitting with a friend on a park bench, digesting the news that she had just been laid off from her starter job at a recruitment firm. Aware of how much she had struggled to find that position, and conscious she had not exactly been raised in the lap of luxury, I asked her what she was planning to do next. Perhaps I expected her to say something about moving back in with her parents or working on polishing her CV. Not at all. Instead, she shrugged, and flashed me a broad smile. 'Who knows! I'm sure something will turn up!'

And, miraculously, turn up it did. Fast forward several years, and almost as many stops and starts and nearly-theres across multiple countries – personal trainer, live-in tutor, master's degree – and she finally landed her dream role as an environmental consultant. No matter what trials and tribulations life threw at her, she bounced back every time. Always smiling through, confident that things would work themselves out in the end.

We can call this sort of breezy, carefree mindset the *Happy Camper*. How might we tell if we – or people we know – are a Happy Camper too? One telltale sign is that we tend to prize having a good time above everything else. We are generally at peace with our lot in life, give or take. We are also prone to letting our imagination run away with itself, getting lost in fantasies and losing track of the real world. We could never be accused of overthinking things, and we are unshakeably sure that we will be able to figure them out eventually. If that sounds even a little familiar, we have good grounds to suspect that we might have a bit of Happy Camper in how we think. But what is going on in a Happy Camper's mind? What goes into creating their mindset?

Happy Campers, as our name suggests, are emotionally **happy** above all else (see fig. 1.1). That happiness is underpinned by a cluster of four personality traits that are especially pronounced in our mindsets – we are a mixture of **emotionally stable**, **extroverted**, **agreeable**, and **careless**. That is not to suggest that these are the only traits we have. Of course, we have our own tendencies to be open or closed to experience, and to be honest–humble or biased–superior as well. But these two generally come out in a much more evenly balanced way in our thinking.

It is worth mentioning that 'happiness' is an emotion that takes many different forms, which mix and match in all kinds of ways with quite a few personality traits, even ones at opposite ends of their respective spectrums. That is why it plays a major role not just in the Happy Camper but also the Jokester, whom we will meet in the next chapter, and even the Cool Cat later on.

If we think of happiness specifically as 'jaunty enthusiasm', then it ties in well with the cluster of personality traits we find here. Psychological studies tend to pick out extroversion as the trait happiness is associated with the most strongly, while its links with the Happy Camper's other traits (emotionally stable, agreeable, and careless) are typically a shade more nuanced. Combining our emotional stability with our particular brand of happiness leaves its mark on the generally contented, upbeat way we think about the world. Our agreeableness underpins the pleasure we get from showing and experiencing compassion to others. Meanwhile, the distinctive effect of carelessness comes into play above all in our occasional outbursts of joy, and our ability to take information that challenges our mental outlook nonchalantly in our stride.[1]

This outlook has a distinctive effect on how we Happy Campers tend to view the world around us, interpret, and reflect on it. We typically prefer information that gives us 'good news' about what is going on. We find a couple of places to get this information from, and hoover up as much as we can – relying on what we are already familiar with, rather than totally fresh, new facts. We generally put a positive spin on things; we can be pretty forward-thinking, and we have a mild tendency to fold in what other people think too. We find ourselves cleaving to our existing views about the world. Finally, we use mental shortcuts fairly generously when we come up with more complex arguments, and largely try to put these in terms that other people will relate to.

	Fig. 1.1: The Happy Camper		
	Personality traits		
MENTAL OUTLOOK	Extroverted		Introverted
	Agreeable		Disagreeable
	Open to experience		Closed to experience
	Honest–humble		Biased–superior
	Conscientious		Careless
	Emotional		Emotionally stable
	Emotions		
	Happy (joyful)		Sad
	Angry		Calm
	Fearful (anxious)		Eager (seeking)
	Disgusted		Desiring

	Information	
	New ▪ Previous ▪ Long-unused	
	Positive ▪ Negative	
MENTAL PICTURE	Personality-congruent ▪ Emotion-congruent	
	High ▪ Low	
	Fast ▪ Slow	
	Selective ▪ Indiscriminate	
	Diverse ▪ Limited	
	Predispositions	
	Pro ▪ Con	
	Emotion-congruent ▪ Reasoning-congruent	
	Compliant ▪ Defiant	
	Revise/revisit ▪ Defend/maintain	
	New ▪ Previous	
	Conservative/reactionary ▪ Progressive/radical	
FORMULATING THOUGHTS	**Reasoning**	
	Heuristic ▪ Non-heuristic	
	Reasonable ▪ Unreasonable	
	Rational ▪ Irrational	

Becoming a Happy Camper

Lying at our core as Happy Campers is a virtually inexhaustible wellspring of cheerfulness. This gives us a solid redoubt of certainty that acts as our lodestar in everything we do. Among the family of thinker-types, we are the quintessential optimists. We hope for the best, and we are upbeat enough that we expect that 'the best' will actually happen too. Almost without fail, we see the people we meet, the things we discover, the situations we enter into from their brightest side. So why should we be anything other than carefree? From where we are standing, we can see clearly and unmistakeably the way things have to go to turn out well. All we need to do is keep our head, and we will reap the rewards pretty much without breaking a sweat.

What social experiences foster such cheerful confidence? To start with, it helps if we are broadly satisfied with the way things are going – in our job, our relationships, at school, with our hobbies. Feeling well-off where we are gives us a deep sense of security in ourselves and appreciation for what we have. This is not just a question of how much income or wealth we have, where 'having more money = feeling more positive' – though as many studies have shown, financial security is a major ingredient of 'doing well' for all of us.[2] Instead, for Happy Campers, the sense of well-being we get from our situation also depends on how closely our life conforms to our idea of what it *should* be like. Unsurprisingly, the better insulated we are from not having enough in a material sense, the more content we feel about our place in the world – but just as important for us is being on the right trajectory, heading in our preferred direction. When our projects are progressing, our sense of self is growing, *and* we have a rock-solid pile of assets in the kitty, we cut loose, and splash out on fun and frivolity.

The same conditions underpin our ability to absorb ourselves in what we do. We Happy Campers derive endless pleasure from creative work as an essential part of our personal flourishing – and we can be indefatigably industrious when we turn our minds to it. But our minds need clarity and ease to lean into our tasks, unimpeded by other concerns crowding in to distract us. It helps if we only have fairly low-intensity schedules structuring our lives. Manageable expectations with plenty of leeway to forge our own paths – from household chores to work deadlines – along with light-touch, hands-off approaches to 'checking in', and a healthy balance between 'time on' and 'time off' let us find our rhythm, and help our self-assured contentment bubble to the surface.

We can also be obliging team players, wholeheartedly happy in more or less any role, deferring to and falling in line with the expectations of those around us, if they feel comfortable and ultimately reward our goodwill. We run with whichever work project we are asked to take part in; we play in any position our team needs us to – as long as others draw on our input and our talents, and make us feel respected and understood. For that, we need more than just honest returns for honest labour, but outlets where we can offload our concerns. Spaces to air comments and questions, channels of engagement and feedback, and opportunities for guidance if we are struggling to work out the lie of the land. In other words, we need good mentors – from managers and teachers to more worldly-wise friends and family members – to give us proper 'role satisfaction' through a carefully calibrated balance of highly immediate motivations and rewards.[3] Over time, we grow a strong sense of attachment to the people we are surrounded by. Steeped in the shared culture we have built together, we develop a kind of magnanimous pride about our place among them.

It might also be that, for us, 'doing well' is tied up with ideas of 'get up and go' or 'putting ourselves out there'. As we learn to throw ourselves with gusto into our day-to-day activities, a kind of assertive fervour may begin to creep into our sense of self. We might find ourselves starting to get a bit ahead of ourselves, haring off merrily down our own path – especially if others around us allow or even encourage us to do so. We have a knack for the extraordinary and a relentless sense of adventure, and we can be headstrong in pursuing them to discover what lies at the end of our quest. We do so even in the face of other people's considerable doubts – like the magical nanny Mary Poppins or the scrappy vagabond Huckleberry Finn, both defiantly indifferent to the forces of convention that struggle to comprehend their spirited approaches to life. This can inflate our sense of self-worth – not enough to actively challenge those around us, but possibly enough to come off a little bit jarring – even if we tend to take the edge off with copious spoonfuls of light-hearted charm.

The confidence we draw from our stability gives us the impetus to put ourselves right at the centre of every situation. For us, it is the 'taking part' itself that makes us happy. Psychological research on how people in general feel when they expend time and effort, money, planning, or forethought on 'special treats' for themselves *and* for others suggests that they get a lot more joy out of experiences than material goods.[4] This is especially true of us Happy Campers, since our well-being is firmly tied to our positive fellow-feeling towards 'our people'. Sure, if we happen to be a hotshot broker, then our bullish eye for a good investment will satisfy us immensely. But for the rest of us, that joy goes up an order of magnitude if we end up nabbing those gig tickets, that dream holiday, that must-have birthday gift to spoil our friends or our partner with. All the more so if our favourite people can benefit too, and we can share our enjoyment in their company.

Projecting our satisfaction

Buoyed up by self-assurance, we Happy Campers erupt effervescently into the world, exhilarated at the sheer prospect of getting stuck in. We instantly detect the opportunities all the roles and situations it presents us with have to offer, and our hesitations recede far into the background. We are convinced that we know precisely what it takes to make the most of them – so all that anyone else needs to do is let us be us. We are irrepressibly genial and unflappable, radiating almost unbearably strong waves of exuberance. Think of Paddington Bear, and the earnest way he tries to help out the Brown family and his other friends in Notting Hill. Or Mei in *My Neighbor Totoro*, whose unbridled delight helps her befriend the forest spirits living around her home, including the gentle giant Totoro. At our best, simply through our infectious high spirits, we win people over whether they like it or not.

In part, this is because we Happy Campers are not-so-secretly extremely ambitious for ourselves and those we adopt as 'our own'. We often go to great lengths to be attentive and amicable towards the world and the people around us – we have a clear idea of what we want for us *and* for them, and we reckon that we are more than self-sufficient enough to go out and get it. But we cannot help being a bit opportunistic while we are at it. After all, we are rather pleased that we have everything so well figured out (or so we believe). We are jubilant, sometimes to the point of complacency, and we are more than willing to jump into things unquestioningly, whereas others might prefer to sit on the fence.

As wonderful as this chirpy assurance might sound, it does contain the potential to become a little bit overwhelming, even insufferable, for those around us – including the people we are trying to win over. Crashing straight into the centre of attention, demanding that everyone's eyes turn to us, can give us a brash, abrasive edge that may be a lot for others to handle. In general, our approach simply gets priced into what we are like: a bit giddy and theatrical, but fundamentally in control. Yet sometimes our dynamism may earn us some flak from the cagier or more withdrawn thinker-types – a brusque Hothead put-down or a spiky Quibbler riposte. To head that off, we need to learn to modulate our zeal.

We Happy Campers are hardly the only thinker-types to be determined and enterprising in pursuit of our goals – but there are times when we need to consciously dial that back a bit. We can conjure up enthusiasm for more or less anything; we know exactly when to step in, what to say, how to persuade anyone to see things our way. Spend enough time in corporate marketing, in communications, as an online influencer, and we become well-versed at selling what we want other people to buy. Little wonder that this can sometimes come across as affected or fake. Our limitless reserves of self-assurance can easily be construed as arrogance, misplaced pride, or sheer egotism. *We* may well buy what we are selling, but not everyone wants to be pitched at hard all the time. And that can be a difficult balance to strike.

Where this self-assurance gets put to the test is when things are no longer 'on our side' – when they start going a bit pear-shaped, then badly wrong, until finally full-blown disaster strikes. Even then, our cheerfulness remains indomitable and resilient. Let things go how they will – we shall bide our time, stay positive, and simply wait. It is the 'Panglossian' mindset that takes its name from the confidently optimistic tutor in Voltaire's *Candide*. The world we are living in is the best one possible, and everything in it is ultimately 'for the best'. Whatever it throws at us, we are convinced we can 'work with' it, and put a silver lining on more or less every cloud. But just because we can eke out some fragmentary positives from our situation does not mean we should just ignore its significant negatives. That, in fact, is the lesson Candide draws from his experiences of military pressgangs, flogging, shipwrecks, slavery, the Lisbon earthquake, and other horrors – that good things will only happen if we tend to them.

A colleague of mine once came into the office and mentioned, almost in passing, that when he returned from holiday, he had found his house had been burgled. Obviously, we all whipped around and offered our sympathies. Was he OK, what a shock that must have been, how devastating to come back to a ransacked home, and so on. 'Well, I did wonder if something was up while I was away,' he said. How so? It turned out that a camera in my colleague's home had picked up some suspicious lights and shadows and alerted him. And then the police had got in touch to say that his bike – safely locked up when he left – had been found abandoned by the side of a local road. Did that not make it obvious that something was up? 'Oh no, I was sure it was nothing too serious.' Was he not worried? 'Not really, I reckoned it could probably wait until I got home.'

At what point does our business-as-usual blitheness and ploughing ahead turn into irresponsibility? We can learn a lesson here from the character Joy in the film *Inside Out*. The fairy-like Joy, breathless and frenetic, exerts a kind of leadership role over the emotions belonging to an 11-year-old girl named Riley. Joy goes to great lengths to keep the other emotions (especially Sadness) in line and, crucially, well away from the 'control panel' to Riley's mind. Conflict between the emotions erupts just as Riley is trying to navigate starting at a new school, which leads to Joy and Sadness accidentally getting 'memory holed', and Riley becoming indifferent, borderline unresponsive. She returns to her usual good-natured self only once all her emotions are back together again, with the twist that Joy becomes willing to hand the reins to Sadness and the other emotions from time to time, symbolising Riley's emotional growth.

The moral of the story? Our Happy Camper mindset may be very good at keeping us going and helping us carry on as before. But it is much less adept at allowing us to change tack quickly and decisively when we need to. For that, we have to let our minds be coloured a little more by thinker-types who do not have quite the same rose-tinted view of the world. It helps us to learn that there is value in entertaining something of the Worrywart's doubt and the Gloomster's resignation about what we can reasonably expect from it.

In other words, we Happy Campers are sometimes too easily satisfied – insisting that everything is fine, sticking with our familiar ways of doing things. We must be mindful that this can get squarely in the way of doing something about what ails us, and remember that the path of least resistance will not always lead us to the best possible outcome. Left to their own devices, things will not *always* turn out all right in the end. To make sure they go well, we often have to get our hands dirty – steel ourselves to get uncomfortable, face what we find unpleasant, to reap the rewards on the other side.

Flexibility and its limits

We Happy Campers are inveterate observers, keeping up a wide-eyed wonder towards anyone and anything we come across. And we relish every chance to get involved, give things a try, have a go at being actual participants too. Like the genial tourist Twoflower in *The Colour of Magic*, we are apt to find pleasure and amusement in chance acquaintances and discoveries, skipping offhandedly from one entertaining new occasion to the next. We are among the thinker-types that are most receptive to finding out and absorbing facts and experiences from our surroundings. Ribbing our friends into spilling the beans about their latest dating dramas. Coaxing out a new colleague's life story on their first day. Losing ourselves in conversation with someone we meet at a houseparty.

This tendency is instilled in us increasingly firmly – or, at least, more easily unlocked – the more time we spend in situations where the name of the game is quickly picking up a broad spectrum of knowledge and skills. We thrive on a rich curriculum, from the classroom to the workroom, from the sports pitch to the studio. We learn to range widely in our interests and preoccupations, developing a remarkable ability to keep adding new ones to our roster – and we can switch with impressive versatility from each one to the next, adjusting like chameleons to their different tones, norms, and expectations.

But our happy-go-lucky demeanour can make it seem as if we do not feel all that strongly about much at all. If we are relaxed and exuberant about *everything*, is there anything we have a special emotional attachment to? Are we only enjoying ourselves because what we need and want sits squarely within 'the rules' that society operates by? Or perhaps because we have never actually fallen foul of the rules or come up against any boundaries, we have the diffuse confidence that comes of knowing, deep down, that they are pretty much always going to be on our side?

We are caught in a bit of a bind here. We have a boundless capacity to enjoy our experiences. We can see things not just from our own point of view but from other people's too – so even if we are not that hot on something, we can see why they might be. Especially if they are 'our people'. We choose to like *it* because we have chosen to like *them* – to our way of seeing things, it becomes an extension of them.

Yet we can give the impression that our wide-hearted satisfaction is either empty or suspiciously pliable. How can we possibly be so universally gung-ho? Do we truly have no red lines, no preferences of our own? Are we that blurry, apathetic, easily swayed? Perhaps when we learned about the world as children — or learned *how* to learn about it — we were taught that the right way of doing so is to keep an open mind and avoid getting caught up in minutiae. 'Don't sweat the small stuff', 'look on the bright side', 'put things in perspective', that sort of thing. Now we are adults, there is every chance that we struggle to tell exactly what, and how much, is at stake — which leads us to see any kind of discovery process as a blanket positive experience.

Our adaptability certainly has its advantages. But it also opens the door to another source of mutual incomprehension between us Happy Campers and other thinker-types. Our versatility and taste for variety can easily manifest as inconstancy. It may look as though we form an unstable, fluctuating series of attachments to an endless, even random array of new people, objects, and causes — what we might think of as our David Copperfield tendency. In part, it might look that way because that is the way of forming attachments we may have had impressed on us — a blend of innocent dedication, groupie-ish fandom, and impressionable loyalties that makes us rove ritualistically from one shiny new thing to the next, mixing-and-matching eclectically between successive fads.

Again, the spectre of emotional ambivalence raises its ugly head. Our attention seems limitlessly malleable. One moment we are delighting riotously in a Shostakovich symphony or a session of *Hearts of Iron 4*. The next we are giggling at the antics of our cat or the latest TikTok reel. Can anyone depend on the fact that we are truly enjoying any of these things — and will *keep* enjoying them? At least if Gloomsters are despondent, we can expect them to stay feeling that way. Whenever Quibblers object to something, we know they *really* mean it.

We have to stay cognisant of how we show the happiness we feel. If we do not, we risk being condemned as changeable and untrustworthy. Politicians profess delight for all manner of local projects, niche pursuits, or novel business ventures. Genuine interest or simply gladhanding would-be voters? Celebrities defend plenty of worthy causes or endorse hot new products. Their actual passion or just a paid partnership? This is the flipside of our charisma. Our effort to present as personable a face as possible, to make as many other people 'our people' as we can, can easily undermine our bid to be taken seriously if we end up seeming performative or fundamentally unserious.

Here, our best qualities can conspire against us. We must avoid getting caught up in so many things that we fail to achieve the goals we set ourselves. That means paying special attention to how we run our schedules: whether (and how often) we miss appointments, lose track of time, or procrastinate. We may find ourselves dashing between so many spinning plates that we unwittingly forget some, give up on others, and end up breaking half the dining set. If that is the case, we should put in the time and effort to make spinning them all actually viable, or – more likely – choose which of our plates we need to put down. It is no good simply maintaining the same air of casual elation at all the fun we are having. If we are so care*free*, who is to say we are not just care*less*, that we even care at all?

Active in our communities

The answer to this conundrum, for us Happy Campers, is unambiguously social. Whether as fans or players, customers or faithful devotees, whatever we 'get into' usually comes with a community in tow. Communal spirit is part of the package of what we believe attachment means, and we feel unalloyed pleasure when we form deep-rooted, intense ties of belonging. Social research suggests that in many arenas – from quality of life and public health to social capital and productivity – the familiarity of being one among many is a major part of what we get out of the things and people around us.[5] Part of why we try to treat those around us as gregariously as we can muster is that we aspire to getting the same treatment in return.

But as Happy Campers, our reciprocity is far from self-serving or transactional. We feel a clannish devotion towards whoever and whatever is 'ours', and we value the times we spend around them. Perhaps the 'birth family' of our parents and relatives has left us with memories of harmony and laughter – raucous games nights, vast, joyous feasts at Christmas, Diwali, or Thanksgiving. Perhaps our 'chosen family' of friends and partners have opened their hearts and hearths to us. Or perhaps we have spent a good portion of our lives searching for a sense of family care and connection. We admire the ability other people have to make us happy – we take it as a compliment, a recognition of who we are. Our attachment to them gives us the sensation of being 'at home'. We may even get a little bit addicted to it, relying on ever more of these benign symbioses for our sense of fulfilment.

In return, we offer those around us as much constructive support as we can – our way of paying forward all the times they showed us they cared about us. Like Lesley Knope in *Parks and Recreation*, we are quite literally *always* happy to help, and more than willing to work hard if there is a chance that it will benefit someone else. There is an extensive literature that studies how we learn to be helpful and generous during our early-years development. Many factors, from our parents' educational backgrounds to experiences of bullying and pedagogical nurture at school, shape how we learn to interpret other people's affection, moral worth, and need.[6] But our 'helpful' tendency also comes from recognising later in life that solidarity is a powerful way to reach out and shore up the communities in which we feel good. We have learned just how pleasant kindness and compassion feel, and become accustomed to their affective warmth as the baseline currency of social interaction – a currency we are glad to spend.

The immense joy we take in putting ourselves at other people's disposal can baffle some of the other thinker-types. Why not just engage in pleasantries but ultimately go it alone, as Jokesters would in our shoes? Surely there is a chance those around us will let us down, as Worrywarts are convinced they will. Our answer as Happy Campers is simple: engaging with other people is a reward in itself. And our capacity to win people over lets us bring them together in ways these other thinker-types would never consider. We can corral them into alliances to get large consensual projects of shared endeavour off the ground, using our cheeriness to coax them into joining us, and pushing our collective boundaries above and beyond.

All this requires tremendous reservoirs of energy. The same hyperactivity that the rest of the world might look at askance when it sees us bearing down on them finds its natural home in the gargantuan efforts we make to keep everything ticking along. We think, just as we live, at 100 mph. It is the way of life, and the way of thinking, we are forced to develop if we want a career that is fast-paced, pushing us over long hours, putting us 'out there' constantly in front of other people. A barrister, perhaps, or an estate agent, a restaurant manager, a performer. Each in their own way may fit the 'work hard, play hard' profile, but each also gives the world 'service with a smile'.

Hope in its proper place

As inveterate optimists, Happy Campers place great store by the indomitable power of hope. Our determination to see the world from its sunniest side is clearly a gamble – one that many other thinker-types might consider absurdly dewy-eyed. We are tempted to cherry-pick only positive facts and experiences to gather and hold onto, and, in fact, we tend to see gathering these facts and experiences as a positive thing. This can lead to our mental pictures of our surroundings becoming so rosy that we blind ourselves to the possibility that they might be grey or discoloured in any way. Of the other thinker-types, only Jokesters come close to our unusually high levels of 'good news' bias, and sometimes Cool Cats when they are at their most relaxed about what is happening around them. We ignore or forget that a truly complete picture would also take this greyness and discoloration into account. In that vein, we should try to see the world a little more through the eyes of Gloomsters or Quibblers, forcing ourselves to imagine 'what if things go wrong?'

I distinctly remember a late January evening when an ex-partner was filling out her online self-assessment tax return. A daunting and long-winded process at the best of times, but she was categorically convinced she would have no difficulties rattling it off shortly before the deadline. Batting away my concerned questions and increasingly urgent reminders, she was confident that she needed nobody's advice, that she could work it all out for herself. 'How hard can it be? They'll definitely have put everything I'll need up online.'

Spoiler: she soon realised, and very suddenly, that the process was much more complicated than she thought. An online account she had to register for. A tax code she needed to submit the form, which could take weeks to get. A pile of paperwork whose whereabouts she did not know. Gripped by the chilling prospect of being penalised for late tax filing, she called me in a panic, along with several of her friends. We sat her down and walked her through the checklist of things to do. We downloaded forms and guidelines, found her the revenue service's phone numbers to ring, more or less held her hand to bring her back onto an even keel. Mercifully, everything came through just in time for her to submit. And then: relief. Almost instantly, she was back to her cheery self. Her 'can do' attitude returned, now bolstered by the news that she actually *could* and *did*.

But we Happy Campers cannot always assume that this sort of forced self-belief will carry the day for us every time. And we also cannot presume that other people will always be there to feed our delusions and smooth the path for everything to work out. If we want to avoid putting ourselves in situations where only a 'Hail Mary' escape saves us from imminent disaster, we have to be more circumspect. We must learn to plan ahead, rather than just trundling along. To take responsibility, but also to be clear-eyed about where our individual responsibility begins and ends – above all, when we need to ask for help. *That* is where thoughtful growth lies for us.

We want to hold ourselves accountable – and to do that, we can partly rely on the responsible goodwill of those around us to help us keep our joyful excesses in check. We may depend on the benevolent oversight of our friends, parents, or partners – gently admonishing and reminding us to eat properly, to study for our exams, to make sure we do not turn up to the party empty-handed. Or, if we have become habituated to the professional interventions of doctors, therapists, or various care staff, we let them act as our external consciences, giving us our 'to-do list', running our day-to-day schedule. We find 'outsourcing' at least some of our accountability an incalculable relief. It validates our decisions about which path we should take. But it also stops us darting off too far down it and dissipating our energies.

When confidence pays off

Being a Happy Camper comes with an aura of winsome certainty that things are probably going to turn out all right. On the face of it, that might sound like a pretty great thinker-type for us to be. But we need to remember that none of these thinker-types are 'good' or 'bad' as such. Instead, we should recognise both our unique strengths and our particular weaknesses – which parts of our mindsets we should cling to, and which we might want to adapt.

On one side, several aspects of the Happy Camper mindset really work in our favour. We are in the fortunate position of knowing what we want *and* having a good sense of how to get it – and we can take most quirks of shifting circumstance in our stride. Some elements in our mindset are particularly promising and useful to cultivate: for example, we are highly attuned to what is going on, and we can 'stick at' something for a long time if we have to, if we really want it. And we are notably generous towards 'our people', always ready to offer them our energy, respect, and support.

We can also point to several characteristics that other thinker-types might find valuable to learn from us. Our endearing charm easily gets others onside – cajoling them without the need for any Jokester intrigue or Hothead incandescence. We see the best in other people's plans and get on board with them, rather than zeroing in on the risks, as Worrywarts do, or dismissing them as wrong-headed, as Quibblers will. Our easy-going nature lets us unspool and have some fun in the world – a useful antidote to Gloomsters' downcast reserve, or Cool Cats' occasional stuffiness.

Yet there are a few aspects of how we think that we would do well to keep an eye on. Though we are generally even-keeled and self-assured, that can come across as overbearing complacency about how well things are going for us. We may appear to lack strong, long-lasting emotional investments – which may make us unreliable, easily distracted, and liable to drop the ball and let important things slide by accident. We are inveterate people-pleasers, courteous to a fault – but often slightly too trusting and diffuse. And we need to have 'all eyes on us', chatting incessantly and irrepressibly, which may come across as superficial or merely a performance.

In this respect, there are a few tricks we could do with picking up from other thinker-types – by paying attention when they are modelling the best sides of their mindsets, and getting pointers for how to plug the gaps in our thinking. We innocently place too much weight on the 'good faith' of those around us – so we need a judicious dollop of Gloomster despondency or Worrywart reticence to give our view of the world a more realistic edge. We too often suspend our critical intuition about what will and will not fly in the projects we are involved in, which we can fix by giving our Quibbler scepticism muscle more of a workout. And we need to plan better rather than just muddling through – which, as Jokesters show us, we can do while still being a force for fun in the world.

All this makes us a pretty handy person to have around – and we make it look easy too. We tend to toddle along casually, like penguins on an ice floe, merrily slotting into line, diving after the glint of shiny prospects on either side. Others can only marvel at how unerringly we join the dots off the flimsiest evidence, and whizz up whole new ways of seeing things they have looked at a hundred times. But we cannot let our imagination run away with us. If we get too lost in whichever castle we happen to be building in the sky, we leave ourselves vulnerable to a rude awakening. If we forget to come back down to Earth, we may find that the Earth has gone on without us. Society depends on us to help keep things ticking over and moving forward – but we cannot let it leave us behind.

CHAPTER 2

Jokester

Every group needs someone who knows how to bring the fun. At university, one of my friends gained a certain notoriety for the pranks she played on the rest of us. An utter menace at games night – always with a crucial piece or card that *just happened* to have stowed away in her back pocket. She would routinely disappear items from desks and shelves, replacing them with instructions for elaborate treasure-hunts to get them back. Several times, one or other of us returned to our rooms to find that everything in them had been turned upside down, wrapped in newspaper, or covered in plastic cups. We always knew it was her, of course. But part of her game was to feign a look of hurt innocence, and deny everything with a quip or a quick retort.

Years later, we found ourselves at a reunion get-together in her flat. A full-blown, multi-course dinner – canapés, cocktails, all somehow squeezed into her cramped inner-city kitchen. As she dashed around, distracted by her fantastically ambitious cooking schedule, our talk turned to old memories – including the pranks she used to play. We spotted an opportunity for a bit of payback. One by one, we quietly snuck out, and saw to it that the rest of her flat was well and truly upended. Nothing too severe – but a pretty thorough pranking all the same. When she realised what we had done, she let out an exaggerated howl of protest. 'But how could you? Not fair! Really, you're all such children!' On the surface, she took the joke well – but a look of genuine displeasure flashed across her face, and a slight shortness crept into her tone for the rest of the night. And it was a while before she offered to host a reunion again.

This kind of behaviour is the hallmark of the *Jokester*. How do we know whether we might be one too? Perhaps we really appreciate the absurdity of the world. We may be uncommonly good at spotting the quirks and bizarre moments that pepper everyday life. We take comfort in humour, we play the resident trickster. We like to have an audience. Or maybe we carry a hard-nosed sense of what is worth*while* and what is worth*less*, and clearly put ourselves on the 'right' side of that divide.

This thinker-type has some echoes of the Happy Camper here and there. But there are places where we could not be further apart (see fig. 2.1). We Jokesters are also led by **happiness**, though our cluster of supporting personality traits is a larger spread of six – **emotional**, **introverted**, **disagreeable**, **conscientious**, **closed**, and **biased–superior**. Unsurprisingly, this makes for a very different experience of happiness than the Happy Camper's jaunty enthusiasm.

We can summarise it as a general demeanour of sarcastic satisfaction. Given that, it might seem odd that it is conscientiousness that has the most durable link to happiness in our mental outlook. Yet we get tremendous pleasure from striving for our life purpose *and* hitting the targets we aim for. Our closedness and introversion make us glad to carve out our own path, and coolly hang back as we dismiss other novelty distractions. Meanwhile, our bias–superiority, disagreeableness, and emotionality are less strongly pronounced, but give us a common underlying pattern of making light of our vulnerabilities, and finding an impatient, triumphant glee in overcoming them against the odds.[1]

Like Happy Campers, we Jokesters pick up on the 'best bits' of what is going on from a tiny set of go-to sources – sometimes only skating over them superficially, but sometimes scouring them in copious detail. Generally, we stick with what we know – though we may suddenly latch onto new things or dredge up long-forgotten ones instead. We oscillate between taking a bright or a dim view of what happens around us, and we do so generally from a pretty conventional perspective. We tend to push back against what other people think, sometimes doubling down hard on the views we already hold. We like a bit of mental corner-cutting too, and we do not mind railroading people into accepting our line of argument.

Fig. 2.1: The Jokester			
MENTAL OUTLOOK	**Personality traits**		
	Conscientious	▮	Careless
	Emotional	▮	Emotionally stable
	Agreeable	▮	Disagreeable
	Honest–humble	▮	Biased–superior
	Extroverted	▮	Introverted
	Open to experience	▮	Closed to experience
	Emotions		
	Happy (joyful)	▮	Sad
	Angry	▮	Calm
	Fearful (anxious)	▮	Eager (seeking)
	Disgusted	▮	Desiring

Mental Picture	Information	
	New ▐ Previous ▐ Long-unused	
Positive	▕▋▕▕▕▕▕▕▕▏	Negative
Personality-congruent	▕▕▋▕▕▕▕▕▕▏	Emotion-congruent
High	▕▕▕▕▋▕▕▕▕▏	Low
Fast	▕▕▕▕▋▕▕▕▕▏	Slow
Selective	▕▕▕▕▕▋▕▕▕▏	Indiscriminate
Diverse	▕▕▕▕▕▕▕▕▋▏	Limited
	Predispositions	
Conservative/reactionary	▕▕▋▕▕▕▕▕▕▏	Progressive/radical
Emotion-congruent	▕▕▋▕▕▕▕▕▕▏	Reasoning-congruent
Pro	▕▕▕▕▋▕▕▕▕▏	Con
Revise/revisit	▕▕▕▕▕▋▕▕▕▏	Defend/maintain
Compliant	▕▕▕▕▕▕▋▕▕▏	Defiant
New	▕▕▕▕▕▕▋▕▕▏	Previous
Formulating Thoughts	Reasoning	
Heuristic	▕▕▋▕▕▕▕▕▕▏	Non-heuristic
Rational	▕▕▕▕▋▕▕▕▕▏	Irrational
Reasonable	▕▕▕▕▕▋▕▕▕▏	Unreasonable

Becoming a Jokester

Deep down, what drives us Jokesters is a powerful sense of relief, which we get from keeping ourselves a little removed from our surroundings. It gives us a kind of settled fulfilment, as if we are nestled into a comfortable armchair in the opposite corner from whatever is going on – and the more firmly we become ensconced, the more affirmed we feel in our independence. Lone wolves, we take ironic joy in the fact that we are unattached to the world at large. Yet, paradoxically, we also fundamentally want other people to appreciate us for who we are. *We* think we are special, but we are deeply unconvinced that the rest of the world shares our view. So we become preoccupied with finding ways to make ourselves more unique, attractive, and interesting to those around us. To stand out to them, and stand apart from them, so they will stand back in awe. We build a ring of clear blue water around us and put the most ornate castle imaginable at its centre, ready to be admired.

We also hive ourselves off from our surroundings because we are unusually conscious of our own weakness. We want to make sure other people appreciate what we have to offer without taking advantage of us. Our fragile sense of self is easily offended, so even as we are setting up our boundaries we may come across as snippy and waspish. We turn everything into a joke as a defence mechanism, hoping secretly to be understood but also simultaneously, crucially, left to our own devices. Of course, that hope is often dashed, meaning that we default to prickly, thin-skinned cynicism. This tendency to self-preserve through jest makes us Jokesters uncommonly keen observers of our surroundings: Lady Bracknells who can see straight through the indecorous foibles and hypocrisies of the (high) society we move among. We are sharp-eyed and quick-witted – with the sort of biting rhetorical flair that is highly prized among the best diarists, essayists, and other literary raconteurs.

Unsurprisingly, the social experiences that steer us in the Jokester direction are somewhat different from those that shape Happy Campers. Perhaps we have found ourselves carrying the can again and again for some truly make-or-break decisions – landing that deal that keeps our company afloat, swinging that case in our client's favour, the impossible shot that wins our team the title. And, against all odds, we nail it every time! We make the right call, we prove our worth. Easy, really – just what happens when we are a born superstar. And so, we can easily become persuaded that we have found our calling, that we know what we are doing. That what we have is a preternatural gift, and nobody should dare to meddle with our approach.

This happens especially if we internalise the idea that we are carrying on a proud tradition that has been entrusted specifically to us. A hallowed family ritual, a philosophy of deep truth, a prestige brand handed down since time immemorial, which only the truly elect fully understand. We owe it to our predecessors to carry the torch onward, to keep the faith – and keep it exactly. Perhaps when we were first taught the ropes, shown the secret tricks of the trade, or inducted into 'our way of doing things', we were also told that any deviation at all in the process might bring the whole house of cards crashing down. Once this is instilled in us, we come to see it as literally ridiculous that anyone would know better, or try to go a different way. Logic is on our side, and success is in our bones, after all – we know which risks to take and which to avoid. Others will come round to our way of thinking eventually. The joke is on them if they do not.

We also learn our acerbic mindsets from situations that reward us for playing the rules to our advantage. An eye for imperfection, mixed with an enthusiasm for expectations to be set and satisfied, helps us spot technical loopholes and opportunities for crafty spin, and thereby play (and beat) others at their own game –

from finessing legal contracts to exam questions. This is an especially useful skill to learn if we have to hold 'the powers that be' to account: as campaigners picking apart flimsy policies, press critics calling out scandals, or comedians lambasting the incompetence of various worthies. Yet our most distinctive Jokester thinking comes out in roles that encourage us to lean more into our protective self-interest – especially through the wheeler-dealing and opposition research that gets 'our side' an advantage instead of 'the others'. Nothing neutralises a rival like making them the butt of a joke. That is what the world of competitive advertising and marketing, negative campaigning, trash-talking, and 'psy-ops' to sow dissension in the opposition's ranks is all about. Spend long enough in that world, creating it or absorbing it, and strategic joking becomes an automatic habit.

But finessing this all flawlessly all the time is stressful, and the thought of what it could cost us if we do not puts us on edge. Getting fired or reprimanded, shut out or told off puts a sizeable dent in our self-image. So trying to see the funny side, and having a laugh at other people's expense, is how we self-regulate. Humour gives us a vent to stop our neuroses brimming over – comic relief in a very literal sense. It works as a kind of balm for our soul, suturing the wounds the world leaves in our sense of self. Social research has repeatedly validated the therapeutic role humour – including 'black' or 'gallows' humour – can play in helping us cope with everything from day-to-day setbacks to personal pain, trauma, and large-scale social disasters.[2] But our turn to fun also helps feed our ego. When our friends or colleagues give us space to mock others, it is our vanity they are flattering. We are *better, more worthy*. What we do is special because we are the ones doing it. If others cannot see it yet, we humour them until they do – and, meanwhile, we just keep doing our thing.

Laughter as the best armour

A significant part of how we maintain our self-esteem and sense of mystique is by holding back the best parts of ourselves, keeping our skills and our wit under wraps. We have too great a sense of self-worth to grab onto everything that crosses our path – our capacity for jest may be infinite, but we do not feel the need to deploy it all the time. We value ourselves too highly to jump straight in; we are reticent, even stand-offish, out of sheer self-preservation. In its low-key form, we are merely trying to set some boundaries around our self-respect: we do not need anyone or anything else to help us value ourselves.

But as this sensibility gets more entrenched, a slightly more prideful element starts to creep in. Actually, we are something of a scarce resource, one of a kind, even – so other people should value us more highly, and make the most of our presence and our time when we give it to them. Psychological studies have long supported the idea that people place a premium on things if they are rare rather than abundant, and are primed to seize hold of them when they cross their paths. We tend to gain this attitude fairly early on in our cognitive development – it is not constantly activated, but can be primed to kick in very easily.[3] We Jokesters play this capacity to our advantage. We withhold ourselves until others show us to our satisfaction how pressingly they need us. The more we internalise this scarcity as a sign of our objective, undeniable worth, the more this aloofness can turn into conceit.

At this point, valuing ourselves independently from the world can make us inward-looking, even wholly self-referential. A potential pitfall of the sardonic individualistic place we carve out for ourselves is that it can transform into more of an isolated – and self-isolating – cell. In this case, we stop noticing other people, stop caring about them, even start to mock them complacently because they are not us. It is a characteristic shared by the haughty landowner Fitzwilliam Darcy in *Pride and Prejudice*, and Hercule Poirot, the brilliant Belgian detective from Agatha Christie's crime novels. Alongside their cool reserve, both have a talent for dry observations that emphasise their differences from those around them – one in his wealth and status, the other in the brilliance of his 'little grey cells'.

As we congratulate ourselves on how thoroughly we have nailed being who we are, we can stop taking anything that is not like us seriously at all. The lifelong habits that we credit for our special status all seem impeccable compared with others' chaotic nonsense. When we get up and go to sleep (bright and early! at a decent hour!), how we brew our morning tea or coffee (loose leaf! French press!), how we pack our bags or fold our laundry. That we studied a proper subject or learned a sensible trade, compared to whatever wishy-washy waste of time other people have chosen. What is 'ours' is interesting, vital, worthwhile. What is 'theirs' is dull, irrelevant, pointless. Against that backdrop, if we do choose to give someone the time of day, it must be because they are worth the effort, deserving of our serious consideration. As for the rest – we seclude ourselves, smile, and let them pass us by.

But we do not have to disrespect other people in order to respect ourselves. So how do we mitigate this tendency? By putting the brakes on our quickness to cast judgement, and being a bit more circumspect about sharing our unfiltered thoughts. It is a lesson both Darcy and Poirot learn. Darcy's humour becomes lighter and more playful over time, especially as his relationship with Elizabeth Bennet progresses, while Poirot grows steadily warmer in the affection he shows his long-time allies Miss Lemon, Captain Hastings, and Inspector Japp.

We need to stop our sardonic side from spilling out all the time and potentially jeopardising our relations with the people around us. If we let ourselves see other people as there only for our frivolous amusement, we will struggle to be anything other than superficial in how we deal with them. That tends to be a lot more transparent than we may think. People typically notice pretty quickly if we dismiss them out of hand – for their political views, for watching *Love Island* or *Star Trek*, for listening to Taylor Swift or Tool. Maybe we are fine with that. But if we mock everyone for everything all the time, we have to be aware that this can fuel their resentment.

We face a choice. Either we stand our ground, double down, insist everybody else needs to get better at 'taking a joke'. Or we reel ourselves back in, keep our most barbed observations as 'inside thoughts', and learn to accept other people's ways of thinking and being in the world, even appreciate them, rather than dismissing them out of hand. Which option we choose comes down to how important we think the people in question are – whether we calculate that their disapproval is likely to matter in the grand scheme of things. But that is a calculation we should make with a lot more caution than we are normally apt to do.

Keeping the comedian in check

When we are engaging in perimeter defence, we can throw ourselves into humour with considerable gusto. The further we take this, the more we turn what began with a concern about our own frailty into an ostentatious show of strength. We start to relish opportunities to display our whimsy. We may actively put ourselves in situations where we can play the buffoon, in the vein of Captain Jack Sparrow relying on his irreverent bravado to survive whatever the Caribbean throws at him. What starts as a peppy, punchy way to fend off threats becomes a deliberate performance. If we grew up using humour as a way to deflect, to evade the attentions of bullies or paper over gaps in our school tests, then we will instinctively reach for it if we ever feel a bit unsettled. We also know that acting the buffoon is generally a pretty reliable way to win people over: they are much more likely to forgive us our trespasses if they fundamentally quite enjoy being around us.

That was certainly the *modus operandi* of one of my grandmother's neighbours. A larger-than-life man, with loud shirts and a louder voice, he was the kind for whom the phrase 'quite a character' might have been invented. A small-town Sir John Falstaff, stalwart of the local brewhouse, who liked to lord it over the residents in my grandmother's apartment block, and prided himself on his cosy connections with the local council. People were largely content to put up with him. Partly because he was an unrivalled source of neighbourhood gossip (and who does not like a bit of gossip from time to time!), and partly because of his hilariously fruitless efforts to command the one resident who refused point-blank to listen to him: his own Jack Russell terrier. But one day, he took it upon himself to pin a pointed note about 'overflowing bins' on the door of my grandmother's flat, while we were clearing out her belongings after her move to hospice care – which earned him a very public rebuke from the residents' association.

Entertaining our way into people's good books works a treat – until suddenly it does not. Eventually, we may find the joke wears thin, and their patience runs out. Non-Jokesters can tolerate our clowning around as long as they do not get the impression we are making light of something they consider too serious to be a laughing matter. None more so than Agonisers and Cool Cats, who struggle the most with what they see as our lack of depth. If that happens, they can turn on us in an instant. The same ebullience that previously drew them in can suddenly become precisely what most puts them off about us – we might then end up being dropped hard, and everything we do 'cancelled' without recourse.

Ironically, in pursuing our dignity so determinedly, we may end up becoming quite the opposite in other people's eyes: boorish, lightweight, and thoroughly undignified. Think of Basil Fawlty in *Fawlty Towers*, whose cutting sarcasm towards the staff at his dysfunctional hotel serves as a – largely unsuccessful – mask of self-delusion about his own ineptitude. So we often need to pay closer attention to how we actually come across to the people around us. What may be little more than a lightly humorous aside in our minds may resonate far more significantly with others. At best, we risk opening up points of tension with precisely the people we are trying to win over. At worst, they may judge us as uncaring, uncommitted, or frivolous.

The two levels of our wit(s)

But these frontline histrionics are only one way we confront the world. That we get into the business of sarcastic witticism at all is because – to our minds – the rest of the world *just will not let us be*, but instead keeps obtruding in on us. That, after all, is why Matilda Wormwood starts to play pranks, first on her neglectful parents, then the sadistic Miss Trunchbull – to get her own back for their cartoonishly cruel and incompetent interference in her life. What we Jokesters find most satisfying of all is actually just enjoying the world's quirks without disturbance, without being called upon to intervene. So when presented with a chance to quietly savour ludicrous people, strange objects, preposterous events, and farcical situations, we do so with great delight. We take simple pleasure in the fact we do not have to have anything to do with them. We are quite happy being left on our lonesome, permitting ourselves a gratified smirk that we can just keep being our singularly excellent selves.

Over time, we may build up a bit of an 'inside/outside' divide. When we are with 'our people' – those who know us best, and with whom we are most comfortable – we typically dial back our comedian act or turn it off entirely. Around people who we have (very carefully and deliberately) 'let in', we tend to take our enjoyment in a far more reactive way. We may sit back happily in our armchairs, lobbing our hand grenades of hilarity. We want to be noticed, yes, and we want 'our people' to be an appreciative audience for our wit. But we also want them to give us space to breathe and shine.

Jokesters are much more thoughtful than our outward appearance might suggest. As much as we may not want to overinvest in the world around us, we are alert to it and intrigued by its goings-on. At the same time, we also muse extensively about ourselves – what we need, what we like, what makes us happy. We find ourselves deeply enthralling. We are not overthinkers, as such, but more than other thinker-types, we must be careful to avoid these internal preoccupations from spilling over into narcissism. Gloomsters and Worrywarts are as focused on themselves as we are – but they do not assume that they automatically matter just as much to the rest of the world too.

We want to stay sensible and proportionate, even if how we respond to events often includes some madcap clowning-about. This sets up an important dichotomy in our character. Outwardly, we can be as snarky, foolish, or silly as we like. Inwardly, however, we are careful, watchful, and relatively sedate. We draw self-satisfaction from internally being as unlike our nonsensical surroundings as we can be. On what matters to us, we hold ourselves and 'ours' to rigidly perfectionist standards. We know exactly how to read our balance sheet or investment report; we precisely fine-tune the specs on our new kitchen renovation or garden extension. When it comes to things we care about, we will pore over minutiae as long as it takes. For what we do not, we are happy to let these standards drop. For all our ironic exterior, we take ourselves and anything we are personally invested in immensely seriously. Of course we do: we are, after all, the best.

That we can be outwardly unserious while maintaining a laser-like focus on what matters to us on the inside is one of the most intriguing findings about our psychology. Some researchers have taken this so far as to probe the links between our humour and 'dark' tendencies, such as Machiavellianism and even psychopathy. Other analyses suggest, more mundanely, that our 'playful' or 'gameful' mindset is how we express our creativity and develop our practical wisdom in the situations we confront day to day. Both indicate that, ultimately, our humour is at least partly a tool we deploy – covertly or overtly – in service of our 'grand plan' for ourselves and what is 'ours'.[4]

We are also far less changeable than our impromptu quickfire wit lets on. Once we have learned the rules, absorbed the by-laws, maxims, and rites that tell us how to live our lives, we stick to them diligently. They shape what we see as normal, rightful, and sacred. In many ways, they decide what it is we are willing to joke about. This is another way we distinguish ourselves from many other thinker-types: we are resistant, even impervious, to being changed in our core. Not for us the Reveller's supple whimsy or the Keen Bean's erratic quantum leaps. When push comes to shove, our core remains firmly anchored to the spot.

This makes us likely to reach for our familiar comedic weaponry, unerringly retell the same gags, rehash the same punchlines. We have learned what there is to learn, what we are doing has worked for us before and will again – so we can afford to rest on our laurels. Yet this can make us far less unique and original than we like to think. If part of our mission is to keep being the most interesting person in the room, then the deadliest sin we could commit is to let the joke grow stale. And that means refreshing our material by opening ourselves up to the wit of other people and understanding what they can bring to the table, even if that does not always come naturally to us.

The power of our charm

What does make us stand out from those around us is that, unlike any other thinker-type, we combine a single-minded inner pursuit of our interests with being outwardly facetious, informal, and above all extremely funny. This unusual combination is one of the most powerful assets we can bring to society. The more serious-minded thinker-types, such as Gloomsters and Worrywarts, let their mindsets shine through palpably in the face they present to the world, while the more light-hearted ones, among them Happy Campers and Keen Beans, are light-hearted all the way down. As long as others' purposes align with our own – which is, of course, far from a foregone conclusion – there are few more upbeat, zealous, and unremittingly devoted allies than us Jokesters. Just by cracking a smile we can pull others back from the brink, ease their stress, lift their morale.

Nobody knows better than we do how to lighten the mood or defuse a challenging situation. And nobody has quite our talent for using our personal pizzazz to advance our interests, especially when there are hurdles or sticking points to overcome. But it is vital not to let that tendency get out of hand. Our self-preservation can turn into self-obsession; our support for our own views and interests can become doctrinaire – to the point that it starts getting in the way of helping us achieve our goals. It is on us to firmly draw the line, to ensure that we do not lose the selves we have been trying so hard to protect.

A former housemate of mine spent a couple of years working for a boss who seemed – at first impression – both brilliant and charismatic. On the face of it, the role was perfect. Decent pay, great exposure, a good mix of responsibility and self-direction. Plus the feeling that her company truly valued her contribution. In the beginning, the going was fairly spectacular. Profits, expansions, new hires. For her, a raise, a promotion, a solid bonus. Then business turned sour. Commissions dried up, sales fell through, contracts ran out. Her salary payments started to arrive late, then stopped coming altogether.

Yet curiously there was no change in tone from her boss. 'It's just the difficulty of running a small business, I know you can turn this around!' Was there a plan? 'We're an expensive outfit, we've got to pull together!' How would they be paid? 'We need to land more projects; I know you'll manage it!' Somewhat mollified, my housemate and her colleagues redoubled their efforts, pulling longer hours, working weekends, pushing themselves to the limit. No change. Eventually, they demanded to see the company books. The profits they had worked for had disappeared into the ether. My housemate handed in her notice within days. Not long after, the company folded.

There is something quite remarkable about Jokesters' ability to pull off this sort of 'magic trick'. After all, it can make all the difference if we can keep people onside through our charisma – if it helps us keep our show on the road even when it seems like that road might be about to run out. Call it the 'razzle dazzle' that the criminal defence lawyer Billy Flynn uses in *Chicago* to save his clients on 'Murderess' Row' from a death penalty verdict in court. If it works, our Jokester charm can help us protect what is 'ours' – even if people suspect, or know full well, that we are driven by a sizeable helping of self-interest. But only if it works. As strategies go, it is quite a high-wire act to choose. We have to learn to play things carefully and not take our illusionist's sleight-of-hand too far. Above all, we need to know when the time has come to drop the mask.

A game of pros and cons

What helps us draw this line is developing a clear sense of what we actually want to achieve. We find it unambiguously fun to imagine all the limitless opportunities we can strike out for. We also rejoice in the process of coming up with life plans, strategies, and pragmatic tools to help us make the most of them. Yet once we have done so, we are relentless and absolute in pursuit of our goals, knowing that achieving them is the only surefire way to push back against the absurdity of the world outside – the only way to keep our lives incomparable. Whenever we do achieve what we set out to, we get a mischievous thrill out of the elaborate, calculating plotting we had to do to get there. Somewhere in between the disruptive pranks and schemes of Loki, the Norse trickster god, and the masked vigilante V's theatrical vengeance in *V for Vendetta*.

We are always on the hunt for glory, and we are happiest when we are operating in the world of tangible achievements and eye-catching 'big ideas'. In particular, we carry inside us the echo of material success, and we are not averse to shamelessly self-promoting to get it. Obsessed with data, we look for the numbers that validate our efforts, black on white. Our promotion trajectory, our perks, our salary. The likes, reposts, and views our content gets on social media. The number of people who show up to our house party, the ratings our big speech gets on TV. Despite our whimsical manner, the achievements we set for ourselves tend to be comprehensive, ambitious, clear, and precise. And we are especially jubilant whenever we hit one of our milestones – because we did so, and because nobody stopped us.

We see ourselves in a position of rivalry with most of the people around us – and we take undeniable pleasure in any way we find to get ahead of them. For us, life is fundamentally a question of zero-sum trade-offs, and we are acutely aware that other thinker-types are after their own achievements too. Cool Cats have their heads firmly screwed on and their goals in view; Agonisers are highly alert to what the world has to offer; Revellers know how to get what gives them satisfaction. How can we jostle past them? Perhaps by making them look staid and boring, or drippy and whiny, or greedy and promiscuous. Is that true? Who knows or cares. Will it *work*? – that is the main question.

It is no surprise that our humour can get fairly combative. Our zingers are not just idle asides, but acutely observed and calculated, expertly calibrated to hit their mark. The more time we spend in 'them-or-us' scenarios, the more integral they become to how we win or lose. Do they land? Then we win. Do they miss? Then the verdict in the room may turn on us. Even if – or precisely because – our humour is piercingly on-point. Are they not entertained? Sure they are, at least for a while. But even our most loyal audiences can grow weary of our barrage of banter. So we have to know when to change the track.

That is a hard calibration for us to make. We tend to take aim at anything that crosses our path, using any weapon that comes to hand, fair means or foul, overkill or not. We may find this quite exhilarating in the moment. But the more we come to rely on that, the more effort it may take us to keep our ironic distance from the world, as antagonistic self-assertion increasingly shines through and bleeds into our jocular façade. If we do not watch out, we lose what makes preserving ourselves worthwhile in the first place. Even if there is much about the world we cannot abide, we are not going to change it merely by tearing it down. If we truly think of ourselves as a model, then we must show the world a reason to be more like us too – a light shining another way.

The space for contrarian indulgence

Being a Jokester can be a highly compelling experience – but one we may enjoy best in isolation. We have a powerful sense that we ourselves, our time and effort, and what we care about are of irreplaceable value – so we bury them deep, hide them from prying eyes, and put up a protective forcefield of hilarity. We deal with the troublesome things we encounter by using our guile and humour to cut them down to size, keeping everything in proportion. Best of all, we can spot what 'fits' and what does not from a mile off, and we are unerringly quick off the mark to call out nonsense in the world.

Other thinker-types have much to gain by being a bit more Jokester in their mindsets. We are extremely attuned to what makes us tick, and we have a clear sense of purpose – which would benefit Revellers careering from attraction to attraction, or Agonisers who routinely put others first and themselves last. We know when, and how, to keep our cards close to our chest – we can plot and plan without being transparent about it, as Cool Cats often are, and without letting slip our displeasure as much as Quibblers do. We cleave consistently to our way of doing things, and we find advancing it endlessly fun, rather than the stressful chore it is for Worrywarts, or the grim necessity it is for Gloomsters.

As with all the thinker-types, we also have our negative sides, which we need to keep in check. The flipside of protecting what we value is that we can be selfish, and shut out what matters to those around us. We take umbrage as soon as things stop going wholly our way, and reach all too easily for our rolodex of put-downs in retribution. Once we embark on that route, we swiftly harden our hearts and slide towards belligerence. At our worst, we come off as aloof and vain, unable to hide that we think our way of doing things is unambiguously better than other people's. By treating everything we do not directly care about as essentially ridiculous, we can seem dismissive and shallow – and risk losing other people's goodwill.

To counteract these characteristics, we can take cues from several other thinker-types. As an antidote to our hair-trigger reactions, we can always try the Happy Camper's more relaxed view of good-natured fun, or take a salutary dose of Cool Cat equanimity. To appreciate other people better, we can take a leaf out of the gregarious Keen Bean's book, or learn to love them the way Revellers do. And if ever leaning fully into the lighter side of our nature seems like the wrong approach, we can learn from Gloomsters, Hotheads, or Quibblers how to be more open about our misgivings.

We walk a high tightrope, and not always out of choice – but it often pays high dividends. We are like jackals cackling on the sidelines of the herd, keeping a safe distance but always primed to jump in for the spoils. Society can be a silly place, and we unfailingly poke fun at the nonsense others may be too blind or blinkered to see. By calling it out, we carve out a space for something better. But the joke has to end somewhere. If nothing is sacred, nothing serious, then we become paralysed, with no path left to turn down. Knock everything down, and nothing will ever get built. Ultimately, society needs us to play the role of jester, but not so much so that the court collapses around our ears.

CHAPTER 3

Gloomster

When the void comes calling, some people are readier to face it than others. A few years back, a friend was trekking around Bolivia with his sister. Against his advice, she took a mountain bike up the Yungas Road – *El Camino de la Muerte*, all hairpin bends and jaw-dropping views – with some other holidayers she had met at their hostel. After she rounded a particularly treacherous turn, her companions suddenly found her stretched out in the road, with a halo of dust and gravel settling around her. My friend got the call from the hostel telling him what had happened. From that moment on, everything faded into a dark miasma. The trip to hospital, the gut-wrenching horror of calling their parents. Seconds, minutes, hours inching by as she hovered between life and death.

Waiting in the corridor, my friend brooded on every choice, every move, that led his sister into the path of the rockslide. He pounded himself with reproaches – had he done enough to warn her, should he have gone with her? – and steeled himself for every possible outcome. Mercifully, after a day or so, she awoke. Aching, disoriented, with acute memory loss – but still in one piece. A long, unsteady path to recovery followed: physio, therapy, endless medical check-ups. And my friend was there every step of the way, wordlessly reorienting his life to make sure he was available to take care of her. Moving house to be just a short drive away. Changing his medical specialism to work more closely on how to treat traumatic injury. Never fully convinced that his sister was out of the woods for good. Never quite shaking off the feeling he had failed her when the moment came.

The best term for this mindset is the *Gloomster*. What are the giveaways that we might be inclined towards this mindset too? Are we the sort of person who expects doom and failure to lurk around every corner? Do we have a tendency to inflate our problems into insurmountable catastrophes? Withdraw into ourselves when we get overwhelmed by the frenetic pace of the world? Feel like perpetual bystanders, passed over while others hog the limelight? Does everything look and feel just a little bit noir? If so, we may well be a Gloomster at heart.

This mindset is palpably the opposite of the Happy Camper's bright technicolour, more or less inverting the fundamental elements of their thinking (see fig. 3.1). As Gloomsters, our main emotional state is one of **sadness**, with a mix of five underlying personality traits – **emotional**, **introverted**, **disagreeable**, **conscientious**, and **closed**. Sadness is another emotion that can align with personality traits from both ends of the various trait spectrums. That is why it plays such a significant role not just for the Gloomster, but also the Agoniser in the next chapter.

When we combine sadness with this cluster of personality traits, what emerges is a certain kind of glum dejection. Psychology typically finds that emotionality and closedness have the strongest association with sadness in its murkiest, most maudlin form. They let us get easily derailed by the negativity we meet in our day-to-day lives – stewing, getting stuck in our morose mood. Our introversion and disagreeableness detach us from what is happening around us, leading us to absorb ourselves in our own inner lives, and quietly opt out of other people's company and concerns.

Meanwhile, our conscientiousness keeps us locked in a cycle of intense mulling and self-recrimination, until we lose the will to break out – which just goes on longer and longer the more the world fails to live up to our expectations.[1]

We Gloomsters pay attention to 'bad news' above all. We also generally absorb it from only a small number of different sources, sometimes fixating on just one or two key details about what is going on – things we have just found out, things we already knew, or things we remember from longer ago. Our view of the world is decidedly cloudy, and we often retreat to safely middle-of-the-road stances, following our tried-and-tested rules of thumb to form our more complex opinions. We tend to engage only reluctantly with other people's views – except if ever we find ourselves needing to rethink our assumptions about the world. When that happens, we latch tightly onto what they think and dwell on it at considerable length, as part of a larger process of 'repairing' what we believe.

Becoming a Gloomster

The Gloomster's mindset is rooted in melancholy. It is an inescapable anchor weighing on us, a pallor draining our surroundings of their vibrancy. Above all, it is intensely private: it hits us deep in our core. Nobody else around us feels it (or so it seems to us), while we are dragged down into the depths. Secluded in our solitude, we survey the world and our hearts falter – as all we expect to see is a morass of infinite, ashen grey. If the sun shines for Happy Campers, then for us Gloomsters, the people we meet, the things we discover, the situations we enter into are often obscured by clouds of thick, dreary fog. They are the stereotypical optimists of the thinker-type family – and we are the pessimists.

The social experiences that shape us into Gloomsters are quite unlike those that underpin a Happy Camper or Jokester mindset.

Sometimes, things just go wrong, and it is not obvious that it is anybody's particular fault – maybe we are caught in a wave of layoffs as our company goes bust, or our whole world is turned upside down when a close relative dies. Perhaps these events were inevitable, perhaps freakish coincidences or sudden accidents. But just because matters are out of our control does not make them any easier to cope with. If things keep piling up – insult upon injury, upon injustice, upon indignity – and we find ourselves powerless to do anything to change our situation, that becomes a recipe for resignation. In the worst case, if the message we keep getting is that there is nothing to be done, then at some point, we will just start doing nothing. We withdraw, lose interest, abstain.

Fig. 3.1: The Gloomster

Mental Outlook			
Personality traits			
	Emotional	▮▮▮▮▮▮▮▮▮▮	Emotionally stable
	Conscientious	▮▮▮▮▮▮▮▮▮▮	Careless
	Honest–humble	▮▮▮▮▮▮▮▮▮▮	Biased–superior
	Extroverted	▮▮▮▮▮▮▮▮▮▮	Introverted
	Agreeable	▮▮▮▮▮▮▮▮▮▮	Disagreeable
	Open to experience	▮▮▮▮▮▮▮▮▮▮	Closed to experience
Emotions			
	Angry	▮▮▮▮▮▮▮▮▮▮	Calm
	Fearful (anxious)	▮▮▮▮▮▮▮▮▮▮	Eager (seeking)
	Disgusted	▮▮▮▮▮▮▮▮▮▮	Desiring
	Happy (joyful)	▮▮▮▮▮▮▮▮▮▮	Sad

Mental Picture				
	Information			
	Selective			Indiscriminate
	Fast			Slow
	Personality-congruent			Emotion-congruent
	High			Low
	New		Previous	Long-unused
	Positive			Negative
	Diverse			Limited
	Predispositions			
	Conservative/reactionary			Progressive/radical
	Revise/revisit			Defend/maintain
	Emotion-congruent			Reasoning-congruent
	New			Previous
	Compliant			Defiant
	Pro			Con
Formulating Thoughts	Reasoning			
	Heuristic			Non-heuristic
	Rational			Irrational
	Reasonable			Unreasonable

That is a fairly extreme scenario, however, even though many of us face it now and again over the course of our lives. More common is that we get just enough taste of disaster that it glowers like a thundercloud on the horizon – enough that we feel guilty if we do not do something to head it off. We are told, or tell ourselves, that something *can* be done, if only we have the wherewithal to do it. We still have a chance to fix the problem as long as we keep our eyes peeled, stay disciplined, and keep doing what we have previously learned to do. If we stop, we will be letting ourselves and everybody else down. Pressure to avoid being a disappointment places a heavy burden on our shoulders. Every time we fail to live up to it, we are reminded of our seeming inferiority – by awkward silences and disapproving looks, critical feedback and corrections to our work. We internalise this, until eventually we can hold ourselves in a certain level of contempt. The danger is that we stop trusting our instincts, and grow too ashamed to keep going at all.

The seeds of this may be planted by our earliest experiences, if our parents and mentors treat even our slightest flaws with exacting severity. We forget our homework and our teacher shames us in front of our entire class. We miss a crucial tackle in the grudge match against our rivals, and our coach cold-shoulders us and drops us from the starting XI. If we receive too many of these 'disappointment cards' in our youth, they teach us to be oversensitive, 'on edge', leaving us prone to becoming moody – whereas, if our elders and superiors use them on us more sparingly, they may in fact sharpen our focus. They can motivate us to be a better child, citizen, or employee, and inspire us to greater diligence and virtue. But they are a risky gambit all the same. If the same people push us too far, if they try too hard to make us feel bad, then we may simply give up. Whereas our other emotions spur us to think and behave in highly specific ways, psychological research has found that one of the major things sadness encourages in us is inaction.[2] We try to find a way out – not by averting disaster, but by washing our hands of it.

More than other thinker-types, Gloomsters incorporate things we learned or lived through a long time ago into how we think today. We reflect on the many moving pieces that added up to create the situations in which we find ourselves – or the myriad ways we have had them imposed upon us. We can revisit chapters from our past in light of recent events; we reopen wounds, plumb yet again the depths of despondency. Every bill we struggle to pay today casts a retrospective shadow over every 'unjustified' treat we splashed out on in the past. Any promotion stymied or raise denied calls to mind the times we last felt stuck in a work rut, with no apparent prospect of escape. We remember every time we felt the oppressive weight of vast impersonal forces beyond our control stopping us from doing *anything* – and making all our options seem to stretch miles out of reach. All of them are grist to the mill, mixing into the greyscale tint we give our image of reality. And each one offers us more clues to answer our underlying question: how did we get here? How did it come to this?

In these situations, we withdraw primarily to regulate how sad we feel – about our present, our past, and the way the two bleed into each other. Our withdrawal takes both an active and a passive form. Actively, we remove ourselves from the situations that make us sad; we disengage and walk away from whatever we are doing and whoever we are with. In the most extreme case, like *The Scarlet Letter*'s Hester Prynne, humiliated and ostracised by the judgement of a puritanical society, we may try to chart a path to dignity and selfhood within the confines of our isolation. Passively, we mope around in a lethargic torpor – unable to summon the initiative to take part in any new projects or relationships. Here, the countervailing extreme is that of Miss Havisham, ensconced in her wedding dress amid the decaying remnants of her house, with only a few dependants to ease her desolation. In both cases, the oppressive weight of our aloneness causes us to turn inwards.

The ever-mounting costs of isolation

In part, we become prone to morbid turns inward because we grow intimately familiar with how stressful it is when we are ripped out of the normal course of events. We know the world is uncertain, and that obstacles will emerge to thwart our aspirations. How deeply we internalise that is down to how far we are convinced that these obstacles are 'owed' to us. Have we earned them through some deep fault of our own, some lax mistake or dreadful oversight? Are we getting the karma we deserve? Is it cosmic payback for that lie we told our parents, those sweets we shoplifted, that dress we borrowed and never gave back? If we always blame ourselves, that can easily trigger us into a series of chronic neuroses.

In turn, this can rattle our sense of self, turning it into a precarious house of cards that the slightest gust can dislodge. We wait with a certain sense of foreboding for the dereliction that will tip us over the edge – to some extent, we already resign ourselves to the fact that some fateful moment will inevitably come. We brace ourselves for the long, slow task of dragging ourselves out of the pit, limb by limb. And the surer we feel, deep down, that there is little we can do to change things, the closer we can slide towards despair. If nothing – no petition, no protest, no vote – manages to move the dial one jot to make the world a brighter place for us, then acquiescence, and lingering private pain, is our only choice.

Once we come to see the world in such a bleak light, this can fill us with an all-encompassing feeling of pity. Pity for the world that looks so dismal and cheerless from our perspective. Pity for other people who cannot see the blackness. Pity for ourselves because we can. Our pity isolates us from our surroundings, and them from us, a glass through which we can only see each other darkly. We begin to operate in a solipsistic reality shaped more and more by our woe. Wretched, smothered into silence, trapped in our own hell, we may no longer feel truly seen by those around us.

This can lead to a feeling of friendlessness, which we experience as an acute rejection. We fixate on all the ways our sadness holds us back, leaves us left out and left behind, with a steady realisation that there is a barrier that some things simply cannot cross. That only we can wrestle with our inner anchor because only we can feel it pulling us down. Only we carry the weight of our aims and aspirations when they are frustrated and crushed, because nobody can quite relate to what the loss means to us. Our hearts grow sluggish, and we create around ourselves a kind of bubble of negativity. The darkened glass becomes thicker, tinted ever inkier colours, growing ever more impervious to letting light out or in.

We may conclude that we are so drastically at odds with those around us that the go-to channels of advocacy or care we might expect to rely on are closed to us. But if nobody cares about us, then at least we Gloomsters will take care of ourselves. And *care* certainly lies readily available at the forefront of our minds. Studies of the strategies people in all kinds of contexts use to combat intense grief or depression acknowledge the prominent roles of self-agency, self-centring, and self-sufficiency.[3] When we feel these pronounced forms of sadness, we may decide that we cannot wait for external support to arrive, and begin the self-care process ourselves. We turn inwards into our private sphere – our household, and those within it – to nurse ourselves, and we look to ourselves to sort ourselves out, give ourselves the support we need. We may cope through journaling, physical exercise, drawing, painting, or other forms of artistic expression. Or our self-treatment can be more psychologically targeted, through meditation or analgesics. In either case, we learn to be autarkic.

Yet in these moments, we cannot hold ourselves so far aloof that we omit, or refuse, to ask for support. Our sadness can confine us in a web largely of our own making, turning us into pallid ghosts, invisible mourners at a party that goes on unabated. If we let it cut us off from the world, we can lose sight of the fact that help is actually available to us – as long as we learn to look for it in the right places. In *The Bell Jar*, Esther Greenwood feels a deep gulf between her and those around her, an undertow of disillusionment she feels they cannot relate to, imposed on her through their stifling expectations. Yet her path to recovering her agency is made possible through her benefactor Philomena Guinea and Dr Nolan, whose sympathetic intercessions – personal and professional – allow Esther to start navigating her way out of her hopeless situation. If we insist on turning inwards, and only taking our own counsel, we risk missing out on the potentially transformative insights that those around us have to offer.

Keeping score of our failures

Whenever we feel as though we have lost control over our lives, floundering under the weight of the obstacles piled up in our path, we dial back to where we do have power – what we *can* plan for, where we *can* salvage a sense of self. First and foremost, we grieve what we have lost. When we say we 'count' our losses, we mean that literally. We dwell, individually, excruciatingly, on each one of the things that sadden us, turning them over and over in our minds. Every life goal left unmet – that coral reef we never dived to, the clarinet we never picked up again, the friend we never got to say sorry to. The inheritance of heartache – archived texts from 'the one that got away', shoeboxes full of letters and old photos, private languages and terms of endearment with nobody to tell them to. We 'go deep' as we acknowledge the half-built edifices of futures that will never come about, extracting every last exquisite ounce of sorrow.

In our grief, we craft our ledger of losses into a narrative, trying to make sense of what has happened. This is the tragedy of Clarissa, the eponymous Mrs Dalloway, plagued by regret over her past choices and the paths she could have taken instead. We think of our lives – how we wanted to lead them, and how they have turned out – in acutely tragic terms. Our fall from grace, our heroic trial, our paradise lost. Our overriding feeling is one of shame. Disconsolate at our abortive efforts, determined to learn from our experiences, we promise ourselves to undertake a wholesale epic odyssey to reconstruct our sense of self. The more we are used to buying into the sources of our sadness, the more we see them as things we ought to fix.

We are especially prone to internalising narratives that present the troubles we face as issues of private fault rather than wider public concern – derelictions of our own that brought us to where we are now. Is the planet dying? Yes, because we put the wrong kind of plastic in the bin, took a flight instead of a train to Barcelona, and ate steak not seitan the last time we went out. Are we overweight? Yes, so we need to count every single one of those calories, do those extra 20 reps on the weights machine, stay on top of our 'sleep debt'. 'Civic duty'. 'Personal responsibility'. Never mind who might be pumping toxins into our air, our food, our land and water supply, and never mind who might be letting them get away with it – we still feel a heavy dose of personal guilt.

Even if we are loath to ask for help from people who seem to navigate the world more successfully than us, we may nonetheless try to learn from them – especially if they are aware of its dark sides too. Agonisers find their own share of heartache in the world, so how come they are able to get on and get by when we find that so hard? What lets Cool Cats keep everything in such well-ordered perspective? How do Quibblers keep putting up with so many things they obviously dislike? And how might we translate those capabilities into our own Gloomster mindsets?

But these scrupulous comparisons only get us so far. If we are not careful, looking too avidly at who else does it better may only make us more depressed. Every good example and positive role model we find is liable to boomerang back to us as a reminder that, if we are ever going to get out, we must be the ones to do it. We feel we owe it to ourselves, because – ultimately – we only have ourselves to blame. But we cannot simply punish ourselves in the right direction. Getting there takes self-sympathy too: turning the pity we feel so intensely into an understanding of where we are coming from.

We need to recognise that along with shame, we also carry a lot of guilt. If only we work hard enough, practise and read enough, make enough notes, we will make the grade and prove our worth. And, of course, we often feel that we could and should be working *harder*, practising and reading and noting *more*. No matter if we want to be a rocket scientist or a rock guitarist – that is the way to get there. And if we do not, that is because, somewhere along the line, we dropped the ball. The best thing we can do is own up to it.

Yet we must also keep this within healthy parameters. We may get so caught up in this process of punitively comparing ourselves with those around us that we essentially forget why we are doing it in the first place. We can get rigidly stuck on beating ourselves up for a whole series of frustrations that might not even necessarily be our fault. We may internalise more than our fair share of responsibility, insisting on holding ourselves to stringent standards. We make ourselves protagonists in our very own disaster movie, castigating ourselves for being neither as good as other people nor as good as we could have been. In the (approximate) words of boxer-turned-longshoreman Terry Malloy in *On the Waterfront*: 'We coulda been contenders.' We parent ourselves in a very austere, narrow way, imposing strict procedures, exacting standards, and firm controls – but with too little of the gentleness and patience that should go alongside.

Avoiding the pitfalls of rock bottom

More than many other thinker-types, we Gloomsters are prone to losing ourselves in our intense self-preoccupation. What makes this potentially dangerous is that we are also more susceptible to extreme emotion – less able to calibrate how we feel, or stop it constricting and wresting control of our thinking. Once we start the descent into our lonely melancholy, it can be very easy for us to keep going until we hit rock bottom. That is the mental skill we need to develop the most urgently. We have to accept and validate the full intensity of what we are feeling, let ourselves sit with it. But we also have to let our minds breathe, pausing on every step rather than rushing headlong into the crypt.

It is important not to mistake our profound sadness for a straightforward case of depression. Current psychiatric scholarship is particularly adamant that we need to maintain a clear difference between the two, so that we avoid under- or over-diagnosing one where the other is more apt.[4] Of course, it is possible that certain shocks in our lives tip us over from a relatively healthy state of grief into out-and-out depression – including extreme cases of loss, such as bereavements or breakups. But it is rare for negative experiences alone to cause this without the compounding influence of a host of other biological and social factors, from diet and physical health to medication and embedded trauma. We are quite capable of running melancholic in response to the setbacks we live through – even over a longer period of time – without becoming catatonic, or seriously jeopardising our ability to engage with the people around us. And the mere fact that we tend to let these setbacks balloon from tiny molehills into gigantic mountains in our minds is not, by itself, grounds for medical intervention.

In part, the key to this is that we Gloomsters do not take the hammer-blows life deals us entirely lying down. We know they are coming, which turns up the throttle on our anguished minds, sending them into overdrive. The longer this lasts, the more we may feel that the only way to survive is by giving vent to our struggles. We placate ourselves with a spending spree, impulse-buying a pile of romance novels, outlandish shirts, chocolates to stuff our face with on the couch. Or we try to shed our lives like an old snakeskin, downsizing our worldly possessions and taking ourselves off to pastures new.

It is one of our most unusual characteristics that we feel our loss before it has actually happened. We may feel 'anticipatory nostalgia' as a much-needed restful weekend draws to a close, or premonitory sadness if we contemplate losing a grandparent or having to get the family dog put down in future.[5] Our pessimistic tendency gives us a kind of advance-warning system, which allows us to pre-empt the actual 'zero hour' itself – to prepare for how we will respond to it, if not exactly mitigate its effects. So we start to plot and plan. What do we salvage when the moment comes? What can we do to try and pick ourselves up off rock bottom?

Our pessimism puts us in the right frame of mind to take such practical steps ahead of time. But left unchecked, this tendency can start to warp how we approach our surroundings. Since we are prone to catastrophising, we see not just shadows lurking behind every corner, but gaping voids – each of which we half expect to swallow us up. Yet at the same time, our pessimism can also block our ability to mentally sidestep these voids or close them down. We expend so much energy preparing for the aftermath of 'zero hour' that we crowd out our ability to think about how we might stave it off: we lose sight of the prevention because we are so focused on the cure (or on its palliation). However much we might try to steel ourselves, in the end, we still feel that have no choice but to let what is happening happen. Our sadness makes us surrender meekly when the moment finally comes, greeting the frustration of our aspirations with bitter, stoic acceptance. If we acquiesce too far to the inevitable, we risk confining ourselves in our own sense of demoralised resignation.

During our mid-twenties, two friends were going through protracted breakups – one after three years with his partner, the other after five with hers. As so often, problems first reared their heads, then grew more serious, then remained unresolved. I asked them both what was keeping them going in their relationships. 'Our lives are just so entwined now.' 'Our families are really invested in us.' 'We're meant to go to the Maldives in the summer.' Prior commitments, expectations, obligations. Ties that bind. But might they be binding them to the wrong person? Could they bind with someone better? 'It could certainly be worse.'

True enough, both had had a pretty miserable run of it. Even little things began to count as progress – a good day here, a kind word there. A lifeline of normality they could cling to, enough to survive the swirling vortex for now, but not enough to escape the chance of drowning. Was this a life he could live forever? 'Well, I guess this is it.' The future she wanted to sign up for? 'It feels like it's the end of the road.' As it turned out, it was not. But they had convinced themselves it was, shrunk themselves into passive witnesses in their own lives. So much so that it took their partners breaking up with them to start them on the road to taking back control.

Our sadness tells us to keep on caring, even as it also tells us to accept the sources of our care. Yet we cannot go through our lives trapped in the logic of permanent triage, wondering if every moment is 'the big one' that will bring our catastrophic fantasies to fruition. If we let this kind of self-sympathising fill up our entire consciousness, we may find ourselves drifting passively through the world in reflective self-seclusion, overawed by the seeming futility of putting up a fight. Existentially disillusioned Hamlets, driving those around us either to confusion, like Rosencrantz and Guildenstern, or distraction, like Ophelia. This can set up a potentially debilitating tendency in our mindsets. The more we mourn our frustrated aims and aspirations, the more we jeopardise our will to pick ourselves up and carry on going. We have to learn to break ourselves out of our interminable loop of dour contemplation. If bad things are coming our way, then they are coming whether or not we linger compulsively over them – and doing so is hardly going to make them any better.

The path through the darkness

So how might we escape the temptation to simply wallow in our resigned isolation? If we become too dejected about our chances in the world, we risk falling into nihilism, a decadent sense of world-weariness that magnifies – and exaggerates – the hopelessness of our situation.[6] The danger is not so much that we take out our frustrations on anyone that comes near us: sadness cannot really sustain outward violence, so it takes quite a lot for us to become hostile. More likely is that we turn our weapons in on ourselves. In a sense, we find ourselves in competition with ourselves – the selves we could have been had we achieved what we set out to, and not suffered any setbacks. Cut off from the world, we can become our own harshest critics, our own judges and juries.

What can save us from this is realising that we are actually *not* alone – that there are people out there who not only want to help us, but intimately understand where we are coming from. A handful of my friends have – like me – lost someone dear to them before their time. Parent, partner, brother or sister, friend. A shattering loss, which everyone goes through in their own way. One, a historian and journalist, processed the loss of his father by writing: articles of breathtaking eloquence, poetry of fragile dignity, a beautiful piece of religious liturgy. He pulled back and found solace in his inner monologue, in part because he found less than he hoped for around him. His partner and family were just wired differently; even their best-intentioned sympathy could not meet him where he was at. The everyday tasks they needed him to do – chores, finances, raising children, the bricks-and-mortar of life going on – became brutal reminders of how alone he felt.

What he needed was people who had been through what he had. So, between us, we formed our own alternative community of solidarity, based on the universally accepted healing powers of food. 'Beef and grief'. 'Fries and cries'. 'Quorn and mourn' (for the vegetarians). We turned our sorrow into a multi-sensory indulgence. We literally dined out on it. We gave it a space where we could visit it, pick it up, hold it as long as we needed it – and then *put it down*. So it would stop casting a pall over every other experience in our lives. So he (in particular) could start to look forward to a life that was more than merely regretful consideration of 'what might have been'.

Finding 'our own' like this is only part of the story. At the heart of why we Gloomsters turn so strongly towards those who get us in this way is that we convince ourselves that the rest of the world has forsaken us. To echo the ruminations of the Ent Treebeard in *Lord of the Rings*: 'We are not altogether on anybody's side, because nobody is altogether on our side.' None of them are quite doing the work we think they should be doing to get familiar with the darkness the world shows them – and not just as a distant prospect or an abstract proposition, but as a constant reality. They have little to say to us, we think, and we have nothing to say to them.

But that is exactly the tendency we need to challenge in ourselves. The others can learn from us – specifically, learn that if something goes wrong for them, it is not necessarily always somebody else's fault. Sometimes, it just *is* our own fault: we recognise that more than most. And sometimes, things just do not go the way we want them to for no obvious reason. So rather than spoiling for a fight, or firing off zingers in every direction, Hotheads and Jokesters could do with adopting a less accusatory, less up-and-at-'em perspective, and give in a bit more to quiet resignation. Our role then becomes to gauge how to bring this insight to the thinker-types who need it. How much of our mournful tale they will tolerate us sharing in one go. How to sell them on our stygian pitch; how to tailor it to the language of grievance, relief, unease, and so on, that each thinker-type is likeliest to buy. So that we may be solemn, but not too solemn for the rest of the world to understand.

At the same time, we need to reconsider if they might not also have a point. Perhaps they are right that not all is darkening in the world, that the way of the future may just as easily lead up as well as down. Or maybe others *are* at fault and we do not have to shoulder all the blame. It is all too easy for us to get overinvested in beating ourselves up mentally, as a way of holding ourselves to account. After all, effective or not, it is only supposed to be a means to an end, not an end in itself. Instead of letting the shadowy tunnel envelop us, perhaps we can let ourselves admit that there might be light at the end of it – and that Happy Campers, Keen Beans, and the rest are not categorically wrong to try and find it.

In that vein, we need to learn to back ourselves. To have more confidence in our ability to leverage our experiences, especially the bad ones, and break the cycle of inevitability between past, present, and future. Even if we assume that all our efforts might meet with failure eventually, that does not mean we should not give them our best shot in the meantime – just to see how far we can take them. This is the logic of contingency planning. We stress-test our portfolios to see what they can handle: asset bubble bursting, sovereign debt default, stock market crash. We wargame how our security services would respond to national threats: cyberattack, superpower invasion, terrorist incident. We push our 'worst-case scenarios' to the point of forlorn hope.

We try to pre-empt disaster by making it less likely that we will end up wishing we had considered this, done that, expected the other. We shore up our defences, mobilise our resources, get things in working order. Perimeter checked and double-checked. Stockpiles fully stocked, with spares in reserve. Every last bit of machinery cleaned, oiled, and primed for action. We know we will regret it if we do not, if we realise afterwards that there was more we could have done. It is this tendency that came into its own for my friend when his sister had her horrendous accident. It allowed him to marshal all his reserves to help her – and himself – come through and out the other side.

Ironically, this is by far one of the most useful services we provide to other people – even if we do so at considerable cost to ourselves. After all, somebody needs to be drawing up the contingency plans. We assiduously work out our fallback positions, our baselines, the minimum functionality that makes us viable. And we will do it for 'our own' too whenever and wherever we can. But they could be doing it for themselves (and for us) too – and learn from us how to do it better. In this respect, at least, *all* the others could do with being a bit more Gloomster from time to time.

The method in our meekness

Being a Gloomster can sometimes feel like drowning in an ocean of darkness that is entirely and solely our own. But more than most, we put our own capabilities into meaningful perspective, and astutely reject the heroic delusion that we can handle anything the world throws at us. Our minds are mobile to the point of overdrive, eking out every last scrap of insight, and we have a rare dexterity at building what we learn into deep, complex narratives. Our gift is to act as society's ready-made warning bells. We are acutely sensitive to costs and losses; we put them into full context, and we plan for the worst possible outcome – not to prevent it, because often we cannot, but to ready ourselves for its arrival.

There is much of value in our mindset. Living in the now – as cheery Happy Campers or offended Quibblers both do – is all very well, but to really clarify where things have gone wrong, we need to pore thoroughly over the past. We must do the work to acknowledge our own flaws, and expend significant effort to repair them wherever possible – a lesson in imperfection that Hotheads and Jokesters would do well to learn. Ultimately, we reconcile ourselves to things going wrong, and adjust to the new reality rather than continuing to deny it – which can help dampen the hyperbolic buzz that Revellers and Keen Beans seem to feel about their every interaction.

But there are also evident downsides to how we view the world. At our lowest, we can become inclined to question whether there is a point to doing anything at all, so convinced are we that whatever we do is doomed. This makes it hard to get any projects of change or improvement off the ground, when we are perennial naysayers pouring cold water on others' hopes. We easily get trapped in self-reinforcing cycles of neglect, and lose the ability to focus on anything beyond our own four walls. This can sideline us as lugubrious shadows, push us to the margins of our social groups. Worst of all, we fixate so much on holding ourselves to account for our past failings that we end up failing all over again now, standing by rather than stepping up.

Mercifully, we are primed to pick up tips on what we can do better, and add new dimensions to our mindsets. To become less emotionally unsteady, to see the negatives without drowning in a flood of feelings about them, we need some Cool Cat sobriety or Agoniser venting. This will help us avoid our murkiest depths, and instead stay nearer the surface – either consciously, like Revellers, or more intuitively, like Happy Campers. Above all, we need to process our concerns and considerations without poleaxing our motivation to do anything about them – which both Quibblers and Worrywarts have cracked in different ways.

We are the archivists of the pain the world bestows on us. We stand vigil, like elephants lingering broken-hearted over their fallen family, returning to visit them long after they are gone. When things simply get too much, we try to detach ourselves from what is happening – 'this far and no further', 'we just want out'. But in detaching, we cannot let ourselves sink without a trace. When even the slightest hurt becomes too much and makes us pull away, we stop being able to discriminate between what we can probably handle and what really is unbearable. If all we offer is despair, it will not be long before others despair of us. Society depends on us to know when things cannot go on the same way anymore – but we must chart the new path together, without falling by the wayside, and not take on burdens that grow too great to carry.

CHAPTER 4

Agoniser

Society needs people who are willing to put themselves on the line. When I was at university, a minor scandal erupted at a neighbouring college: contraceptives, freely available in all restrooms, were being damaged en masse. Punctured, ripped, put beyond use. Every time they were replaced, it happened again. The college authorities were unmoved. 'Nothing to be done – an internal matter for the student body.' Outraged at their indifference, one student took matters into her own hands. She organised a network of volunteers in every student house, each with a safe stash of contraceptives. The network grew into a support group. Anti-harassment, relationship mediation, sexual health advice. It spread to other colleges, welfare teams across the university threw their weight behind it. At the centre was the student who began it – cajoling, collaborating, giving impromptu talks and sending sternly worded emails whenever needed.

But her role did not go unnoticed. Senior figures in her college quietly suggested that her activities were getting in the way of her studies, and her tutors were considering remedial action. Anonymous hate mail began to arrive, drink-sodden abuse, crude misogyny, religious zealotry. Undeterred, she pushed on. She negotiated with her college to make interfering with sexual welfare a disciplinary offence. She pushed her student council to take over the support group and write it into its constitution. Finally, encouraged by supporters across the university, she ran for the student union. Her mission: roll out what she had started across the whole student body. The students duly rewarded her with a crushing victory.

The intense, pained sensitivity that gave her the impetus to take such a fraught situation and find a way to help those who needed it, no matter the adversity she faced, belongs to a type we can call the *Agoniser*. What might mark us out as members of team Agoniser too? Do we find ourselves caring, strongly and in detail, about a huge range of causes? Are we highly attuned to the world's endless supply of suffering? Do we have a powerful, easily wounded sense of justice and fairness, stubbornly refusing to accept that things must be a certain way because that is just how they are? And does it eat away at us if we think we have let other people down?

This thinker-type, which rounds out our opening foursome, resembles something of a turbulent emotional maelstrom that tugs at us from every side (see fig. 4.1). We Agonisers are **sad**, sometimes profoundly so, with occasional flashes of **anger** and **fear**, underlaid by an asymmetric blend of three pronounced personality traits – **extroverted**, **honest–humble**, and, especially, **open**. This is one of the most complex emotional combinations of the whole thinker-type family. It is predominantly 'led' by the intersections that sadness has with these traits. But a few key parts of it emerge from specific moral associations that anger and fear gain when our care and grief are focused on those around us.

From our cocktail of emotions and personality traits arises an attitude of sympathetic distress. Openness tallies above all with this cluster of emotions, slightly more with sadness and fear than anger. It gives us an urgency about finding our authentic purpose in the world – a niggling sense of frustration that makes us find new and unexpected ways to throw ourselves into the breach. As we do so, our extroversion and honesty–humility together lead us to turn to others for a guiding 'steer'. We bring their concerns out into the open and take them on as our own source of motivation.[1]

We Agonisers focus on the worst news available – new, familiar, or ancient. The judgements we come to about it are complex, soaring to exalted heights one moment, plunging to the dingiest depths the next. Sometimes we cleave to what others believe, sometimes we veer sharply away – but all in all, we are broad-minded, willing and able to update our views fluently when we need to. How we contemplate our way to fully developed opinions is just as intricate and nuanced. We are equally capable of absorbing others' views as pushing back against them, and we mix our favoured mental short-cuts with fairly systematic logic as the occasion demands.

Fig. 4.1: The Agoniser

MENTAL OUTLOOK

Personality traits

Open to experience		Closed to experience
Extroverted		Introverted
Honest–humble		Biased–superior
Conscientious		Careless
Emotional		Emotionally stable
Agreeable		Disagreeable

Emotions

Angry		Calm
Fearful (anxious)		Eager (seeking)
Disgusted		Desiring
Happy (joyful)		Sad

AGONISER

MENTAL PICTURE	**Information**		
	Selective	▐▐▐▐▐▐▐▐	Indiscriminate
	New ▐▐▐ Previous	▐▐▐▐	Long-unused
	Personality-congruent	▐▐▐▐▐▐▐	Emotion-congruent
	High	▐▐▐▐▐▐▐▐	Low
	Diverse	▐▐▐▐▐▐▐	Limited
	Fast	▐▐▐▐▐▐▐▐	Slow
	Positive	▐▐▐▐▐▐▐▐	Negative
	Predispositions		
	Emotion-congruent	▐▐▐▐▐▐▐▐	Reasoning-congruent
	New	▐▐▐▐▐▐▐▐	Previous
	Revise/revisit	▐▐▐▐▐▐▐▐	Defend/maintain
	Compliant	▐▐▐▐▐▐▐▐	Defiant
	Pro	▐▐▐▐▐▐▐▐	Con
	Conservative/reactionary	▐▐▐▐▐▐▐▐	Progressive/radical
FORMULATING THOUGHTS	**Reasoning**		
	Heuristic	▐▐▐▐▐▐▐▐	Non-heuristic
	Reasonable	▐▐▐▐▐▐▐▐	Unreasonable
	Rational	▐▐▐▐▐▐▐▐	Irrational

Becoming an Agoniser

Agonisers' essential experience of the world is marked by an acute, sudden, and excruciating feeling of torment. It invades our minds, obstructing whichever paths we were determinedly pursuing before. Our sadness, inflected with fear and anger, manifests as crippling doubt that spreads spasmodically into our chests, at times even choking the breath right out of our lungs. And we strain against it, fighting the suffering that threatens to engulf us. We Agonisers are highly attuned to what is going on around us. We are constantly on the lookout for causes of concern. It is when things are looking troubling that we spring to life and get on our guard – the moments when our strength and resilience are really put to the test.

The social experiences that awaken this mindset within us are ones where we confront situations of moral urgency that demand a prompt salvific intervention. Emergency services dealing with the fallout of a natural disaster, public authorities simmering down a civil disorder – or parents seeking treatment for a sickly child. This is especially the case where the solutions are not quick and easy, but require complex thought and effort. Perhaps they are too much for the victims in the situation to handle themselves – they may be helpless, injured, or lack some crucial resources. Or perhaps they are beyond any one person's scope and require a 'coalition of the willing' to address them, such as a team of dedicated professionals. In both cases, it is because we are in a position to help that we are called upon as a catalyst for resolution. The more such situations we face, the more we may start to internalise our professional obligation as a sense of personal responsibility. We may begin to feel that it is always morally incumbent on *us* to do something, and that everyone is relying on *us* to rise to the occasion.

As a result, we Agonisers can become drawn to anyone or anything that tugs at our heartstrings, insisting we ought to care about them too. We firmly believe that others' pain will continue until we find a way to stop it, and we may begin to apply that logic even when our help is not formally required. There is always another budding victim of catastrophe, one more 'damsel' or 'dude in distress' we encounter as we go about our lives. We are prone to feeling instinctively that we are neglecting them, doing them a disservice, if we insulate ourselves from their concerns. We measure our value in how alive we are to the sorrows of our surroundings, and we convince ourselves that this is how others measure it as well. We each carry inside us our inner Ma Joad (*The Grapes of Wrath*), our own Úrsula Iguarán (*One Hundred Years of Solitude*), always ready to steer 'our people' through their relentless crises – especially those of their own making.

It is not just experiences of dire need in front of us that can steer us towards this conclusion, but also roles in which we are trained to prepare for emergencies in advance. As mentors and teachers, carers and confessors, counsellors and HR staff, we are drilled into being always alert, on the lookout for new situations that demand our attention even before they emerge. We learn to extrapolate 'the possible' from everything we know about what else is happening now, and what has happened in the past. More than other thinker-types, we Agonisers absorb and leverage all the information we can discover about our surroundings. Memories of sad times we once had. Difficult events we lived through recently. And every other hurtful thing that is still going on as we struggle to overcome our current disquiet. Our sadness pre-emptively infers the damage such events could wreak if they took place again, sharpening the concern we feel towards those who might be exposed to them.

But this training also trades on the power of our imagination. It encourages us not only to discover creative solutions to the problems we already face, but also to find new potential problems that demand to be solved in their turn. Even as our bodies live in the present, our minds strain – and are encouraged – to live in the future. We Agonisers take this on to a particularly powerful degree. We feel sadness vicariously – even about things that have not happened yet, and which may never happen. Perhaps we work in public health, with a commanding view of how many lives will be affected with every service that gets cut, every programme that is defunded, every aid project that is cancelled. Or maybe we are doctors and hospital managers during a disease outbreak, watching our scarce resources get depleted – fully aware of the life-threatening consequences if they run out. Every person becomes a potential data-point, every situation a calamity waiting to happen.

But that sort of fatalism under the weight of evidence can also be matched by similar disconsolation where evidence is entirely lacking. We become so accustomed to dealing in hypotheticals and improbabilities, so well-versed at forecasting future decline, that we find ourselves imputing urgency and moral quandaries to situations that may never exhibit them. As new parents, fretting about every cough and gurgle our newborn lets out. Or looking after elderly family members, worrying that every minor incident is a major accident, convinced that every prolonged silence spells disaster. We may be desperate not to do anything to jeopardise our charges – but fundamentally unable to tell what we can and cannot plausibly do something about.

The danger is that, in our zeal not to miss anything out of inattention, we can tip over into paranoia, scanning the world incessantly, apprehensively. We grow used to doing this prophylactically – not least because we soon realise that actually doing something to solve an even halfway complex problem or manage an emergency takes time, and needs a high level of coordination. Especially if people cannot (or will not) do it on their own behalf. We become convinced that we will be called upon to lead the charge and organise the mobilisation. So the more we are 'on top of' what is coming towards us and those in our care, the more effectively we feel we can discharge the responsibility other people have imposed on us. We conjure up worlds of suffering that play out entirely in our heads, speculating what we would do if something did happen, and gaming out how we would respond.

The ups and downs of hypervigilance

Above all, it is what is unknown that concerns us. What we already know, we can handle. If we are going to be dismayed, it will be by something that provokes our vigilant curiosity. We are primed to be distracted by any scary new stress or strain in our lives. Not just distracted – we are ready to let it cognitively change and develop us.[2] Psychological studies suggest that our brand of sadness helps us accurately remember the new things we discover around us – which is why we go on to reconstruct our beliefs and judgements about the world, and the goals we pursue, off the back of them. Our sadness is protective, warning us immediately when things we want to save are at risk.

This leads us down the path of radical candour, of being frank about what the world is like, where others might prefer to remain in denial. We greet the world with clear-eyed honesty. We expect neither well nor ill of the world; we expect it to do neither well nor ill by us. What we expect is that the world will not leave us be. If that is an ominous picture, it is one we feel equipped to handle. What we resist in ourselves, and what wounds us when we see it in others, is the cocky, guileless delusion that sends them skipping straight into the lion's maw.

This is essentially why we are so tender-hearted and tenacious. We are well aware that everything *can* be all right, that everything *can* ultimately come out in the wash – but that making that happen means conscious effort and a hefty dose of realism.

For us personally, it may also mean pricing in a significant degree of sacrifice. We have the capacity to let our causes consume everything about us, until all that is left are our moral principles. We 'volunteer as tribute', just as Katniss Everdeen does to save first her sister Prim, then her District, and eventually all of Panem from the oppression of the Capitol and its brutal Hunger Games.

In small doses, our creative phobias are not to be sniffed at. Where Gloomsters dolefully brace themselves for the inevitable, we cover our bases for the possible. It is hard to think of a better weapon we could have in our arsenal. But however great the energies we devote to what might be, we cannot let ourselves fixate on that entirely in place of what is. We possess such a precious ability to stay sensitive to our surroundings that we cannot afford to lose ourselves wholly in our thoughts, or undermine ourselves by lowering our defences. We need to keep returning to the surface for air, to make sure we are not actually zeroing in on the wrong thing.

If something happens to catch us off guard, we are bowled over straight away. Our minds run away with us, and we twist this way and that trying to shake off what has assailed us. Gone is any sense of pity, or sympathy, or even redemption. Caught in the whirl of 'what is', frantically recalibrating our sense of 'what might be' – all we want in that moment is to survive. This is when we are most in danger of lashing out. In this mode, we seize on any opportunity we can see to steady the ship.

Talking the pain away

What we reach for depends on what we are used to trusting. A comforting parent or partner who can swaddle us in reassurance and stability. The refuge of mindfulness or prayer, helping us self-regulate and bring order back to our provoked sensibilities. The impersonal clarity of a bureaucratic edict or court judgement, the lodestar of a principled ethical code. In those moments, we demand answers, solutions, anything that can adjust us to the imperfections of a flawed world. We hurt, deeply, until sometimes our hurt is so great that we simply cannot contain it inside. It erupts out of us, whipping us up into a frenzy of nervous despair. We cannot stay silent. We wear our hearts on our sleeves.

We have learned that putting what torments us into the light is the first step to processing it. Like Willy Loman in *Death of a Salesman*, recounting his failures and frustrations to anyone who will listen, we need a circle of friends and counsellors to lament to – and who can bear witness to what has happened. If we need to recover from addiction, maltreatment, or trauma, then sitting in a room of fellow survivors, sharing our vulnerabilities, is what will begin to heal us. So, perhaps, will talking therapy that gets us to vocalise and explore out loud unhelpful patterns in how we think and behave. If we have done something wrong, then our inclination is often to confess our sins – to those we have hurt, to a priest, or direct to the divine – as a crucial stage of repentance. It is how we learn to affirm ourselves, to find succour and support for our position. We want to better comprehend our sadness and find validation for it in equal measure.

For a process of healing and rebuilding to work, we know instinctively that we have to share, to talk everything through. 'No greater agony than bearing an untold story inside us.' If we stay still, hold back, how will anyone ever get our point of view? Even if they have been through the wringer just like we have, how will they know? If they have stayed unscathed, why would they ever think we have a point? Whether we are looking for closure, forgiveness, or simply understanding, engagement holds the necessary key that unlocks the door to truth and reconciliation. It is the only way we feel we stand a chance of finding our balance again. We deal with our pangs by reflecting them back out into the world.

We refuse to take any disappointments, great or small, simply lying down. Although our sadness is a part of us, we can still feel embarrassed that it has captured and disabled us – and rather than hiding our suffering, we broadcast it, determined to hold (and be seen to be holding) ourselves fully accountable. Crucially, we internalise (and externalise) how 'out of character' these disappointments are – and, paradoxically, make our reaction to them an essential part of our character. We learn to lean in, own our mistakes, and redouble our efforts to keep going.

Finding ways to get stuck in

If we Agonisers have found ourselves wanting, what we look for is not just a chance for redemption, but an opportunity to take back control. We realise that creating this chance means doing some quick and creative thinking to turn our situations around. Clearly, we have work to do: we have been tried and found guilty, whether by the impersonal verdict of events or the court of wider opinion. So trying to come back from our mistakes is about rebuilding bridges and reintegrating ourselves with those around us.

Criminology research has explored how 'reintegrative shaming' can offer restorative alternatives to traditional punishments for a range of crimes, petty and serious. Evidence suggests that encouraging offenders to see themselves as fundamentally good people who have done specific bad deeds works better than blanket stigmatisation in prompting remorse, promoting reconciliation, and avoiding recidivist reoffending. But if we find ourselves in that situation, those around us also need to be willing to forgive us, heal in concert with us, and put our mutual conflict permanently to rest.[3]

We Agonisers think along similar lines when we try to (re)connect with those around us. The prospect of getting a fair hearing helps us (re)assert ourselves, pull ourselves together, and throw ourselves back into the breach. As we plead our case, for ourselves and the things and people we care about – 'A second chance! Have mercy!' – someone standing by us is like manna from on high. An amicus brief from an unexpected ally. A new witness called for the defence. A gaggle of supporters with placards and slogans: 'Free *them*', 'Save *that*', 'No justice, no peace!' A word in our favour is worth its weight in gold. We latch onto it as a sign of (re)acceptance.

Yet if we decide that it is not only our self-image that is flawed, but quite possibly everything we thought we knew about the world, we are often motivated to urgently get ourselves a better perspective on things. Deep down, we believe that we will find a way out of our predicament ourselves – that we will overcome. There is always a new angle we can try. That motivation is the main thing keeping Holden Caulfield going in *Catcher in the Rye*, as he tries to fill the hole left by his brother Allie's death by starting up a series of conversations about his teenage insecurities with everyone he meets – from his sister Phoebe and several friends and classmates to the sex worker Sunny and a group of nuns.

The point drilled into us by the social situations that demand our intervention is that we should never stop participating in what is happening around us. Rather than accepting our ostracism, as Gloomsters might in our shoes, we Agonisers always find new ways to get involved again – and continue fighting for what we hold dear. Even when waves of pain wash over us, we pick ourselves up and force ourselves to keep going, step by step. We are on a mission. As we push ever harder, if we do not find allies to stand alongside us, we can grow acutely conscious of feeling alone. In these situations, our ambitions are set against the world: nobody else is as invested as we are. Certainly not Jokesters or Hotheads, who view our turmoil with a kind of bemused *schadenfreude* or borderline irritation. Nor Quibblers or Worrywarts, who are too preoccupied with their own discomforting, terrifying concerns.

No problem, we will make them care! We reject their rejection. So we become louder and more ostentatious, overbearing, even overpowering, radiating more and more of our sorrow at those around us. Our separation from them turns into our unassailable armour. Behind it, we try to regroup and reclaim our strength. We jump on every chance to put ourselves back out there. Whichever cause we champion, every space we enter becomes a townhall debate-in-waiting. The poor and downtrodden need a voice? We shall advocate for them. A compromise needs striking – on pay, on tax, on who does what to whom? We will do the bargaining. Critics and objections to overcome? Let us do the persuading. Our struggle becomes an entrepreneurial project; we learn to leave no stone unturned on our way to find favour.

Our ambitions grow with the scope of our care – even more if we find ourselves facing resistance. Sometimes, we merely aspire to survive our everyday lives, amid a handful of the people we care about. Yet with a larger view, and greater possibility open to us, we expand the horizons of what it means for us to prosper. We are like Elphaba Thropp in *Wicked*, who tries to harness her growing magical powers in her own idiosyncratic, quasi-utopian way, at first to fight for her own acceptance, and then to rectify the mistreatment of the talking animals in Oz –

in stark contrast to the manipulations of the deeply mediocre Wizard (a Jokester) and the breezy naïveté of Glinda Upland (Happy Camper).

But we can take this too far. We do not have to upset those around us just so they take seriously how upset we are. And diffusing every feeling we have everywhere all at once is not guaranteed to get the message across in a way that they will understand. Better we keep our counsel until we have a bit more to say, like Gloomsters and Hotheads do – though perhaps with less gravity or force. Better yet, feed in some Cool Cat dispassion, so we can translate what we want to say into a language that people who do not feel as we do can still grasp.

Carrying the weight of the world

As well as projecting our sadness into our surroundings, we Agonisers are just as prone to absorbing it from them. It is not only our own pain that can overwhelm us – we are equally sensitive to that of others. We develop an acute sense of when other people's setbacks and struggles are burdens they cannot carry by themselves – when it feels as though we are the only ones available, capable, or simply willing, to help them out. We train ourselves to go beyond sympathy every time, to make their cause our cause. We express our care for them by expressing their need for care on their behalf. We add our voice to theirs, take charge of their hurt and loss.

However, the danger is that we devote so much effort and energy carving out a space for others that we forget to do the same for ourselves. Clinical medical research has studied this with a view to helping doctors and nurses cope with the bad news they often have to give their patients, and creating guidelines for how they can deliver it in a sensitive way. It has found that people do this best when we balance our empathy with an appropriate measure of distance. We cannot absorb the full spectrum of other people's emotions, but nor can we become wholly emotionless, defaulting to simply spouting facts. Instead, we should aim for a healthy midpoint: building rapport, practising reflective listening, and offering support that targets what others need – as well as opening ourselves up to what they feel on *their* terms rather than through our own projections.[4]

A relative of mine, an aspiring actor working as a carer in small-town Austria, once told me he felt his life was slipping through his fingers. He was trying so hard to meet the needs of people around him that, bit by bit, he was giving up on his own. Social workers whose incompetence kept depriving him of much-needed time off. Friends who dumped their problems on him over reams of texts or voicenotes, but were mysteriously absent if he ever asked them to repay the favour. Overbearing parents who kept weighing in on his life choices, his politics – and vetoed his early dreams of going to dance school in Paris.

Time and again, he put others first and himself last. On call all hours of the day and night, literally losing sleep over problems they had outsourced to him. He was always skirting close to snapping under the strain: at one point, he was even hospitalised for chronic stress. He had taken on too much, opened himself up too far, and it was threatening to engulf him. What he desperately wanted was support to help him become the person he could be. What he found instead was cage after cage to stop him doing exactly that. This moment of acute candour was also a plea – not for help as such, but for permission merely to take up space. Approval that what he wanted, what he felt was good and just and right, was a legitimate thing for him to stand up and fight for, rather than something he should speedily abandon.

The risk for Agonisers is that we can internalise the idea that wanting to individuate is an antisocial thing to do — that taking up space for ourselves means taking space away from other people. So often this comes in the form of duties of service that are imprinted on our minds, sometimes from an early age. Helpless younger siblings or seniors we have to advocate for, struggling friends and colleagues to support, constituents and parishioners to dedicate our time and energy to. This may start to go further than service and in fact become self-abnegation — just as it does for Jane Eyre, as she is relentlessly pulled between the successive demands of her aunt, her school, and eventually Mr Rochester (a somewhat brusque Jokester). It is not enough that we help others; we also have to deny ourselves. We can feel deeply ensnared in networks from which there is no extricating ourselves. How could we even dare to try turning our back on them? That, to us, would be the worst kind of betrayal.

What we have to do is shake off the gnawing concern that if we choose to strike out on our own, then we are to blame for anything that happens to those who leaned on us for their care. The easy slip we make is that everything that follows *after* whatever we decide to do must also be a consequence of it. If we cannot alleviate others' pain, we convince ourselves it must be our fault. Needless to say, that is a logic we should work to dispel from our thinking: simply put, we cannot help everyone, and we will collapse under the load if we try to go above and beyond every time. Yet this is also exactly the kind of mental and emotional labour that other thinker-types could do with taking off our hands. Many of them take far less notice of their own feelings than we do — and none at all of ours. We Agonisers can help them see when, and how, they can help others more. But that sort of mentorship should be part and parcel of helping us do it less.

Too many plates to spin

As Agonisers, the sheer volume of what we take on means our lives become a constant flurry of activity. We can often struggle to avoid being taken over by sadness, searching the world for new concerns, see-sawing back and forth from rejection to dependency in our relationships. We are constantly trying to read cues from other people to see whether they still accept us, constantly trying to align ourselves with the 'mood of the room' on quite how much we can vent our feelings, and how much support we should expect to offer and receive in turn.[5] Yet we are usually too twitchy to sink into melancholy, as Gloomsters are prone to do. There is simply too much for us to do. We are always 'on', multitasking, spinning plates, juggling responsibilities.

A few years ago, I was gathering article submissions for a blog I edit about the study of ideology. One scholar I signed up, a geopolitics expert, promised me what sounded like the perfect piece. Exactly what I needed to plug a major gap in the field. As the deadline approached, an email landed in my inbox – five paragraphs of apology. A previous project had overrun, the leader was cracking the whip – could he have an extension? No problem, push it back a month. A month rolled by, then another email. Seven paragraphs this time. Caveating, hedging, more apology. Departmental drama, funding crisis – another extension? Sure thing.

Another month, another apology screed. Even longer, more urgent. A definite breakup, a possible breakdown, a likely breaking-apart of the global order – one more extension? Of course, but is everything OK? I asked him. If things are getting too much, should we forget about the article? 'No no no, not at all, it'll be with you soon!' More emails, some texts, a call, a long chat over coffee, all spelling out a painfully lurid picture of the hyper-complicated web of intrigue that was my colleague's life. He could barely even think of the article without cringing with embarrassment. Did I think worse of him? Did I believe his explanation? Was he taking up too much of my time? Again and again I reassured him, only for him to reappear with a new concern. Eventually, we drifted out of touch. And his article never came.

We Agonisers are highly susceptible to adding more things to our to-do list. We take evening classes in calligraphy and improv, boxing and salsa. We volunteer for local schemes and enterprises. We run a YouTube channel as a side-hustle alongside our office 9-to-5. We struggle to let anybody or anything go, especially once we have spotted any problems heading their way. Our sadness invigorates us. It is not exactly that we thrive on it, but we do take a new lease of life from the febrile mindset our anguish puts us in. It gets our blood up, gives us a new test for our mettle. Ours may be a 'quiet war', like the one Esperanza Cordero wages on behalf of her Chicano neighbourhood in *The House on Mango Street*. Or we may wage it as visibly as possible, like Atticus Finch's risky and ultimately doomed trial defence of Tom Robinson in *To Kill a Mockingbird*. We see our saddening experiences as a challenge, a question we need to answer. And we back ourselves to answer it. Though we may call on the world for aid, we cannot be assured that it will always respond.

If Gloomsters are the picture of silent withdrawal, we Agonisers are practically garrulous in our willingness to say how we feel. Sadness, for us, is a two-way street of conversation and exchange. But what happens if we are the only ones sending traffic down it? If we offer ourselves to other people, but meet with rejection? If we are Cassandras, blessed – or cursed – always to issue dire warnings about the sufferings looming on the horizon, but nobody is willing to hear or heed our concerns? Again, we find ourselves conflicted, permanently caught between our minds and the world outside them. In these moments, we never shake off the doubt that we are really alone. But how else should we keep our torment at bay?

The moment for a moral compass

At times, being an Agoniser can be like fighting our way up a very steep hill with a force nine gale whipping into our eyes. At first glance, our mindset seems fraught with tension – but it has several sides that we can play to our advantage. Perhaps our greatest strength is that we are such expressive communicators, articulate and eloquent, naming exactly what agitates us. We channel our incredible capacity for imagination into endless ingenious solutions to the problems we find. Threading these together is our drive to wrest control of situations and fix them – and enlist other people to do this in tandem. We are society's 'horizon scanners', putting together a syncretic view of everything we see and remember. Sincere to a fault, we strenuously avoid deluding ourselves or other people with too positive or negative a verdict.

There is much that other thinker-types can take from us and adapt to their own purposes. We are highly attuned to other people's pain, and we rarely hesitate to take on their burdens as our own – which puts Gloomsters' passivity and Jokesters' airy dismissiveness in the shade. We recognise how much we all depend on each other to get through the vagaries of life – not just to give each other the frisson of novelty or satisfy one another's appetites, as Keen Beans and Revellers tend to think. Above all, we cleave firmly to the conviction that things will only turn out well if we get stuck in, and put our own minds and bodies on the line – rather than expecting them to happen by themselves, as Happy Campers and Worrywarts are variously inclined to do.

Yet some of our best characteristics cut a very different way if we do not keep them on a tight leash. That we externalise our feelings rather than bottling them up can give us a tendency to overshare, which makes it harder to meet the obstacles we face by gritting our teeth and suffering in silence. Though we are attuned to others, we can still wrongly assume they are wired the same way, which means we are taken aback if they do not reciprocate, are unwilling to share, or have no time for our feelings. Meanwhile, our push to stay on top of everything can lead us down the road to doom-mongering, and blind us to new opportunities. Our overactive minds jump too quickly to 'panic stations' and 'survival mode' – and we throw our whole selves at a problem in one go, rather than working through it incrementally.

Perhaps our biggest temptation is to become submerged under other people's problems, twisting ourselves out of shape for them entirely. Here, we could do with a firm reminder to carve out enough space for ourselves, what we want and value, as Quibblers and Jokesters do without hesitation. It helps that we are inclined to look for ways to rid ourselves of our emotional hang-ups – like Gloomsters, and decidedly unlike Hotheads. And if our ties to those around us have been disrupted, we need to avoid seeking permission to be let back in, and instead use some Keen Bean or Reveller initiative and simply reach out first.

Altruistic to a fault, we open our hearts and minds to become society's consciences, for no other reason than that it is the right thing to do. Like humpback whales, protecting their smaller aquatic neighbours from orcas and other hunters, carrying them to safety, taking on their fight to let them escape. We recognise both the good and the bad that the world has to offer. Yet as we become others' lodestar, we cannot risk losing our own footing. When we offer ourselves as everybody's heroes, as targets for every sling and arrow they face, we are in danger of taking on more than we can bear. If we are always there to save the day, have we saved enough for home? Society needs us to keep it on the straight and narrow, but it cannot test our limits so far that we fall into the ravine.

CHAPTER 5

Hothead

Some of us stand by what we believe, come hell or high water. One time in North Wales, on the morning after a wedding, a group of us were milling about in our hotel trying to decide where to go for breakfast. On our phones exploring the available options, we managed to whittle it down to either a hipsterish café or a fairly inoffensive chain pâtisserie. All of a sudden, one of our group chimed in: 'I think we should go *here*.' Where was here? A Belgian waffle house, an early casualty of the whittling-down process. Why? 'Well, for a start it's closer.' Seems a bit much of a muchness, really? 'No, no, it's closer.' Some quick tapping on his phone, and a maps app held up triumphantly. 'See? They're 825 metres away, this one's only 8*10*.'

And what was the big deal with this place? 'It's the only place here that does proper coffee *and* they have amazing pancakes.' Surely we could get halfway decent coffee elsewhere? 'No! I know the roast blend they use, it's the best, I guarantee you.' And what if we want something other than pancakes? 'What?! You *have* to try these pancakes!' Oh, very well then. Fast-forward to the waffle house, and a hapless barista turning to us with a solemn look. No coffee, the machine was broken. And the pancakes? Sorry, not on the menu anymore. Cue a sullen trudge back to one of our original choices. 'Well, if they *had* had them they *would* have been better.'

That feeling, writ large, is what it means to think like a *Hothead*. What might indicate that we share this mindset? Maybe we are very attached to our pernickety 'just so' way of doing things. We might get disproportionately worked up about everyday inconveniences, or spend a lot of time thinking about how to get back at people who have hurt or harmed us. We are prone to a 'red mist' that blinds us to what is *really* going on, and what people *really* think of us. Or perhaps we are the first to bravely charge in when the fight is on, with scant regard for our own safety.

Not for no reason do Hotheads have a reputation for a forceful temper (see fig. 5.1). We are generally **angry**, and occasionally extremely **eager**, supported by six traits – **emotional, introverted, disagreeable, conscientious, closed,** and **biased–superior**. This is a thinker-type that shares its primary emotions with several others on the thinker-type roster. Anger in particular also has a role to play in the Agoniser, as we learned in the previous chapter, and the Keen Bean, as we shall see later on – although its undisputed epicentre lies in the Hothead mindset.

Putting this anger-led combination of emotions and personality traits together gives us a core of excitable frustration. Perhaps unsurprisingly, emotionality pairs the most closely with our anger – it is why we are so readily provoked, easy to get a rise out of, and liable to impulsively jump in and fight back. Whenever we do, our disagreeableness and closedness play a vital supporting role in making our feelings last past their initial spike. They build our momentary irritation up into sustained hostility, turning nuanced disagreement into absolute refusal, which keeps us butting heads with other people. Alongside these, our conscientiousness and bias–superiority allow us to suppress our rage, and channel it into tenacious plotting about how we can get our way. Meanwhile, our slight introversion makes us keep a rigid, frosty silence, cold-shouldering the world in between the times when we lash out.[1]

We Hotheads mostly take notice of 'bad news', even if we only come across it in a couple of places here and there, since it does not take much for it to grab our attention. When we do, we get up to speed as quickly as we can, relying heavily on what we already know, with barely any room left over for new facts or ideas. What we make of the world runs the full gamut from raucous approval to shrill disapproval, but our views are usually fairly orthodox – and we double down on them, even (or perhaps especially) if that puts us at odds with those around us. We jump to our conclusions faster and more urgently than many other thinker-types. We cut corners, make spectacular leaps of logic, and blast straight past what others believe to get to our opinions.

Fig. 5.1: The Hothead		
Personality traits		
Emotional		Emotionally stable
Conscientious		Careless
Extroverted		Introverted
Honest–humble		Biased–superior
Agreeable		Disagreeable
Open to experience		Closed to experience
Emotions		
Angry		Calm
Happy (joyful)		Sad
Disgusted		Desiring
Fearful (anxious)		Eager (seeking)

MENTAL OUTLOOK

MENTAL PICTURE	**Information**		
	Selective	▮▮▮	Indiscriminate
	Personality-congruent	▮▮▮	Emotion-congruent
	New / Previous / Long-unused		
	Fast	▮▮▮	Slow
	High	▮▮▮	Low
	Positive	▮▮▮	Negative
	Diverse	▮▮▮	Limited
	Predispositions		
	Conservative/reactionary	▮▮▮	Progressive/radical
	Emotion-congruent	▮▮▮	Reasoning-congruent
	Pro	▮▮▮	Con
	New	▮▮▮	Previous
	Revise/revisit	▮▮▮	Defend/maintain
	Compliant	▮▮▮	Defiant
FORMULATING THOUGHTS	**Reasoning**		
	Heuristic	▮▮▮	Non-heuristic
	Rational	▮▮▮	Irrational
	Reasonable	▮▮▮	Unreasonable

Becoming a Hothead

We Hotheads carry inside us a pent-up bitter wellspring, ready at a moment's notice to swell up in our chests. Anytime we detect its roiling currents stirring inside us, we instantly recognise what they are telling us: there is a grievance that we must redress — or a potential grievance we must head off. Bit by bit, this bitterness subtly distances us from our surroundings, filling us with sanguine certainty that there is something amiss about them, which it is utterly imperative to fix. And every time it surges within us, we rear up with it, freewheeling away, as if we have been unleashed, even liberated, from some constraints. We brim over with self-assured conviction, ready to hurl ourselves against anyone and anything without any hesitation, brooking no compromise.

To understand how we become shaped into Hotheads, we need to look at a different set of social experiences to those we have for the other thinker-types up to now. A dog-eat-dog bidding war, a protest and counter-protest rally, a title-deciding final can get us properly fired up. When there is a race to be run, a competition to be won, a prize that either *our side* will get or the others. For us, *nearly* is about as good as *not at all* — either we make that tackle, land that punch, or we get trampled in the dirt. So we had better gear up. Locking eyes with someone across the halfway line, the negotiating table, the security cordon, time after time (serious? again? back for more? not taking no for an answer?), can bait us into becoming ever more embittered and annoyed. At our worst, we can let the urge to lash out consume us. 'Really asking for it now.' 'Settle it once and for all.' We see the path down the road of tit-for-tat and we strain to rush headlong down it.

So much of what we learn as children is about the self-mastery we should exercise over ourselves in moments of tension such as these. Asking politely if we can have that new Lego set, leave the table after dinner, or stay up late to watch TV, and swallowing our frustration if and when we cannot — instead of simply bawling our eyes out, throwing a strop, or storming into the next room. Specifically, we learn how to make this choice more deliberate, how to get a handle on our anger – how to either repress it or express it in a measured way, how to let it go and settle ourselves down. Everything we learn afterwards in life builds on the rudiments of this early socialisation, adding contextual nuance and refinement.

But at the same time, there is also another lesson these experiences may teach us: that just playing nice is for losers, and winners need to know when to get their hands dirty. People in all walks of life may rely on us to go the extra mile, push ourselves past our limit, want to beat the others no matter what it takes – from our clients in court to the performers in our troupe, or the soldiers in our squad. Not quite at all costs, since it will be a short career if we leave everything on the field straightaway. But through these expectations, we steadily become more willing to take on other people head-on. We learn to see the race, the competition, as a matter of morale. We grow used to rehearsing the customary tropes and nostrums to shore up our side's integrity. What is right and wrong, good and bad, true and false. And, eventually, we develop the skills to win the almighty tug-of-war with our feelings. To not just let our anger go, but channel it in a particular direction.

As Hotheads, the cardinal virtue we learn is knowing how to strike the proper balance: *when* to repress and *when* to express our anger as our situations demand. There is a time and a place to let our fury course through us. Sometimes, nothing will do us quite as much good as a proper catharsis, as simply letting it all out. In part, we can find 'our people' among those who let us lift the suppressing weight off our anger – who take our side, and join us as we plunge into the trenches or rush to storm the barricades. We only need a little encouragement to let anger galvanise us, give us the impetus to strike out for what we want. Not too much encouragement, though, else we may go overboard and do something fatefully rash.

The longer our embitterment stays with us, the more pronounced it becomes, turning from a temporary state into an ongoing characteristic of our thinking. After the first sudden flash of fire has passed, our temper recedes into the cooler but more durable red glow of coals burning quietly in the background – and every new grievance we face casts another coal into the brazier. Eventually, it solidifies into an exceptional detachment and remove, tailored to the grievances we object to and the people we blame for them. Rather than fighting what provokes us, we just want to separate ourselves from it: our self-reservation becomes self-preservation. We convert our natural sense of distance into withdrawal – just as in *The Iliad*, Achilles pulls himself and his Myrmidons out of battle during the siege of Troy, out of rage that Agamemnon has taken 'his' war prize, the captive Briseis.

Our bitterness can also slip into scornful dismissal – setting us not just apart from others, but above them. The more we learn about them, the more convinced we may become that we are more deserving, better qualified, vastly more enlightened – that our side is not just the right side, but that the rest have nothing to offer us. Then, our blame turns to arrogance, even intolerance. Psychological research sees anger as strongly linked to a sense of entitlement: we jealously defend making our ire the centre of our own and other people's attention.[2] We insist that what matters to us should be all-important and taken seriously by everyone around us as well. The more space we let that take up in our minds, the less inclined we may become to factor in – or even notice – whatever anyone else cares about. Does it happen to align with our irate sensibilities? Yes? Then we co-opt it as 'our own', and grow increasingly resentful the longer it stays unacknowledged and unresolved. No? Then we relegate it to our lowest tier of concern.

The uses and abuses of rage

As Hotheads, we grow used to deploying our anger to guarantee that other people will turn their focus onto our problems. From our earliest years, we can become enraged if we are exposed to discomfort and uncertainty – especially if it seems to us that we unfairly have to put up with either of these, while others do not. Here, even well-worn paths of managing our anger have their limits: if asking politely does not get our parents to pay attention or understand what we want from them, then as toddlers and teenagers we still sometimes launch into an almighty tantrum. Even if they shout and snap at us in response, at least we are now on their radar. What we glean from this is that a well-placed outburst can get us exactly what we want. The indulgence of those around us, above all 'our people' who know and care about us, creates space for us to get angry – more than 'propriety' might normally allow. And part of us owning our displeasure means finding the limits of how much they will tolerate from us, and pushing on them to make sure we are seen and heard.

Letting our anger play out is our way of taking up the space we feel we are owed and validating the intensity of what we are going through. As a result, we Hotheads live continually on the cusp of a complete takeover of our mindsets by whichever grievance happens to be our concern *du jour*. From one moment to the next, we can erupt with little warning: our inner Kali, our inner Ares, are only ever a provocation away. We become tetchy and unusually thin-skinned: what sets us off really gets us going. And just as quickly, we can simmer all the way back down again. The sheer speed with which our anger can flare up and dissipate leaves us grumpy and somewhat unpredictable.

Susceptible as we are to getting fired up like this, Hotheads are more exposed than many other thinker-types to the ever more sophisticated ways the world is evolving to 'flick the switch' on our emotions. We are often first in line to hoover up the emotional appeals of leaders and orators of all kinds. We tend to develop strong opinions on politicians in the public eye, while podcasters and radio presenters whisper in our ears, and tabloids and TikTok reels blare into our vision. Social movements often harness anger to make people take part in riskier activities they would not otherwise consider – especially when what they want are some fairly major changes to the social order. Demos against poverty or war. Rallies across the spectrum from hard left to far right. Standing on picket lines striking for better pay and pensions. Every one of them is likely to have a sizeable portion of Hotheads among their number. And every mass action we take part in riles up our energies and wears down our emotional barriers.

Needless to say, this is not a comfortable state of mind for us to be in. We cannot keep our anger flaring at full blast all the time. Instead, it usually settles in a midpoint state somewhere between active and passive, keeping us on the edge of our seats, alert and determined, willing to fight for justice, for order, for proper closure – and ready to burst back into flames if our grievances are left unaddressed. In its less intense form, our anger gives us prodigious motivation. It can help us power through setbacks and stresses, and survive the high expectations, fast pace, and late hours that others impose on us in our day-to-day lives. We have to fortify our nerves, and protect our reserves of incandescent energy, which means we must be judicious about when, and how, to give our anger free rein. This makes us cagey: we look around us, straining to tell where the next thing to provoke our anger will spring from.

At a low level, this kind of relentless watchfulness is a useful learning tool we often pick up during our later years in education. Getting irritated by something makes it likelier to linger in our minds – especially where our indignation at struggling with an exercise or skill we are determined to master makes us furiously practise it all the more. If simple interest will not help us get it into our heads, then annoyance is a decent second best! In this respect, we are prepared to give in to our anger far more than many other thinker-types are to their emotions, precisely because we have learned to appreciate the less obvious ways it can be a positive force in our thinking. But at a higher level, our watchfulness can easily tip over into expectant neurosis – and we may become hostile, even militant, about whatever provokes us. This is probably the thing about us Hotheads that stands out the most to other thinker-types, especially those – like Happy Campers, Keen Beans, or Revellers – who cannot summon the same level of emotional tectonics. When something gets on our nerves, we positively fizz with rage, glowing with an intimidating intensity of feeling.

When the heat starts to rise

Because we detach so instantly from our surroundings, we are always a little at risk of losing control of ourselves. Our irascibility is like a coiled spring, waiting to be released – with no real knowing where or how far it will launch us when it is. This is less of a problem in contexts that challenge us to be a bit daring – if we slide in for a crunching tackle, just within the bounds of the rules but still a little bit too gung-ho. But there are other situations where this impetuous tendency can have far more serious consequences, such as if, when our anger is roused, we blurt out something liable to cause actual damage or genuine hurt: sensitive information, false suspicions, spurious accusations, insults primed to cut deep.

A few years back, I met a development economist at a conference who told me she was in the middle of moving jobs. Nothing unusual about that, as such. But when I asked what prompted the change, my innocent question triggered a minor volcanic eruption. 'Oh, it's just a snakepit. Everyone there is toxic!' Cue a high-speed exegesis of everything wrong with her old institution. Bullying, sabotage, skulduggery, one story after another. *Him*, a creep. *Her*, a chronic plagiariser. *Them*, always blocking other people from applying for grants. And herself, misunderstood and undervalued, her ideas sidelined and shot down. 'They just don't want someone like me to succeed! I've seen their type before.'

I started to get the sense that everyone was part of the problem. What about the people who were just trying to survive? 'They're the worst! They'll encourage you to speak up, but if you do, they'll never back you.' Had that happened to her? 'I got them to call a special exec meeting, asked for a full external investigation.' And? 'They just sat there looking blank. One even said I was being too extreme!' Had she tried getting any of them onside? 'Not a chance! Honestly, the whole place needs burning down.' Well, good that she had found a way out. Was that the end of the story? 'Depends, I'm considering taking it to the *Guardian* . . .' Was going public the wisest thing to do? 'Oh, so *you're* a coward too!'

Clearly, her wounds were still raw. Yet, angry as she was, there was something in her that was not-so-secretly thriving on the towering height of indignation she had reached. When we act up like this, it can be a formidable sight to behold – and, if we are honest with ourselves, we know that quite well. When our anger is sparked, we become truly ferocious, a classic 'loose cannon' – a Tybalt, or a Sonny Corleone, ready to lay into and launch ourselves at our nearest target. But deep down, we actually get rather a kick out of being a bit too hot to handle. It reminds us of the sheer power that lies embedded in our feelings: even if there is no end in sight to the grievance that has caused them, we can always give them a freer rein to reclaim and assert a space for ourselves in the world.

Yet sometimes, there is simply too much of our anger to focus in any direction – it can overflow and spill everywhere, diffusely, spontaneously, and, above all, dangerously. Sassy backchat to colleagues when we just cannot bite our tongues, losing our cool in a debate, screaming matches with our parents or partners. To take the pressure off those moments, we learn to find smaller, less explosive ways to blow off steam and stop ourselves champing at the bit for too long. Venting our neuroses down the pub with our best friends, in the safe space of a student welfare group, on our therapist's couch. All ways of reaching out more gently to the world around us, which Agonisers and Keen Beans – who, after all, partly share our anger – can help guide us towards. The more of these ways we find to release our anger manageably, little and often, the better a prophylactic we have against fully losing control.

Stewing in our thoughts

Of course, we do not generally go about the world whirling our anger around us like a flail. Instead, we wait, alertly, for it to be unlocked. We can withhold our reactions to our surroundings – ignore them, even – until they provoke our total outrage. It is the same cold, fanatical intensity that drives Daenerys Targaryen in her protracted campaign to recover the crown of Westeros in *Game of Thrones*, earning her first the loyalty, then the betrayal of decisive players such as Jon Snow, Varys, and Tyrion Lannister (broadly, a Gloomster, Cool Cat, and Jokester respectively). Bolstered by an unshakeable sense of righteous justice, she only unleashes the full force of her rage at key moments as a strategic choice.

When our outrage is provoked, our instinct is to respond immediately: our proverbial fuses are as short as they come. But voicing our anger judiciously means wielding it decisively. It is a precious emotional currency we should not spend too lightly. However we express it – sweary shouting, a venomous barb, a strident phone call to customer services – it has to work. If we get it wrong, if we do not calibrate our anger precisely, it may soon lose its impact – which can lead those around us to dismiss us, sending us further into a rage spiral. Instead, most of us learn to manage our temper, keeping just enough of it on show, peeking out from below the surface. The raised eyebrow, the warning glance. Stopping dead in our sentence mid-flow. The briefest of coldly raised voices. No need to reveal more than that, most of the time at least. Those who know us know full well what will happen if we blow our top.

We Hotheads may have a reputation for shooting first and asking questions later. But in truth, we spend more time than most pondering, dissecting, picking apart what is going on. It is just that we do so in a state of exasperation. It stands to reason that we would not be so attentive to the things that set us off if we were not a little bit fascinated by the world. We dwell on our grievances, studying them so hard that we become experts in the exact wounds the world has dealt us, or threatens to deal us. We are all Heathcliffs, consumed by the idea that we have been wronged by those around us, with endless energy to plot our vengeance on them – even and especially the besotted Catherine Earnshaws (Revellers) throwing themselves at us.

This works on a couple of different levels. Remember that sense of distance we get when we first notice bitterness growing within us? That also clicks our brains into gear. Our anger makes us coldly analytical, treating every minuscule fact with a sharply critical eye. For as long as it remains settled, festering within rather than erupting out, we turn our minds to data-gathering, scanning our surroundings, searching for clues. Anger gives us the endurance to keep wading onwards, maintaining our focus, staying closed and removed enough to collect our thoughts. Just as in *Gone Girl*, Amy Dunne spends months gathering the materials and planting the evidence she needs to frame her husband Nick for her murder as retribution for his infidelity.

When we object to somebody or something so much that we get angry, we also fixate on them in a remarkably tenacious way. We cannot live in ambiguity of the sort that Cool Cats thrive in, which both Agonisers and Quibblers are reluctantly resigned to in different ways. We are much more like Gloomsters and Worrywarts, who are chronically liable to caving in to their darkest moods. But unlike us, they have both internalised the idea that things will not always go their way – in fact, they often expect them not to. We can afford to learn something from our affinity with them. We could cultivate a bit more give, a bit more tolerance for an imperfect world, so we do not immediately jump to 'all or nothing' conclusions – either complete victory or utter defeat, with nothing else in between. The needle we have to thread is to find a way of bringing our anger back under sound management, without turning it back on ourselves – without allowing self-criticism to rear its head, accusing us of not taking ourselves seriously enough.

This particular challenge is one we cannot avoid. If we go all in on our anger, letting it grow unchecked, it can perversely shut our minds off to what is actually going on around us. As we persist in our annoyance, the world moves on – but we are too busy being mulish to realise it. Perhaps ironically, the whiter the heat of our anger, the greater a chilling effect it has on how we think. A sense of relentless purism takes over, a pathway of righteous 'mission creep' stretches out before us. We may become obsessive about allocating blame, hunting for 'enemies' under every rock, or finding more and more things to offend our sensibilities – far more than whatever first provoked us. The danger is that we may start to live for our exasperation, and stiffen, entrench, and narrow our sense of what is right.

Firing up our inner engine

Yet our testy obstinacy also has another side to it, which motivates and spurs us on. Anger is not an emotion that fades easily or quickly from our consciousness, even after its initial burst has simmered down. The afterglow of its embers often far outlasts whatever it was that made them catch alight in the first place. This is why we must try to learn ways to keep it managed and settled, or reel it back in once we have unleashed it. Once we take the plunge, it may feel as if we are riding the raging torrent right to the bitter end. But we have to keep reminding ourselves that we are the ones at the wheel. We alone decide how much fire we spit, how far the sparks fly.

On the plus side, since we are on the dogged hunt for solutions to remedy what irks us, anger attunes us to the shortcuts that may get us there – and, crucially, gives us the guts to seize on them when we find them. We do not generally have the patience, or the wherewithal, to come up with complex and subtle new ways of getting the outcome we want. A tight budget to sift through, line by line? Equipment costs, personnel costs, expenses, indirect overheads – more, less, the right amount? No way, the thought alone we find unbearable.

But we can instantly spot the tried-and-tested options and draw up ways to capitalise on them. Here, we draw on our experience of how we dealt with things that frustrated us previously. We may essentially copy and paste what we did last time – minus this here and that there. Or we do the opposite of what went wrong, and get ready to front it out if that fails to work. Either way, we never give up on the idea that the world should adhere to some kind of rules, which should yield us decisive results – and yield them quickly. After all, we crave order and regularity, and we find it profoundly aggravating if for any reason we cannot have them.

Hotheads believe in a final closure, a definitive resolution, in much the same way that Revellers have a 'forever after' in view. In large part, this is because we believe in *ourselves* to assert our aims and boundaries in the world – a self-belief that we can help other thinker-types discover for themselves too. We may recognise that this will not always happen. But there is a strange positivity about the way we develop our approaches to the world, based on the assumption that our anger will bring us the outcomes we want. It is tied to our stubborn certainty that how we think will see us through – a 'causal closed-mindedness' that tends to simplify our cognitive processing, reduces our receptiveness to new or 'disconfirming' lines of argument, and imprisons us in what we consider 'the right way to think'.[3] If we batter hard enough at the door, surely society will change itself to accommodate us?

In short, we do not plan to be angry forever. And it is a failure of other people or the world at large if we end up that way. But, arguably, by thinking like this, we are setting ourselves up for disappointment. Our ambitions may make us reach further than the world is prepared to give. So we can hardly be surprised if we get some pushback – not least from other Hotheads, who are equally unwilling to concede any ground. We have to learn to moderate our expectations, and expand the timeframe over which we assume our plans will be realised. Like Thanos in *The Avengers*, we may think we are inevitable – but we must expect that other people will have their own convictions and agendas too.

Taking no prisoners

In the end, we Hotheads expect that most of our experiences will boil down to some sort of fight, which someone will eventually win, and someone else will therefore lose. Our boundaries are our castle, and we are more than prepared to sally forth in their defence. In one respect, this is quite a clarifying realisation. It takes courage to set yourself up at cross purposes to your surroundings – and courage is something we certainly have in spades. Strong, confident, gutsy leadership is what gets things done, as far as we can see, anyway. It keeps our business afloat in rocky times, betting big on new materials, new tastes, new tech, and backing ourselves to see it through. It keeps our borders and streets safe; it sweeps away mediocrity and waste; it drags us out of decline and into prosperity. Nothing worthwhile ever comes to fruition if we simply concede at the first sign of resistance. And we are pretty sure we will be proved right in the end anyway.

In that light, doing something about our frustrations usually means asserting ourselves over somebody else. Whoever our opponents happen to be, they sink in our estimation: they are at fault, which means they are simply no longer our equals in our eyes. We raise ourselves to a higher status and belittle them as lower status. That opens the door to tribalism and 'emotional fundamentalism' – not just taking up space for ourselves and 'our own', but denying it for anyone else. Psychology and sociology suggest that if we internalise the values of 'our' group to an extreme degree, we become more willing to use violence against people who do not share these values.[4] We take the fact that they reject our norms as a sign of personal disrespect and collective humiliation – an insult that must be avenged.

The danger here is that we may develop a ready-made 'us versus them' dynamic, which we deploy against all comers. Social theory is awash with analysis of how and why humans 'other' those we see as falling outside our groups – infinite binary permutations of 'like' and 'unlike', 'identity' and 'difference', which often encourage a hostile fixation on those who do not 'belong with' us.[5] On our side lie fellow-citizens and friends, on their side aliens, adversaries, or enemies. This can be a destructive mindset to become locked into, particularly for Hotheads, as it gives us a distinct and damaging route down which to channel our anger. The more it consumes us, the further it pushes us to take extreme steps to satisfy it – which lowers our qualms about how poorly we are willing to treat other people.

This is undoubtedly the biggest risk of the Hothead thinker-type. At our most entrenched, we can grow used to imposing our ever-expanding demands on others. Or we antagonise them whenever it suits us, using them as a metaphorical punching bag for no better reason than that they happen to be there. To us, these things might be justifiable, or seem so in the moment. But requiring other people to accept and pander to our strident worldview, living with it without complaint, is little short of gaslighting.

Someone I know found herself thrown into an extended dispute with her estranged father. By all accounts, he was a difficult man at the best of times – rude to staff in the restaurants they met at, which she carefully picked as neutral ground, and prone to glaring at fellow diners, stage-whispering his disapproval. He came ready with new prejudices to blurt out, specially calibrated to provoke her, only to lose his temper when she refused to pander to them. After one of these meetings, he sent her a long, accusatory diatribe in the post. She had neglected her duties as a daughter for too long: from now on, he expected her to support him. 'I paid for your upbringing, now it's your turn – so cough up!' A masterclass in intimidation and mind-games, and an almighty headache for my friend.

This may be an extreme example, but it captures an essential point: when we Hotheads pick fights, we tend to give no quarter, steamrolling right over people instead. After all, we are driven to get to a decision faster than any other thinker-type. We want to put a stop to the causes of our frustration, and we want that *now*. No matter the cost, we can always dial up the temperature that extra notch. And we may lose patience with deliberations that drag on without resolution. So we are quite ready to crack down on other people – to shut them up and shut them out if we have to.

The problem we do not always fully anticipate is that those around us may not be on the same wavelength. If we push them too far, they may simply stop trying to reason with us – and instead, simply try to defang us, walk away, meet us with a flat 'no'. Our flaw is that we are just not all that interested in what the people around us think. In fact, we tend to insist the hardest on those of our views that sit the most at odds with what they believe, as part of carving out our space among them – which is where we earn our reputation for being grouchy and unreasonable. No matter what we are arguing for, we can make it easy for others to dismiss us as bloody-minded and wrong – even in situations where our anger is broadly righteous, and we actually do have a valid point to make.

To allay that, we need to develop the mental muscles to dam or diffuse this tendency. That means picking up a couple of tricks from thinker-types who can model a more muted emotional approach – perhaps Jokesters and Quibblers, who may be inclined to take our side, but are better at voicing it in a less heavy-handed way. They can show us how to siphon tension away from the full-frontal assault we are otherwise gearing up for. We should learn to find 'safer' options for confrontation, looking for points where we can open up a bridge between us and the other side, and explain whatever happens to be annoying us in terms that people outside our immediate circle can relate to. For Hotheads, our boundaries may be our castle, but we must be able to raise the portcullis and lower the drawbridge now and again.

Harnessing the strength of our resolve

Being a Hothead is hard work, and requires us to be hard, often drawing on reserves of resistance in the face of a world that seems determined to thwart us at every turn. The greatest strength our mindset offers us is how effectively it prevents other people from crossing our red lines. We effortlessly spot problems in what lies around us — giant neon signs over what is wrong — and we keep our focus on them until they are gone. We find and seize on quick fixes, giving us the impetus to just get on with it. We know instantly when harm befalls us or one of 'our people', and we mobilise a determined sense of right and wrong to restore order and justice to their proper place. Above all, we have the courage to own our feelings, and make space for them, rather than denying or repressing them.

Perhaps unexpectedly, our emotionality is the side to us that other thinker-types could benefit from the most. We make a clear link between how we feel and the purposes we want to achieve — unlike the slightly scattergun brightness of Keen Beans or Happy Campers. We do not automatically lead with our emotions, but deploy them reactively, strategically, and we can grow quite accomplished at walking our inner tightrope — neither showing our true feelings too soon, like Quibblers, nor hiding them away, like Jokesters. Though we may be explosive, we are undoubtedly consistent, responding as other people would expect, not with anything like the Reveller's infinite shifting constellation of emotional investments.

At the same time, we may be too quick to batten down the hatches and cut other people off out of hand – which lends itself to an exaggerated 'us versus them' mentality. We are too prone to spoil for a fight, which jeopardises the personal boundaries we are so determined to police. If we are tightly wound all the time, that may only fuel the distance between us and those who choose to keep us at arm's length. And when we are really blinded by our anger, we tend to pass over things that do not confirm or justify our heightened emotional state – which means we can see the world as an endless cavalcade of annoyances.

This is where several other thinker-types can help us. They show us that there are other ways of taking up space than simply letting our emotions run amok – reaching out inquisitively, or expressing them to let off steam, as Keen Beans and Agonisers do. We need to stop our emotions from filling up our consciousness entirely, keeping them more as background 'mood music', closer to the role they play for Happy Campers. Above all, we must stay in control even when we do decide to let rip, so we can still break ourselves out of our emotional cycle before we spiral into oblivion – a mixture of Revellers' emotional self-possession and Cool Cats' ability to will their affective ecosystem into submission.

We stop at nothing to get our way, no matter the toll it takes on our energies. We are as frenzied and relentless as terriers, chasing the objects of our rage to the ends of the earth if we have to. We are virtually unbeatable when we get going, leaving others trailing behind in our wake, as they pause, speculate, or second-guess themselves. But we cannot keep our agitation up indefinitely.

Sooner or later, if we cannot bring ourselves back off the boil, we either hit a wall or burn ourselves out – or career off an emotional cliff in a blaze of (in)glory. If we do, the road to recovery is slow and uncertain. In short, we are a thinker-type that society certainly needs but cannot afford to overuse, or it will use us up entirely.

CHAPTER 6

Cool Cat

We all need an anchor we know we can rely on. Some years ago, after a relationship had gone south, I found myself stuck in London with nowhere to stay. After milling about aimlessly, with the possessions salvaged from my ex's place in tow, I rang a friend to tell him what had happened. 'Oh I'm sorry! No problem, come crash at mine.' So I trundled up to his flat, to be greeted by a hug and a beer. 'So what do you want for food? Something comforting, maybe pizza?' As we ate, he listened patiently to my disjointed telling of what had gone down. At the end, he smiled. 'You know, better a horrible end than endless horror!' What more was there to say?

A few weeks later, he called me to check in. How was I holding up? OK, all things considered. 'You'll be all right!' Could I come crash again? 'Sure, but give me a heads-up when – we'll need to schedule!' More calls, more stays, more stories. The highs and lows of dating and singledom, the soap opera of self-rediscovery, with my friend as the unflustered fulcrum for my drama to turn around. 'Told you you'll be all right!'

We can call this way of thinking the *Cool Cat*. What might be the subtle signposts that we align with this mindset? We may value moments of stillness when we can sit back and decompress, carving out a 'safe space' we can retreat to, to shut out the drudgery of the outside world. Perhaps we like to help other people be their best selves. Or we tend to take things as they come and deal with them at our own pace. And maybe we have an eye for the big sweeps *and* the little details, and let our minds meander in pursuit of them both.

As Cool Cats, ours is a mindset of reflective detachment, shaped – like Agonisers – by a complex cluster of emotions (see fig. 6.1). We are highly **calm**, occasionally **eager** and **happy**, with a supporting roster of five personality traits – **emotionally stable**, **extroverted**, **agreeable**, **open**, and **honest–humble**. Just as the Hothead has anger at the core of how they think, calmness plays the same role in the Cool Cat mindset. Meanwhile, the tinge of happiness gives us a slight overlap with Happy Campers and Jokesters, whereas the inflection of eagerness means we share some common ground with Keen Beans too.

This constellation of emotions and personality traits gives rise to a disposition of contented repose. Central to this are our emotional stability and openness. One gives us the composure to keep our impulses safely in check and meet the world with mellow tranquillity. The other underpins our capacity for imaginative exploration, and for adding all manner of new self-actualising strings to our bows. Agreeableness lends us an enquiring warmth towards people we trust – compassion for their preoccupations, along with a good-natured willingness to help out. Slightly more in the background, we owe our air of benign authority to our extroversion and honesty–humility. We are a powerful presence in any group we join; we carry weight, even if we only ever use it to bring other people to the fore.[1]

We Cool Cats rove far and wide in the details we pick up about the world, collecting them from an eclectic range of different places and piling them up to add to our considerable breadth of knowledge. We tend to err more towards 'good news', but we try to balance what we have already learned with the new things we find out. All of these we treat favourably, with a consistent experimental and inventive streak, prepared to change tack if our experience demands it. We elaborate our opinions very systematically, with only a few erratic moments, engaging carefully with the views of those around us, and considering when and where to cut some corners in our reflections.

Fig. 6.1: The Cool Cat

Mental Outlook

Personality traits

Open to experience	Closed to experience
Agreeable	Disagreeable
Extroverted	Introverted
Honest–humble	Biased–superior
Conscientious	Careless
Emotional	Emotionally stable

Emotions

Happy (joyful)	Sad
Disgusted	Desiring
Fearful (anxious)	Eager (seeking)
Angry	Calm

Mental Picture	**Information**		
	Personality-congruent	▮▮▮▮▮▮▮▮	Emotion-congruent
	New ▮▮▮ Previous ▮▮▮		Long-unused
	Diverse	▮▮▮▮▮▮▮▮	Limited
	Selective	▮▮▮▮▮▮▮▮	Indiscriminate
	Positive	▮▮▮▮▮▮▮▮	Negative
	High	▮▮▮▮▮▮▮▮	Low
	Fast	▮▮▮▮▮▮▮▮	Slow
	Predispositions		
	Revise/revisit	▮▮▮▮▮▮▮▮	Defend/maintain
	Pro	▮▮▮▮▮▮▮▮	Con
	New	▮▮▮▮▮▮▮▮	Previous
	Compliant	▮▮▮▮▮▮▮▮	Defiant
	Emotion-congruent	▮▮▮▮▮▮▮▮	Reasoning-congruent
	Conservative/reactionary	▮▮▮▮▮▮▮▮	Progressive/radical
Formulating Thoughts	**Reasoning**		
	Reasonable	▮▮▮▮▮▮▮▮	Unreasonable
	Rational	▮▮▮▮▮▮▮▮	Irrational
	Heuristic	▮▮▮▮▮▮▮▮	Non-heuristic

Becoming a Cool Cat

One major feature that distinguishes us Cool Cats from the rest of the thinker-type family is that the central sensation that motivates how we engage with the world is one that we would almost describe as not a definite sensation at all. What lies at our core is a laid-back collectedness – a feeling of being partly released from feeling, as if we have had our emotional capacity slightly dialled down. An island of peace and quiet amid the lurid emotional torrents that swirl around us. We are somewhat set apart from other thinker-types because we are to some degree parted from the motivating role of affect and emotion in how we think.

Several different walks of life profess the Cool Cat mindset as their ideal, the Holy Grail of how we 'should' be. The austere philosopher surveying the world from their ivory tower, the unflustered civil servant negotiating the quagmire of vested political interests, the elite high jumper composing themselves before their record attempt. But far more than the particular requirements of bespoke roles such as these, it takes a specific set of circumstances to bring about Cool Cat thinking. It is when everything is kind of fine, when nothing is going exceptionally well or badly, that brings it out of us best. All quiet on the front, operations proceeding to plan and on schedule, all systems normal. When things are settled around us, when we are able to settle into them, we can plug into everything that is going on without skewing our concern in any direction. We can work effectively and efficiently through anything that crosses our path – and it is up to our teachers and mentors, figures of authority of all kinds, to put us at our ease, to make us feel secure enough to put our head down and just get on with it.

From our earliest years, we are raised to see our everyday experiences as a journey of discovery. Lifelong lessons in morality, 'teachable moments' that show us how to be a better son or daughter, a more constant friend, a more upstanding citizen. We understand life as a quest to realise our best self, in public and private, through hobbies and pursuits that elevate us that little bit higher. To us, the world and its infinite possibilities come imbued with an unshakeable quiet beauty – waiting for just the right glimmer of light to strike at the right angle for their magnificence to be revealed. We often find in this a consolation that may elude other people. We can be touched by things without becoming too entangled, invest without becoming too invested. We engage with what is happening around us, yet we stay fundamentally independent.

This gives us Cool Cats a remarkable ability to take on and work through facts and experiences about the world. More than any other thinker-type, we are insatiable omnivores. We hoover up any information we can lay our hands on, and we regularly go out of our way to look for more. We are always ready to open up our thinking to new angles on our experiences, with the same innocent wisdom and wonder as the planet-hopping Little Prince – convinced that our investigative questioning is just as important, if not more important, than the answers it delivers us. We can do this because our calmness is a source of tremendous conviction for us. We trust ourselves not to lose our temper – and specifically, to answer any and all challenges in the same even-tempered, good-humoured way. So let us put ourselves out there, make the most of what the world has to offer! We can face it all with cool aplomb.

Psychological studies show that our calmness and openness to novelty are mutually reinforcing, setting us on an upward spiral of positive engagement with the world.[2] If we relax, we can better focus our attention, sharpen our awareness, and visualise what lies around us. Witnessing the world in a consciously non-intervening way helps us connect with it, and makes us more receptive to what it has to offer. This gives us our capacity for 'deep learning' – all being well, our executive functioning gets stronger, our intuitions more refined, and our thinking more innovative. This sense of peace is especially important when we have limited time available in our daily lives. It fosters our psychological development and growth, while lowering our stress levels and boosting our mental and physical health.

The contexts that offer us this zone of remove, allowing us space for careful observation and deep reflection, are precious and rare in day-to-day life – which is precisely why we try so hard, and train ourselves so diligently, to find them. It is the place of spiritual respite that mindfulness encourages us to access and accentuate with considerable practice, detaching ourselves from our worldly ties and transcending our preoccupations. More prosaically, it is also a coping mechanism we may have to develop growing up in a particularly boisterous family. Perhaps we have tearaway younger siblings always on their PlayStation, radio blaring in the living room, the constant clanking and whirring of washer-dryers and hoovers and kitchen mixers – an assault on our senses that we yearn to escape. We learn to tuck ourselves away in our hidey-hole, blot out the racket, and find some semblance of inner peace.

Against a backdrop of stresses great and small, from cataclysmic shocks to the strains of the everyday, calmness lets us channel patience, constancy, and consequence in how we think. It dials down noise and perturbations, and slows down our pace. Specifically, calmness lets us opt out of the incessant pressure that other emotions put on us to find new ways of increasing our pleasure and decreasing our pain. Our affective centre of gravity tends to lie in a state of Arcadian serenity. It is the oasis we find ourselves returning to, the emotional waystation where we can recharge from our forays into the intensity of the world outside.

Our unshakeable sense of self

To those around us, we Cool Cats stand out for our unusually firm resolve, and for how glacially we react to the emotional provocations of our daily lives. What is the use – the actual *purpose* – of flying off the handle? It hardly helps us to get anything done, and saps the energy we need to save for what really matters. We are quietly, durably confident that we can respond to anything that comes our way without losing our head. We project an impassive charisma that encourages the people around us to trust us. And we welcome their trust, taking their admiration in our stride as fuel to feed our self-conviction.

But the real achievement is to think like this when our immediate experiences are telling us not to. Keeping our head in a crisis, carrying on as if things are fine, and not letting triumph or disaster knock us off course. To get ourselves to that point, we have to build up enough experience of how to think when everything is going as normal to tide us over when normality goes out the window. Everyday life presents us with any number of ups and downs that might derail our normality – births and bereavements, breakups and hookups, freak weather events and stock market volatility. No matter what comes our way, our Cool Cat mindset give us the resilience to keep our sense of moderation firmly in place.

Our ability to do this increases all the more if we have comfortably seen off a low-key crisis or three in our time. We learn to check our thoughts by framing our experiences through a wider perspective – insisting that things will even out over time, 'this too shall pass', 'it will all come out in the wash'. Like Mma Ramotswe in *The No. 1 Ladies' Detective Agency*, we face every new problem in a spirit of forbearance – perhaps with a cup of redbush tea in hand – rarely letting stress get the better of us. At the same time, we also see the value in sharing, and comparing, our experiences with people who are in a similar situation. We become well versed at regulating and reducing our emotional burden (positive or negative) by pooling it with others, working on it together rather than wrestling with it alone. A feeling shared is a feeling halved – or dissipated.

Quite simply, the world does not generally faze us in the way it does many other thinker-types. No matter who or what we encounter, we are never short of ways to find solace, for us and for others as well. We got this – so sit back and relax! Ultimately, this is about having the confidence to consciously and deliberately let out what we feel. Letting go any 'excess' until what we are left with is manageable, and just enough to keep us motivated. Until we internalise that doing well and getting things done is not just about knuckling down, but about knowing when, and how, to reach out to those around us.

We are often sympathetic ports in a storm for our family and friends, buffeted by the fierce eddies life throws at them. We keep their febrile feelings earthbound, dispensing dollops of Cool Cat reassurance. But as magnanimous as we might be towards other people, the key to understanding our mindset is a determined drive for self-fulfilment. The ease with which we grow interests, our stakes in various pursuits, or forge links with others, ultimately comes back to our own individual richness and versatility. Our poised self-possession, which keeps us emotionally set apart from our surroundings, is above all a marker of a strongly autonomous side to our character.

Being less governed by emotions makes us more self-governing, physically and mentally. This can cut one of two ways. Either our high-minded stillness lets us get on with the tasks society expects of us without getting distracted. Or, in a more abstract way, we get there by steadily carving out a framework of expectations and rules that we feel comfortable within. In both cases, we feel that our ambitions are authentically our own, liberated from the affective burdens other thinker-types carry – from Hotheads' overwhelming fury to Revellers' bursts of inflamed passion, and even Jokesters' need to look at things from their most ridiculous angle. We are our own enterprise, to be pursued resolutely and with purpose. Ours is precisely the defiant independence and intellectual prowess that Aunty Ifeoma shows in *Purple Hibiscus*, carving out a space for critical thought and free-minded discourse in her home.

Even the most thoughtful thinker-types have much to learn from us here: they all need to step back, take stock, and get a sense of the bigger picture from time to time as well, and we Cool Cats can show them how to turn those moments to their best advantage. However, so determined is our enterprising venture into the world, like a battleship sailing head-on into a storm, that we can lose sight of the nuances of what is happening around us. We are so concerned with realising ourselves and our achievements irrespective of what is going on that we may become self-absorbed and even a little haughty. Whoever we engage with, whatever we experience, we do so a little from 'on high', watching the everyday commotions wash around us far below.

Our unyielding resilience, so often an object of admiration for those who are more prone to being rattled, such as Gloomsters, Hotheads, or Worrywarts, can become a mark of our obstinacy. In *A Man for All Seasons*, the high-minded Sir Thomas More refuses to swear the Oath of Supremacy acknowledging Henry VIII's role as head of the Church of England – which initially wins him the praise and respect of his contemporaries. Yet as he persists in his stance, the costs of his decision to his family's livelihoods and mental anguish gradually become more and more extreme – raising the spectre of wilful selfishness over his conscientious deference to canon law.

We cannot let our untroubled Arctic cool become insensible coldness towards those around us. We need to either dial up our empathy for them to a point of genuine warmth, as Agonisers do so well, or rouse our reserves of enthusiasm on their behalf in a more Keen Bean vein. Above all, we have to offer something more than just 'our way or the highway'. Perhaps we cannot hide that everyone else's way is somewhat alien to us in its emotional intensity, but we should not allow our attempts at understanding them to come off as patronising. Otherwise, our viewpoint becomes at once too navel-gazing and too lofty, too universal and too generic, too obtrusive and too vague.

A flattened view of the world

Perhaps our preeminent characteristic as Cool Cats is that we can take control of our affective impulses. We absorb the push to be professional, smart, well put-together, to leave a good impression. We tend to plan our dress code to the nth degree. We map out how we should enter every situation, how to circulate, and how to take our leave. We always have the apt or courteous thing to say up our well-tailored sleeve. We have instilled in us a deep expectation of self-control. We quite literally compose ourselves, building our mindsets from the lower floors up. And the central part of our architectural plan is that we stringently delimit the role of emotion in our intellectual edifice.

We train ourselves to hold our nerve, and signal that we are subtly satisfied with the world and well-intentioned towards it. This clear but delicate mindset translates into a specific tendency to treat those around us with a default sense of grace. Our charisma has a positive aura of comfort and consolation for all –

of 'doing as we would be done by', of reciprocity as the essence of our ideal relationships. The sense of community we aspire to is shaped by a kind of equality of peace among its members. The link between calm and benign peace is one that research has found in many contexts, from classical philosophy to international politics to workplace engagement.[3] The consensus is that calm as a 'low-arousal positive affective state' is the best way to conserve our resources and create space to communicate with other people.

By clamping down so firmly on the emotional currents that – in our view – only serve to pull others from one histrionic escapade to another, we buy ourselves a far more restful existence. We refuse to see nameless threats or sickening evil around every corner, as Worrywarts or Quibblers do. We do not share the Agonisers' taut sensitivity, nor the freewheeling thrills of Jokesters' ongoing quest for entertainment. At times, though, that may blind us to the true nature of whatever it is that crosses our path – we either take it too seriously or not seriously enough.

In grad school, I asked a department faculty member – a brilliant theorist, unfailingly generous with her time and advice – how to navigate a particularly intractable part of my thesis. It was a proper 'no longer seeing the wood for the trees' moment: tonnes of reading, acres of notes, with no idea how it all fitted together. Worse, the longer I stayed stuck in my rut, the more impostor syndrome began to set in. Eventually, I asked for help. We met in our department café. She strode in and perused me carefully. 'So, are you struggling?' Yes. 'I see. You have my sympathy. Now let us see what we can do about it.'

Two hours of intense feedback later, I reeled back to my desk. Certainly, the solution to my thesis was coming into view. But somehow I felt no better about it. Not that I was looking to be coddled – but I had been hoping for something a little bit less *cerebral*. I struggled on. Later that term, an email. 'I made a note to myself to check in. Are you making progress?' Yes, but something still felt off. Instant reply: 'OK good. I've been reflecting on the problem you raised. As I see it, there are five possible ways forward . . .' Five ingenious suggestions, each better than the last. 'I hope that gives you what you need?' Again, yes of course – but then again, also . . . no? 'Just keep at it. I am confident your argument will clarify itself soon.' Analysis 1, affect 0.

In other words, what we Cool Cats may think of as thorough care may come across as quite a dry, managerial way of dealing with other people's concerns. We treat them fairly, but in a way that squarely aligns with our own sense of 'how things should be done'. We must not forget that what looks manageable to us may feel vast and overwhelming to them – and it is not just the facts we have to take care of, but their feelings too. If we let ourselves dial our own feelings all the way down to zero, we become far less able to understand, and relate to, the affective load that other people take on as a result of their experiences.

The danger is that other people interpret our unruffled sobriety as straightforward indifference. That tendency is the Jedi Order's undoing in *Star Wars*, when the Jedi Council fails to comprehend how far the young Anakin Skywalker's ambitions are driven by his urge to avenge his mother's mistreatment and death. Their lack of sympathy leaves a gulf that Chancellor Palpatine is ready to exploit – leading to the collapse of the Republic into the Galactic Empire, and Anakin's own transformation into the Sith lord Darth Vader.

Cutting down on our affective experience also cuts us off from an important dimension of how we become and remain aware of what is going on. The more we muffle, or even silence, the triggers that would otherwise unleash our emotions and turn on our creativity, the more monochromatic and faded our view becomes.

To get the colour back, we should draw judiciously, selectively, from the other thinker-types' emotional palettes. Adding a tinge of Keen Bean technicolour here, a shade of Gloomster noir there. Even allowing ourselves a bit of Hothead infrared, so we can capture the full variety of what we come across. From our position of 'gearstick neutral', we need to let ourselves inhabit other thinker-types' mindsets – not just comprehend them, but lean into them – so that they start to make sense to us.

If our sense of the world is flattened, we can become apathetic and diffident. Our charisma collapses – we become mannered, pedestrian, sterile, and at times, even boring. In our efforts to leave no room for strong feelings, we risk retreating to the safety of a sanitised inner world. It is the same self-distancing that the wealthy but passionless Sir Clifford Chatterley undergoes in *Lady Chatterley's Lover*, preoccupying himself with writing and business pursuits – leading the far more progressive and sensual Constance (Reveller) to seek sexual satisfaction in her affair with the gamekeeper Oliver Mellors (Jokester), whose sarcastic intelligence masks a deep, tender-hearted appreciation for beauty both human and natural.

If we are not careful, treating everyone and everything with the same lightly positive affect can trap us in a noncommittal bind. We may end up denying ourselves the ability to come out swinging for or against anything, or have anything meaningful to say at all. We cannot put our own convictions so far on the back burner that we – and everyone else around us – lose sight of them entirely. After all, it is in our character to hold them firmly and with a strong sense of truth. So we should not hold our cards so close to our chests that we never reach out to play them at all.

Letting our minds flourish

This tendency threatens to jeopardise the other distinctive feature of our Cool Cat mindset: our determination to puzzle through every perplexing aspect of the world. We are, at heart, phenomenally inquisitive. We thrive on immersing ourselves in what we pick up – always at a certain safe distance, of course – from the currents that whoosh by our contemplative island fortress. From our earliest years of education, we see the road to our self-fulfilment as paved with myriad incremental discoveries. First basic chords and scales, then harmonic theory and standard repertoire, and eventually some jazz improvisation of our own.

The sheer complexity of life means we are best off spreading our learning across a variety of unrelated areas, the more unusual the better. Diligent, quizzical engagement with the world is a key component of our sense of self, and how we aim to carve out a way for ourselves within it – through career 'pivots', hobbies outside our comfort zone, new sources of intellectual spice. This is not just a way for us to function, but the best way for us to flourish. Our serene, intellectual 'safe spaces' work a bit like a courtroom. We do not just examine our surroundings, we cross-examine them. In doing so, we exhibit a level of patience and dedication that few other thinker-types can hold a candle to, motivated less by relentless persistence than unyielding endurance. Like the eccentric detective Sherlock Holmes, we apply our strictest logic to 'deducing' the truth (however improbable) of what is going on – although, in our case, perhaps not fuelled by quite the same reliance on morphine, pipe smoking, or frenetic violin practice.

This is one of our key strengths. We are prodigiously industrious, which psychological research tends to attribute to our ability to keep our emotional state in check – carefully poised and intelligently deployed.[4] Our peace of mind is closely tied to taking a clear run at our to-do list: a very specific interpretation of 'keep calm and carry on'. It also makes us more effective team players, helps us swiftly and adaptively pick up the skills to get things done, and raises the threshold for how well we can complete the workload expected of us. Pretty quickly, we come to associate working hard with cutting out any distractions that might throw that peace of mind into disarray. We aim to channel our energies into labour rather than emotional processing – and we consistently deliver the goods.

We have the untroubled tolerance needed to take on any experience that comes our way, and the resourcefulness to look at it from every angle. But working well includes not only working hard but also working smart. Just because we trudge unhesitatingly onward does not mean that we will get where we are going the fastest. So we need to carefully manage our time, structure our work, and save our labour wherever we can, to make sure our effort is applied effectively.

As thinkers, we develop views that are complex, detailed, and often startlingly original – which can compensate for their occasional lack of sparkle or sparse emotional colouring. The flipside of this is that we are also intellectual wildcards. Our thinking is so heavily determined by case-by-case, in-the-moment flashes of ingenuity that it is often hard to tell where exactly it will take us. This sets us even further apart from the other thinker-types, especially those susceptible to intense instincts and feelings, whose response to any given situation we can probably predict with reasonable accuracy. Others might see us as a bit confused or scatterbrained, but for us, it is a question of intellectual integrity. The key is our essential equanimity, our indulgent even keel.

We realise that there are any number of social problems we could advocate for or mobilise around, and that we can never predict all the potential hiccoughs and hurdles we might face. From that, we may draw the conclusion that we have to stay ensconced in our somewhat removed vantage point, just so we can keep our attention trained on every possible approach. We are not suspicious, as Quibblers are – quite the opposite, we like retaining the option of connecting with anything that crosses our path. We do not want to deny ourselves what could be a golden opportunity. We flatly refuse to differentiate between the things we glean about the world as good and bad, right and wrong, true and false, before we have had a chance to consider them. All of these options go into our great thinking vat.

I spent some time at a small research centre, a rarefied, rule-bound place. While I was there, winds of change began to blow that forced this centre to reexamine its history. Awkward questions were asked about former members, bequests and inheritances, legacies past and present. Attention fell on a painting in the lobby. To some, it was a Ruritanian idyll; to others, a scene of brutal exploitation. Debate soon stretched to the people in it: national heroes or murderous monsters? Controversy reigned. So the centre did what these bodies do best. It set up a forum to deliberate on the issue, overseen by a committee, which tasked a working group to prepare options for what to do.

Behind the scenes the war raged on. Some wanted the painting gone; most wanted it 'contextualised in place'. Those who wanted neither threw the kitchen sink at them. Cultural vandalism! Dereliction of stewardship! Disruption! Prohibitive cost! The rest countered right back. Accountability! Moral expectation! Opportunity for leadership! Reputational imperative! Things came to a head in a special centre gathering. Polite yet devastating recriminations flew back and forth. In the end, a vote was called: should the painting stay or go? Incredibly, the result was a mathematical tie. Eyes turned to the centre's chair. His eyes screwed shut, he slowly rose, intoning gravely about collegiality and procedure. No majority meant no mandate. That meant resolving the tie in favour of the status quo – so he cast his deciding vote for the painting to stay.

To Gloomsters or Hotheads, or any other thinker-types whose emotional investments lie nearer the surface, this sort of approach can seem wilfully obtuse. How can we possibly be so bloody-minded as to have no view about what matters and what does not? It is not hard to see why, in these moments, we may stand accused of failing to consider other people's concerns. It is what happens if we tend to treat all experience and information as insight, which we pick up and ferry back behind the walls of our scholastic bunker. We inspect them insouciantly, at an 'objective' distance, like curios in a museum. Other people may not be able to stomach what can look like such a bloodless, noncommittal approach. To them, we are either forgetfully or deliberately obscuring why we think about the world at all. At best, we are being thoughtless. At worst, psychopaths.

The force of our social presence

It goes without saying that we Cool Cats are not trying to be either. And it is easy to forget, given our tendency to hold back, that we are actually fundamentally inclined to be friendly to those around us. We want to give people the benefit of the doubt, be accommodating and merciful, see them as innocent until proven guilty – and we want them to know this. We may not be as gregarious or hungry for interdependence as some other thinker-types. But that does not mean we are stand-offish. That, after all, is precisely the hurdle that our empathetic aura is designed to overcome.

For us, society is a project of providing salutary service to others, showing them personal tenderness, and addressing their individual needs in a charitable way. We try to assist them in a way that plays to our strengths. We take tasks off the hands of people who are incapacitated or overwhelmed, drawing up rotas, handling their accounts, sorting out their sickness cover. We pursue goals on their behalf, litigating their cases for them, negotiating contracts, putting policies in place. We do our best to facilitate their purposeful presence in society.

This raises a potential paradox. How should we square our vast capacity for this kind of animated commitment with the fact we are fundamentally so detached? How can we be both fortresses *and* juggernauts – immovable objects *and* unstoppable forces? The answer lies in our equilibrated centre of emotional gravity. It allows us to keep a firm lid on our emotional impulses while also exercising a large degree of purposeful choice over when and how we deploy our intellectual efforts. Studies have found that our calm-driven mindset gives us the option to respond to stressful stimuli in a variety of ways – choosing to 'rest and digest', distract ourselves, or reframe how we see the situation, rather than react impulsively.[5] Our motivating energy may be high, but it is potential rather than kinetic. We are live wires, humming placidly until the moment of connection.

For us, feelings are, more than anything else, a source of vulnerability – so our starting point always ultimately has to be holding back the tides of emotion. We see how they can be wielded to wound others, and we are hesitant to weaken our own armour and let others wound us in the same way. We internalise the idea that achieving security means keeping emotions, jointly and severally, within firm parameters, subordinating them if need be. That way lies the path from Arcadian serenity to Elysian bliss.

At this point, the other thinker-types will be looking at us with utter incredulity. A world of clockwork, without any sharp edges, where nothing seems to *matter*? How would we ever find anything interesting? What would excite us to find out more? Why would we ever get invested one way or another? Where, in short, are all the emotional prerequisites for us to think at all? Not a world without emotion, we answer, just without *too much* of it – a world where feeling is kept in its proper place. Clarifying, not bewildering; useful, not disruptive. Spurring us to engage, but not so intense that we get lost in the weeds or wander off track. Emotion can help us navigate the ever-growing deluge of information to find out what we actually care about – but we should not rely on it so much that we get stuck, or derailed by situations that tug at our heartstrings.

When to stay in control

Being a Cool Cat carries an aura of indomitable grace, like entering a vast temple, magnificent but deserted. Our most powerful asset is our sense of balance. We can usually find respite from more or less anybody or anything, no matter how they provoke us. We are acutely aware of the sheer complexity of being in the world, and how challenging it is for us (or anyone) to forge our way through. This gives us deep reserves of patience and stamina, which enable us to keep going and make the most of the many opportunities the world has to offer. We are extremely adept at examining ourselves and what lies around us, always coming up with novel ways of looking at things. And there is next to no danger that our emotions might exercise an outsized influence on our thinking.

These mental facilities have much to offer to other thinker-types. Opening our minds to different sources, taking them as they are, ensuring that emotions do not crowd out our reflections is as much a salve for Hotheads' red mist as for Revellers' rose-tinted spectacles. That meticulous planning does not stop us from being accepting and courteous towards those around us is an insight that Jokesters and Quibblers could take on board, so they do not needlessly poke holes in other people's lives. And being at least partway on top of our emotional inner life helps us to be seen as safe and trustworthy – a reminder to Gloomsters and Worrywarts not to let their concerns become their only calling card.

But even our balance can go too far. By insisting on taking the world as it is, looming above it like an impartial umpire, we may fail to fully grasp what has gone wrong. That is particularly true if giving ourselves space to self-reflect turns into self-preoccupation, limiting our ability to understand other people's perspectives and situations, and causing us to grow insensitive to their concerns. If we never let loose, we are shearing away the profoundest aspects of the human experience. We may get too caught up in minutiae and lose any sense of what really matters on the bigger stage. This can make us unreliable allies and unsatisfying companions for others in need – since our 'interesting take' is less valuable to them than our sympathy and support.

Several other thinker-types can come to our assistance here. We must avoid coming across as didactic and 'holier than thou' – if we think our way is best, then we could sometimes keep that to ourselves, as Quibblers and Jokesters do. We should lean into our benign inclinations more, echoing the prominent place Happy Campers, Keen Beans, and Revellers give their agreeable traits in their mental edifices. We also need to get better at imposing priorities on the things that intrigue us, by finding a 'positive' equivalent of the concerns that Gloomsters, Hotheads, and Worrywarts all beeline for in their surroundings.

Society gives us an onerous role as its sentinels and moral clearing-houses, a role we usually take effortlessly in our stride. We inch along like giant tortoises, shyly docile yet imposing, sedately gleaning whatever they find scattered about in their surroundings. We know how to keep things in perspective, consider them all thoroughly, range widely in our tastes and encounters – and keep our senses and memories whirring in the background. But if we hold back too far in reserve, we risk other people passing over our wisdom. If we accept the place of benevolent arbiters, validating every pathway, 'both-siding' every dispute, we lose our standing. We cannot play the part of judge so assiduously that we abandon our own judgement. For society's sake, though we keep its cacophony of voices in more perfect harmony, we must not let that prevent our own voice from being properly heard.

CHAPTER 7

Keen Bean

We all have that person in our lives who always seems to be on the move. Mine is an old musician friend, a talented singer turned graphic designer. Always newly returned from her latest hiking trip – Cairngorms, Dolomites, Patagonia – or about to scoot off on the next one. Covid-19 hit her soul like a hammer blow. As everywhere barriers went up and everything shut down, to stop herself from going spare, she poured her creative juices into a mammoth art project. It was a record of every date (in-person or virtual) she went on as the world oscillated in and out of lockdowns. Part-concerto, part-diary, part-installation, a proper *Gesamtkunstwerk* involving 16 pianos, one for every date, complete with unique nicknames and personalities.

But dreaming this up was only the start. As soon as restrictions lifted, she rang round everyone she knew. Venue booked, pianos rented, performers found, adverts shared. Within months, she had a small army of creatives at her beck and call, and a performance date in the calendar. Her social media became a tidal wave of 'sneak peeks' and behind-the-scenes content. A local newspaper interviewed her and filmed the rehearsals. Through word of mouth, even friends of friends of friends came to the event itself. One asked her out. A few years later, they got engaged – and where else but at a hotel piano, relaxing after a long day's hike.

This wide-eyed, effervescent style of thought belongs to the *Keen Bean*. What clues might we search for to see if we share this mindset? Maybe we have an endless capacity to get hyped up about anything new that crosses our paths. When we focus on something, we tend to forget everything else and let it blur into background noise. We often find ourselves racing ahead while everyone else struggles to keep up. Perhaps we are always first in line and last to leave. Or we find ourselves living in the future, anticipating and speculating about what comes next.

It is a mindset of relentless thrills, which sees our lives as puzzles to be completed (see fig. 7.1). We Keen Beans are generally **eager**, very occasionally **angry**, and back this up with a cluster of five traits – **emotionally stable**, **extroverted**, **agreeable**, **careless**, and **honest–humble**. The Keen Bean is the primary home of eagerness in the thinker-type family – though, of course, we saw in previous chapters that it partly characterises the Hothead and Cool Cat mindsets too. Meanwhile, its light tint of animated anger contrasts with the tormented and embittered forms of anger we find in the Agoniser and the Hothead.

The intersection of these emotions and personality traits creates in us a kind of ardent expectancy. Eagerness is most powerfully associated with extroversion and, perhaps surprisingly, emotional stability. One gives us our infinite reserves of social energy – it makes us determined to do everything, speak to everyone, pay attention to all of them, and earn their attention in return. The other bolsters this with the self-confidence to do something if we believe in it, and *stay* doing it, but not be too fussed if it does not quite go as expected. Our carelessness adds a large helping of spontaneous flexibility and devil-may-care élan – the 'wild child' edginess that keeps us on our toes (and other people on theirs). Agreeableness and honesty–humility are more of an undertone, but generally help us get along with our surroundings, to the point of glossing over any little wrinkles that threaten to spoil the excitement.[1]

We Keen Beans are highly adept at picking up both 'good' and 'bad news' about the world, though once we get excited about something we tend to stop looking for new angles and simply hover over what we have just found out. Our judgements are often favourable but sometimes flip quite firmly in the opposite direction, and it is anyone's guess how far we ultimately align with the people around us. We are consistently willing to be free-minded, and as oddball as our views might be, we tend to double down on them, come what may. That said, our arguments are not always the most rigorous – sometimes even outright erratic and gappy – with intermittent flashes of both taking on board and rejecting other people's views.

Fig. 7.1: The Keen Bean

MENTAL OUTLOOK

Personality traits

Extroverted	▮▮▮▮▮▮▮▮▮	Introverted
Agreeable	▮▮▮▮▮▮▮▮▮	Disagreeable
Honest–humble	▮▮▮▮▮▮▮▮▮	Biased–superior
Open to experience	▮▮▮▮▮▮▮▮▮	Closed to experience
Conscientious	▮▮▮▮▮▮▮▮▮	Careless
Emotional	▮▮▮▮▮▮▮▮▮	Emotionally stable

Emotions

Angry	▮▮▮▮▮▮▮▮▮	Calm
Happy (joyful)	▮▮▮▮▮▮▮▮▮	Sad
Disgusted	▮▮▮▮▮▮▮▮▮	Desiring
Fearful (anxious)	▮▮▮▮▮▮▮▮▮	Eager (seeking)

Mental Picture	Information		
	Personality-congruent		Emotion-congruent
	Selective		Indiscriminate
	High		Low
	New / Previous / Long-unused		
	Fast		Slow
	Positive		Negative
	Diverse		Limited
	Predispositions		
	Pro		Con
	Emotion-congruent		Reasoning-congruent
	Compliant		Defiant
	Revise/revisit		Defend/maintain
	New		Previous
	Conservative/reactionary		Progressive/radical
Formulating Thoughts	**Reasoning**		
	Heuristic		Non-heuristic
	Reasonable		Unreasonable
	Rational		Irrational

Becoming a Keen Bean

As Keen Beans, when we experience the world, we get a piercing spark of assurance, a sensation of crystalline brightness that cuts through any fog. We feel supremely aware of our surroundings, attuned to them, even aligned with them. We intuitively grasp how we fit into the bigger picture. And we instinctively turn to face the world with a clear-minded sense of purpose. It comes brilliantly, luminously into focus, and we cast our vision as far as it will reach. At our best, we find ourselves sure-footed and self-possessed, a sense of trust in ourselves growing in our hearts – we can, we will, we believe. As this spark keeps burning, settling into a longer-lasting glow, it pushes us to reach outwards – to go proactively out of our way to engage with whoever and whatever happens to be nearby. We want to draw our surroundings to us, and to extend ourselves into them: we are spoiling for a certain closeness to them. We have reserves of dauntless energy that we simply have to release somehow – and the most promising release we can find is to get stuck in.

Creating social situations that set our spark alight *and* keep it burning fiercely for long enough that it turns into a habit of our thinking is a tricky task. We have to be eager on some level about the things we are expected to do if we are actually going to become *and* remain motivated to do them. The activities our parents have planned for the holidays, the products we hawk to passers-by, the pathbreaking research our lab has just won funding for. The world in front of us has to not just pique our interest but also hold our focus, keep us moving ahead and reaching out – so we will seek it out and stay seeking it. This is a difficult needle to thread, between attracting and distracting our attention. If all we learn is to be constantly on the hunt for excitement and novelty, this can spill over into making us easily sidetracked – we get lost down warrens of procrastination tunnels, and caught up in the tiniest, most incidental details.

The everyday situations we find ourselves in may offer us external motivations to keep up our energy and engagement. The roles we are expected to play can have scope for continuous growth and self-direction built into them – and even give us leeway for incremental innovations of our own. But adhering to the expectations of our company, our country's laws, our research field, or our religious creed is only half the story: to get anywhere, we need to internalise them, convert them into inner drives. We must get used to seeing the causal chain from one outcome to the next, so we can start to identify every next milestone to head towards. Over time, this gives us forward momentum at a pace we can handle – not so fast that it sweeps us off our feet, not so slow that we grow impatient and diffuse. Part of how we learn this is by linking our sense of opportunity to our sense of responsibility. Being a top-tier athlete or scholar, doing a decent job as a management consultant or a financial advisor, means staying sharp and being on the lookout for new chances to take a punt on.

But it is no good doing that in a heedless and scatty way – or we may flounder about indecisively and derail the whole enterprise. We Keen Beans need to know what project milestones we have to hit, what latitude we have to improvise and speculate, and how to make the most of the means at our disposal. And the way to ensure that we hold ourselves accountable is to tie our responsibility to other people we either look up to or look out for. We learn to see everything expected of us as a chance to do something with, or for, 'our people', the ones we are accompanied or surrounded by. This is reinforced through contracts, oaths of allegiance, promises, vows, and other commitments that bind us over time, steering our attention towards them and holding it in place. Eventually, we blur the two together. Our orientation towards what we do and towards others becomes one and the same.

Once we internalise this orientation, we Keen Beans can take it in two powerful directions. For one, when we take on this sense of mutual belonging, our craving for connection can turn into a craving for ownership. Merely being attuned and aligned with our surroundings stops being enough for us, and we may insist on something more intense: a way to make whoever and whatever we invest in durably 'ours'. Perhaps unsurprisingly, social research suggests that this possessive eagerness is strongest in the world of consumer business and finance – driving the rise of bubbles in asset price markets, and the push not just to rent property but to own it.[2] Living our best lives in the sales, hunting for an armful of bargains – and coming home with a second armful of impulse purchases too. If something wakens our excitement, we may conclude that the only way for us to sate ourselves is by acquiring it. And beyond the immediate novelty of acquiring it, we become emotionally attached, increasingly seeing it as an extension of ourselves. Whoever or whatever we are keen on, we learn to treat them as an integral part of our personal 'endowment'.

At the same time, it can soon come as naturally as breathing to put ourselves right at the centre of whatever enterprise we happen to be involved in. We take on board that if we do not get stuck in, and give it every last scrap of our energy and effort, any connection we value may end up withering on the vine. So we find ourselves taking more and more of a leading part, placing ourselves increasingly at the head of things. And we let ourselves become ostentatious and theatrical – bold in a good-natured, go-getting, primary-colour way. If we see the next big thing, a route to preferment, we demand to be noticed, to be picked – like Jo March in *Little Women*, straining every sinew to make her mark as the successful writer she has set her heart on becoming. We look for the camera to jump in front of, the crowd we can work, the troops we can entertain.

The risks of overreach

We Keen Beans carry within us a highly entrepreneurial sense of self. There is nothing hesitant or clandestine in how we set loose our will upon the world: everything in our thoughts and actions becomes geared towards making our presence felt. Irrepressible, flamboyant, and daring to a fault, we tend to tackle our surroundings with the adventurousness of a cocker spaniel. We are the ones who pick up the phone unprompted to check in on our friends and family. We plan the hen and stag parties, the city-break excursions to clubs and castles. We set up the WhatsApp groups, organise the shared drives, and insist on that extra selfie at the dinner table.

This also means that our conception of what success looks like is quite simple and linear: we do well when we get some, and better when we get more. Like the scrappy upstart Alexander Hamilton in Lin-Manuel Miranda's musical reimagining, we seize upon every chance presented to us to get ourselves seen and our opinions heard – not a single shot thrown away, our legacy in mind, always giving the eye of history something to see. Even if that means clashing with the sober statesmanship of George Washington (Cool Cat), or the slick charm of Thomas Jefferson (Jokester), or the self-withholding machinations of Aaron Burr (Quibbler).

Yet beneath our determination lurks the possibility that we will overdo it. In a previous job, I found myself line-managing a new colleague, hired to give my team much-needed extra capacity. At first, he was a welcome breath of fresh air. Dynamic, well-motivated, great at getting things done fast and on time. Always first to volunteer for new responsibilities, always with 'yes, and' suggestions to explore. But after a while, cracks started to show. Drafts came back riddled with errors, key bits of analysis missing, irrelevant details in their place. 'I thought that was actually a more interesting point to make!' Triumphant updates after every sales call promised imminent deals that never materialised – while would-be clients were put off by his obvious exaggeration of what our company could deliver. 'But they seemed so keen when we spoke!'

Instead of adding extra capacity, he produced a dizzying array of new initiatives that piled more work onto what we were already focusing on. 'I think what we really need to be doing is . . .' Each idea was negotiated fully under his own steam, often well beyond his brief, while our guidance was left unfollowed and painstaking comments unanswered. He remained convinced he knew exactly what he was doing, and impervious to our increasingly forceful attempts to rein him in. The crunch point came after six months, when he demanded a grandiose new title and the raise to go with it. Not this time, sorry, we need you to knuckle down and focus on our core projects. Soon after, his resignation landed in my inbox. 'I feel my skills will be better appreciated elsewhere.'

In other words, for all our vibrant energy and relentless enthusiasm, we Keen Beans can become a bit of a handful. What starts as enterprising determination and relentless enthusiasm can flip into overbearing arrogance. Worse still, if we leave it unchecked, it can balloon into entitlement, the insistence that others drop what *they* are doing and give us and what *we* are doing their full focus, simply because we have asked for it. If we are not careful, we may even start to get a little hazy on the boundaries between 'us' and 'them', 'ours' and 'theirs'. In fact, 'theirs' may start to figure less in our understanding of things, to be replaced with 'could be ours' and 'should be ours'.

That is a fast-track to confrontation, because this side of our thinking is almost custom-made to rub several other thinker-types firmly up the wrong way. Hotheads and Worrywarts, for instance, may be highly allergic to having their boundaries crossed – especially if we do not try to understand what makes them so protective of what is 'theirs' in the first place. Cool Cats and Gloomsters, meanwhile, may read our demeanour as reckless abandon, while Jokesters and Quibblers might think of us more as wearingly naïve. We must avoid coming across as though we are transparently instrumentalising the people we meet. They cannot be left with the impression that our aim in engaging with them is purely to subsume them into our grand portfolio.

Although this is a risk, as a general rule, we are fairly good at keeping a handle on ourselves. After all, we have to find ways of sustaining our efforts over time. It is no use getting put in charge of something if we abandon the responsibilities we volunteered for at the first sign of something new on the horizon. Without some object permanence around our various prior commitments, our eagerness becomes self-defeating. We have to stay the course. This makes us not so much flashes in the pan as slow burners; we have the Duracell bunny stamina and the resolve to sate our need for immediate gratification.

Finding the bright sides

There is a relaxed, good-humoured side to us, which is one of our greatest assets. The bright light of our eagerness – our Anne Shirley-ish conviction that 'tomorrow is a new day with no mistakes in it yet' – bathes everything in a golden glow. We notice how effective our enthusiasm can be, as long as we use it just the right amount. And if we can get a handle on our inclinations, we can be very choosy about when we deploy it. Like Santiago in *The Alchemist*, we can satisfy our curiosity through our everyday adventures *and* holding in view our deepest dreams – which we see reflected in our immediate surroundings.

We may not always have been the most assiduous learners at school. Likely enough, we were the ones running a note-passing operation in the back of the class. Nor may we have been the most disciplined in training at the gym or on the field. But as we have kept coming across little titbits of excitement – a skill we want to achieve here, a medal contest we want to go for there – we have usually weaned ourselves off any temptation to be lazy. We actively want a challenge, a new bit of handicraft we can turn our fingers to. Part of our genius is in attuning ourselves to our environment: we harmonise our purposes with the contexts in which we want to assert them.

We quickly learn how well we can hold the world's attention by keeping it guessing. Our pupils never know when we might put on *Death of Stalin* or *Gladiator* or *Saving Private Ryan* for the rest of our history class. Our children are never sure when we might produce a bag of Haribos for them to devour, or pile them into the car for a surprise trip to Disneyland. All they know is that we might. That little soupçon of cultivated randomness lets us tread the careful line between being confident and in charge, and at the same time approachable, relatable, and human.

Part of what makes us (self-)assured enough to act like this is that we can find a good side to more or less everything we see – and, in turn, approach it all with best intentions. If we see loneliness, we offer attention, care, and affection. If we see flaws or problems, we immediately also see ways to relieve and remedy them. We discover ways to see the miraculous in the mundane, the wonderful in the awful. We are eager to please, to be pleasant, to be pleased. Our courtesy and considerate generosity can help us defuse virtually any tensions or frictions.

This can give the impression that we Keen Beans are a little biddable and bloodless – which makes us liable to be exploited by those around us. In *Piranesi*, the young journalist Matthew Rose Sorensen's blithe curiosity leads him to fall for the occultist Valentine Ketterley's trickery – despite copious warning signs, which he dismisses – and become trapped in the otherworldly halls of 'the House'. Research from several disciplines has highlighted the 'toxic positivity' that this indulgent side of our character can lead to.[3] Since resilience and emotional strength is so tightly bound into our mindsets, we can put up with a lot more pressure than most other thinker-types – perhaps all bar Cool Cats. Time and again, we affirm, on trust if not through experience, that there must be a way through, if only we strain hard enough to find it. We do so even in the face of refusal and hostility from the people we are trying to help – all in the name of keeping everyone's spirits up. We may find ourselves carrying a torch into the oppressive dark long after other people's lights are extinguished. Then, our determined reaching-out can become increasingly an act of dull faith.

Our eagerness may give us the fortitude and force of will to cope with everything life sends our way. But it can also make us milder and gentler than we rightly ought to be – too inclined to let things slide. Bluntly, not everything is uniformly exciting. Some things are horrifying, scary, and upsetting. If we let our eagerness reach excessive levels of positivity – insisting that we can always find a bright side – it can start to come across as disingenuous or forced, and damage us in the long run. It is unwise to be unquestioningly wowed by the world, and unrealistic to expect to control whatever it throws at us. We must not let one of our greatest strengths turn into our greatest weakness. We sometimes need to down-regulate our eagerness for pleasure, to allow the rest of our rich inner emotional life to come out.

Our retort to this may well be: is it *really* so bad if we are not struck to our core whenever we feel something about the world?

We can feel and carry on going, without turning every experience into a moment of existential import – something other thinker-types should integrate into their thinking too. True, what in us might come across as cocksure nonchalance is often a sign of how stable and tractable our emotional arcs typically are. People are likely to meet us in a sanguine frame of mind. When we seek something, we generally do not waver in our commitment. Rather, we bide our time, expecting that we will eventually achieve it – we lie in wait, readying ourselves to pounce when the right moment presents itself. We are more inclined to try and ambush our targets than charge in headfirst, guns blazing in every direction. We are eager, but we remain thoroughly in control.

Stocking up in the sweetshop

Perhaps the most emblematic element of our mindset is how easily we Keen Beans can become captivated by the world. Finding things miraculous or wonderful is too *passive* for us. We want to truly believe in them – and for that, we have to immerse ourselves fully, be captured by them, mind, body, and soul. We can become fascinated by pretty much anything that crosses our radar. This makes us adaptable and versatile in social situations, as we can switch gears fluidly and without a large outlay of conscious effort on our part. Fascination for us is unforced, a spur-of-the-moment response that, like Alice, we are willing to follow down every rabbit-hole to Wonderland – or straight through every looking-glass.

The downside is that we are prone to getting easily diverted. We can be too spirited, too vehement in the way we pursue what attracts us. In part, this is because we embrace our sense of playfulness. This is by no means a bad thing. Research has shown that playfulness has a wide range of beneficent effects – fostering secure attachment in children and better cognitive health in older people.⁴ It also raises our job satisfaction, improves our learning outcomes, and helps create healthier, safer public spaces. Yet, still, when we Keen Beans play, we need to be careful about allowing ourselves to get dragged so far off-piste that we lose our train of thought and forget about our core purposes. So we should try – where we can – to only indulge those distractions that (perhaps counterintuitively) look like they might align with what we should be focusing on. We need to actively choose which way to turn, which prompts to respond to – but we cannot choose them all. We cannot have our cake *and* eat it. Every road we take means a road *not* taken.

I was once on holiday with some family friends who were determined to show me a picturesque little town on the shores of Lake Como. No sooner had I dropped my bags than they unleashed a deluge of plans for the long weekend I was there. A parade of fondues, pastas, seafood on the promenade. Cable cars into the mountains above Argegno, a hike back down. A day trip to the Liszt house in Bellagio. The botanical garden at Villa Carlotta. Gelato tourism in Colico. It was all I could do not to get entirely overwhelmed. One evening, they pressed an old Baedeker guide to the area into my hands. 'You were saying how much you love old books! Here's something for you to get stuck into before we head out tomorrow!'

All the while, they kept up a whirlwind of conversation, orbiting around their favourite topics. The best-designed hotels in California and Nevada (one was an architect). The cutthroat world of Second World War stamp collecting (the other was a philatelist). The ins and outs of researching their family history (a passion they both shared). And, vicariously, the perils of online dating, with a compendium of stories sourced from their 20-something daughter. They seemed quite content to have me along for the ride, explaining a reference here, an in-joke there – but otherwise just carrying on while I sat back and played the passenger.

This sort of behaviour may give us an air of mercurial irresponsibility. Coupled with the unsentimental vibe we Keen Beans project, we might appear not to be all that fussed about anything around us whatsoever. Our sheer outward-facingness can give our preoccupations an air of being only skin deep, rather than something we draw from deep within our souls – especially compared to the drama of a Hothead, or the gravity of a Gloomster. This is a contradiction we see at the heart of Holly Golightly's capricious restlessness in *Breakfast at Tiffany's*, as she chases an idealised life of fabulous elegance. Her eagerness is transparently performative – but it is also a genuine survival mechanism, as she awaits moments of bona fide connection that offer the possibility of new beginnings and a place to belong.

Our seeming lack of deep concern is a false impression. What others may experience as psychological overload (as I did with my friends) is just the breakneck pace at which our intellectual metabolism works. We can squeeze any number of hobbies into our schedules – banjo here, watercolours there, beekeeping over on the allotment. We may be busy, but we still make sure everything has its proper time slot – short, maybe, but intensely sweet. The more we do this, the better we get at picking things up, getting the value we want out of them, and then putting them down again when it is time to move on. That is how we keep the overload at bay. The risk is that what we focus on gives us only an incomplete, muddled, or myopic view of what is actually going on – above all, by hastily skipping past other people's priorities if we happen not to share them. Our ability to be a jack or jill of all trades is a useful skill to have, but one we should use circumspectly. Experience will teach us many of the lessons we need to learn – but that is no good if the shortcuts we take along the way lead us into thickets we cannot extricate ourselves from.

Finding ourselves in company

We Keen Beans live much of our lives in a state of sprightly anticipation, fuelled by our urge to be close to those around us. When we seek out other people, we are not just curious about them – we want their company. Like Saleem Sinai searching for his fellow 'midnight's children', we can feel an almost telepathic link to a nebulous group of 'our people', and we make it our lifetime's project to find and claim them as 'our own'. The kid next to us in chemistry class who becomes our closest friend for life. The stranger in the bar or on the dating app we go for drinks with, kiss, sleep with, move in with, buy a house and a pet with, marry, have kids with, grow old and retire with, and eventually fall asleep next to for the final time. For all of us, entire life trajectories come down to a moment where we reach out instead of drawing back. And because we Keen Beans want as many of these connections as possible, we err on the side of being positive and sociable whenever we get the chance.

We look out for, and look forward to, the intriguing chaos that interacting with others brings. We are gregarious and animated, waiting for new opportunities to get to know them. It is through exchange that we really get the most out of people. Gifts given, gifts received. Swapping late-night gossip about our school crushes. Pausing for more than just perfunctory pleasantries with our office reception staff. We scoop people up, we make them 'ours'. We are quintessential social butterflies, receptive to all manner of convivial or collaborative engagement. We may frequently embark on schemes that rely on us pooling our resources with others in some way – start a band together, plan to cowrite articles, concoct outlandish holiday adventures. No matter if we do not always see them through before we move onto the next one! Above all, we like joining forces with thinker-types who are similarly cooperatively minded. Revellers for their ardent yearning, Agonisers for their activist motivation, Happy Campers for the sheer pleasure they take in being along for the ride – together with them, what we can accomplish feels limitless.

We Keen Beans want attraction, connection, proximity – not just a little, but in spades. And we cannot wait to keep crafting our narratives, making ourselves the protagonists of another chapter in our epic saga – like Lyra Belacqua in *His Dark Materials*, headstrong and rebellious, drawn into one adventure after another to save our friends and discover the truth about the world. The danger is that we go out of our way to find people to call 'our own' at any price, tolerating whatever we need to so we can get along. We risk compromising on what we value, sacrificing what makes us *us*, selling off our prized assets, just to find the belonging we are looking for. We may let other people eat away at us, sometimes pandering to them too far – friends who make us the butt of their jokes, or partners who take out their bad days on us. We are apt to brush this off, sweep it under the carpet, refuse to notice it enough to let it dampen our excitement.

But we must remember that, for our reaching-out not to be lopsided, it has to go both ways. It is all very well for us to be forthcoming and approachable towards the people we encounter – they need to be the same to us in return. We often discover who we are, forming a stable conception of ourselves, by belonging to several social groups.[5] So we must not let the prize of belonging to one come at the cost of forging links to any others – since that sort of overinvestment may ultimately fail to give us the quality and quantity of connections we are looking for.

We get our self-actualisation from being accepted by the people around us. We are eager to learn how to connect with them individually, and how to play a meaningful part in the group as a whole. For us, that involvement comes above all through self-expression, by sharing what we believe and know – and we expect that others will share their thoughts with us in exchange. We are usually just about patient enough to keep a tight rein, bottling up our eagerness until the right moment comes to release our effusive energy. But 'our people' will be the ones who can carve out space for the fervent way we tend to express ourselves, and let our boundless capacity for fascination explode out of us from time to time.

Every time we find this acceptance, we feel as though we have come home. The idea of a 'chosen family' perhaps resonates better with us than with many other thinker-types – the possibility of finding a group that will cherish us, nurture us, raise us into the most brilliant beings we can be. Sometimes we may discover that this expectation was misplaced. But our belief that connection, fellow-feeling, and embracing other people are the things in life that are most worth pursuing remains unchanged.

The value of fervency

Being a Keen Bean tends to be high-risk, high-reward – a profile in courage, and in having the sheer brazen wherewithal to see how far we can push our luck. Our mindset is highly empowering and energising. It drives us to go out and get what we want – not just get involved, but step to the front, take charge, and make things happen. We are flexible and spontaneous: we always spot something that piques our excitement, and we give ourselves space to pursue it as far as possible. And we have the stamina to stick with whatever we commit to. Our feelings are not just transient inclinations; they stay with us steadily for a long time without overwhelming our thinking.

Several thinker-types might profit from adding a bit of Keen Bean to their mindsets. We know how to see opportunities in the world rather than threats – a useful counter for Worrywart suspicions, but equally appropriate for Gloomsters' and Hotheads' morbid confrontations too. We have an intuitive gift for discovering what is precious and special about the people around us, and the best way to approach them – which Quibblers struggle with, and which may soften Jokesters' catty mockery as well. In general, we embrace the crazy unpredictability of getting to know people well and deeply, which can help Agonisers and Cool Cats to 'loosen up' and join the fray.

But we must also remain sensitive to the less positive effects of our personas. We recklessly say yes to too many things. We overreach and hoard – we cannot give everything the attention it deserves, but we also cannot always let it go. We may end up putting off precisely the people we try to win over if we railroad them and chronically overstep their boundaries. We get so caught up in the thrill of the chase that we struggle to differentiate between 'good exciting' and 'bad exciting', since everything stimulates and interests us. Together, this risks cheapening the connections we build, giving the impression that we are not all that invested in them – and may lead to us forming an inaccurate view of what is going on based mostly on its shiniest sides.

Thankfully, other thinker-types can help us offset this. To avoid getting side-tracked, and to better aim our effervescence at what matters most, we can learn from the affective 'targeting' that comes more naturally to Hotheads and Revellers. We also need to be less acquiescent, and avoid compromising on our sense of self just to be accepted, a lesson few thinker-types can teach us better than the exceptionally boundaried Jokesters and Worrywarts. Tying these together, we can grasp how to find a home in ourselves rather than the things and people around us – seeing *ourselves* as ongoing projects of improvement, in the way that Gloomsters and Quibblers typically do.

In many respects, we hold the key to what it means for us all to be a society. Inquisitive as meerkats, we pop up to keep a beady eye on the horizon, chittering vivaciously if something turns up. Few can rival our agility as we move from one thing to another, then the next, then the one after that. But we must not let ourselves get carried away, or we may waste our energies on fleeting attachments that go nowhere and ultimately leave us unsatisfied. If we keep chasing off to broaden our horizons, we may end up disappearing over other people's horizons ourselves. We are an active, essential ingredient in the encounters and interactions we have – but we cannot let them dominate us to our own detriment.

CHAPTER 8

Worrywart

For some of us, the only way to face the world is to treat it with the utmost seriousness. At drinks one time with two former colleagues, talk turned to a massive tranche of spending cuts being debated in the House of Commons. One, a welfare economist, was unequivocally against. 'It's an act of national self-harm! People *need* these services; without them, they'll literally die!' The other, a lifer at the business department, was just as resolutely for. 'We don't have a choice! The country's broke, the markets will ruin us if we don't cut *something*!' Watching them disagree was disconcerting enough – their views were usually in near-lockstep on everything. Worse was the sheer agitation they were spiralling towards, when both normally kept their cards firmly to their chests. 'You're just doing the extremists' dirty work!' 'And you're paving the way to societal collapse!'

They both swiftly excused themselves from our meet-up. Within minutes, my phone buzzed with a slew of messages. 'Sorry you had to see that.' 'Did I go too far?' 'Is he annoyed with me?' 'Should I text her?' Both worried they had crossed a line, unsure how to straighten things out, all ears for any advice I had. I told them it would probably blow over. They each had good reason to think what they thought, and they liked and respected each other enough to make up eventually. 'Yeah, I mean I *did* do an economics master's . . .' 'I *do* have a decade-plus of policy experience . . .' Exactly. A professional disagreement. 'So you don't think I'm the one who's mad?'

This is the mindset of the *Worrywart*. What are the signs that we might be prone to this kind of thinking too? Do we see risk and danger wherever we look? Find our mind easily paralysed by concerns, conjuring up ever more lurid worst-case scenarios? Do we cling to a litany of careful plans to help us navigate problems – or cower and hide from conflict, making ourselves small to take up as little space as possible? Or will we do anything to make threats go away, even sacrificing our dearest principles?

This is a mindset of shy uncertainty, which makes us 'turtle up' whenever we meet what we do not know (see fig. 8.1). We Worrywarts are highly **fearful**, which we accompany with a mixture of six personality traits – **emotional**, **introverted**, **disagreeable**, **conscientious**, **closed**, and **biased–superior**. The Worrywart is the main 'home' of fear in the thinker-type family – although, as we saw previously, fear also plays a part in the Agoniser mindset, which creates a degree of mutual approachability between these two thinker-types.

Our fear combines with these personality traits to produce a mental outlook of troubled concern. Of all our traits, the trifecta of emotionality, introversion, and closedness have the strongest relationship with fear. The first of these puts our nerves on edge, sharpens our sensitivity to nearby shocks and spooks, and pushes us to react to them quickly and abruptly. The other two ensure that this reaction is not one of pushing forward but pulling back. Introversion makes us freeze up and withdraw to the safety of our private corner, while closedness puts us into lockdown, cagily taking stock of our options. Meanwhile, conscientiousness motivates us to get on top of our situation, marshal our resources, and work out what we need to do. Our disagreeableness and bias–superiority keep up a drumbeat of suspicion towards the world, reminding us to maintain our distance – and never stop looking after number one.[1]

We Worrywarts regularly gravitate towards the 'worst news' about our situations: things that have just happened, or the long shadow of things that took place a while ago. Our reactions to them vary from extreme disapproval to (less often) strong approval, in both cases from a position of resistance to change, even full-on intransigence. We are prone to going back over and tweaking our views in light of our fearful experiences, though we are reticent about letting other people tell us how to think. Our reflections can jump almost at random between highly ordered and somewhat chaotic, and we have particular shortcuts we like to rely on – sometimes factoring in other people's opinions, sometimes firmly rejecting them.

	Fig. 8.1: The Worrywart		
	Personality traits		
MENTAL OUTLOOK	Emotional		Emotionally stable
	Conscientious		Careless
	Agreeable		Disagreeable
	Honest–humble		Biased–superior
	Open to experience		Closed to experience
	Extroverted		Introverted
	Emotions		
	Fearful (anxious)		Eager (seeking)
	Happy (joyful)		Sad
	Angry		Calm
	Disgusted		Desiring

MENTAL PICTURE	**Information**		
	Selective	▮▮▮▮▮▮▮▮▮	Indiscriminate
	Personality-congruent	▮▮▮▮▮▮▮▮▮	Emotion-congruent
	New ▮▮▮ Previous ▮▮▮		Long-unused
	High	▮▮▮▮▮▮▮▮▮	Low
	Positive	▮▮▮▮▮▮▮▮▮	Negative
	Fast	▮▮▮▮▮▮▮▮▮	Slow
	Diverse	▮▮▮▮▮▮▮▮▮	Limited
	Predispositions		
	Emotion-congruent	▮▮▮▮▮▮▮▮▮	Reasoning-congruent
	New	▮▮▮▮▮▮▮▮▮	Previous
	Revise/revisit	▮▮▮▮▮▮▮▮▮	Defend/maintain
	Conservative/reactionary	▮▮▮▮▮▮▮▮▮	Progressive/radical
	Pro	▮▮▮▮▮▮▮▮▮	Con
	Compliant	▮▮▮▮▮▮▮▮▮	Defiant
FORMULATING THOUGHTS	**Reasoning**		
	Heuristic	▮▮▮▮▮▮▮▮▮	Non-heuristic
	Reasonable	▮▮▮▮▮▮▮▮▮	Unreasonable
	Rational	▮▮▮▮▮▮▮▮▮	Irrational

Becoming a Worrywart

The core sensation we Worrywarts feel is one of disorienting unease. It can come upon us without warning – a quivering question-mark appearing over our sense of what is and what is not, getting in the way of our ability to feel or focus on much else, or perhaps lodging minutely in the back of our minds, growing ever larger in our consciousness, almost without us noticing. It might feel like a lurch in our stomachs, a sudden shudder piercing our hearts, or even a clammy vice that clamps our whole bodies in its grip. When it appears, we learn to disengage on instinct – we strain to draw back, impelled by an overriding drive to protect ourselves.

The social experiences that realise this mindset within us are ones that challenge and destabilise our sense of how much in the world we can treat as normal and guaranteed. For all of us, so much of who we are and what we do rests on an unspoken assumption that we have some degree of personal control and oversight over what is going on. We assume that anything we deal with is broadly consistent, familiar if not totally predictable. We also assume that it falls within our wheelhouse enough that we can do something about it. But every so often, we find ourselves colliding abruptly with some things outside our control, which we cannot necessarily cope with – because they are just bigger than us. Acts of god and *force majeure*, grand strategy by global corporations and superpowers, but also the wilful decisions of our family members, friends, and neighbours. Something wicked this way comes, that *is* Birnam wood coming to Dunsinane! We know its name as clear as a bell: danger, threat!

Our relationship to threats can develop from an occasional 'turn' into a permanent feature of our thinking in several ways. A short-lived, present-focused shock may trigger in us a sense of alarm, and an instinct to escape or evade: a formal warning, a raised fist, a smashed window. We may develop longer-acting, future-focused caution towards non-specific threats that are often at most shadows on the horizon – the putative judgement of 'the markets' or 'the voters', global catastrophes such as climate change or war, or simply 'what our parents would say if they knew'. Or perhaps we have spent time on constant alert during situations of chronic stress and difficulty – living on or near the breadline, caught between day gigs and nightshifts, wondering how far the next paycheck will stretch. All of these in their own ways can prompt us to become more vigilant, and prioritise learning more about whatever is causing us fear and anxiety.

More existentially, our Worrywart unease can be activated by moments in our day-to-day lives where *what is* is haunted by *what should not be*. Cultural theory has developed many ways to understand situations where what we think is going on gets punctured by something that does not fit the pattern.[2] Unexpected events that challenge our reality, 'wrong answers' that send us scurrying back to check our working out. A bit of rogue data our equations cannot account for, some outlier event our probability distribution cannot fathom, a glitch in the system. Spectral traces of previous events and experiences, or scars from past ordeals, perhaps, which never quite fade away. Alternative ways our lives might have been can occasionally feel like they haunt how they actually are – the partner we might never have met if we had not turned into that bar on a whim, the accident we might have been caught up in if we had not hesitated a split second longer crossing the road. These remind us that all is not what it seems, that what we think of as our stable foundation is really resting on the finest sand.

It takes being exposed, repeatedly and over a prolonged

period, to circumstances that disconcert us in these ways for us to develop a Worrywart mindset. The more we find ourselves in situations of instability, the more our worries about them grow to fill the space available in our minds, steadily crowding out our other priorities. Memories of pain during our most formative experiences, from passing scratches to deep traumas, permanently rewire how we deal with the world – while any and all disruptions can fuel our underlying wary uncertainty about our lives, even more so if they continue to remain unresolved. Fundamentally, we grow aware that we cannot be as sure of ourselves and our surroundings as we thought. In these situations, we come to the view that all we can rely on is our ability to think our way through – and out of – our predicament, although we would not speculate on how easy, or plausible, it will be for us to make that happen.

As a result, more than most other thinker-types, Worrywarts are prone to seeing the world as a hostile environment, divided into 'ours' and 'not ours', 'victory' and 'defeat', 'gain' and 'loss'. We worry that it is filled not just with bad but with outright evil – malevolent people, baneful things, adverse events, menacing situations. Cosmic horrors and chthonic nightmares that assail us from all sides. All we can do is fall back on what we have – like Jonathan Harker, gradually reconstructing his grip on reality after discovering the true vampiric nature of Count Dracula and his bloodthirsty brides, and barely escaping with his life and sanity intact. We rally around what is safely 'ours' – the flag we follow, the patches of land that stay steady underfoot – and fortify ourselves with rights and razor wire. This is how we become wary, taciturn, withdrawn. What do we trust, who can we command? Only ourselves.

All alone in the unknown

More than many other thinker-types, we Worrywarts are intensely preoccupied with ourselves. This is not a matter of narcissistic self-absorption, but a far more timid, reclusive drive for self-preservation. We feel an overwhelming, relentless apprehension towards the prospect of our own injury and death – and we deeply internalise warnings from our surroundings about the risks of pain and hurt that might jeopardise our mental and bodily integrity. Even the slightest stirrings of fear in our gut, the merest suggestion of a scare on the horizon, can be enough to put us on edge. We lie at the hypersensitive, ill-at-ease end of the thinker-type spectrum. If at any point we grow selfish, it is because we feel vulnerable – and because we know that, above all else, we must look after ourselves. Because we cannot be sure that anybody else will.

This sense of vulnerability puts our guard up, and makes us fall into a somewhat suspicious frame of mind. We feel a pressing need to retreat to somewhere that can give us a sense of safety, so we circle the wagons around us and 'our own'. Anybody and anything outside the perimeter we draw around our little encampment is not only not with us, but (potentially, at least) against us. It is not that we do not care about anyone or anything around us – quite the opposite, they concern us *a lot*. It is more that we can distinguish quite firmly between the protective concern we show towards those on our side of the boundary wall, and the defensive concern we feel about the rest. Those on the outside are neither near enough to belong to us, nor far enough away for us to be certain that they are not a threat – so we feel far too detached for them to count as 'ours', and we want to *stay* detached from them, to stop them getting to us.

At times, we may feel a particularly acute pang of isolation – a cold conviction that there is actually very little that genuinely lies in our control, on 'our' side of the perimeter. If that happens, we can start to panic about how much possibility there is 'out there' for evil to impinge on our lives, and harmful things to happen to us. This is the gateway where conspiracy thinking can come screeching in, when we start to think in increasingly stark terms of 'us against the rest'. We may even reduce whoever or whatever we meet to a simple, one-dimensional calculus: 'ours', safe; 'not ours', dangerous. It is a logic that can freeze our thinking, as we trap ourselves into defining everyone and everything we come across in these binary terms. As long as we remain uncertain about them, we assume the worst. When someone or something new appears in our surroundings, we take a while to thaw ourselves out of our frozen fear – and in that time, we remain distant and frosty towards them, keeping them at arm's length.

If we start to see threats everywhere we look, we can drive ourselves witless with fear of anything unknown, even give ourselves over entirely to mind-bending paranoia. All our time and space is out of joint, all we see is weird and incongruous, there are only clumsy sutures where the pieces of our reality fit together. If things that *should not be* are now on the menu, then that is all we can fixate on. Yet we need to stop our minds from running riot at the darkest end of the spectrum of possibility. If we do not, once unleashed, our minds may keep whirling down this path until they spin out entirely, and we lose the ability to pay proper attention to what is really going on.

To self-preserve and shore up our psyches in the face of this uncertainty, we often cast around for instructions. We want to know where to turn, which authorities we should listen to, so that we do what is expected of us rather than jumping off the beaten track in fright. We need something we can depend on: an anchor, a foundation, a map that lets us navigate the world. Our pastors and teachers, company policies, government guidelines, and house rules help us learn how to cope – presenting us with ready-made solutions and guidance. We gravitate towards frameworks, laws, and structures that we can take for granted. Agendas, routines, and timetables tell us what is coming next; aide-mémoires let us predict what is going to happen based on what we remember happening before. Even just the reassuring presence of our friends gives structure to our lives – as it does for the chronically nervous Piglet in *Winnie-the-Pooh*, propped up by the easy-going Pooh (Happy Camper), the excitable Tigger (Keen Bean), and even the eternally pessimistic Eeyore (Gloomster).

But in our vigilance, it matters that we pay attention to the right sort of information from among all the advice we get from the people around us. If the warnings they give us become too dire – if they do not also come with suggested remedies and clear paths forward for our situation – we risk becoming completely paralysed or succumbing to sheer panic. Meanwhile, if we detect even the slightest sign that we received bad advice, we grow defensive, push back, resist, turn down aid. It is not that we become complacent or overconfident – after all, the threats are still out there, and we are far too self-disciplined to dial back our alertness. Rather, the danger is that we become hesitant to trust solutions that would make our day-to-day lives easier, and withdraw so far behind our walls that we disengage from those around us. Our anchor becomes unmoored, and we dismiss any mental map that is not 'our own' as an unreliable witness.

Unhelpfully, this suggests that we need conditions to be perfect every time we cross paths with anyone or anything we do not already count as 'ours', or we will refuse to put ourselves in that position again. Yet that sort of perfection is vanishingly rare. We need to channel a little of the Agoniser mindset here. They take their fears as seriously as we do, but they are also open enough to give second chances if things do not work out first time. And even if we do not share blither thinker-types' comfort with what is going on, we can at least take on some of their proactive determination. Sure, the world is a scary place. But it will not become any *less* scary for us hiding away from it. Better to seize the initiative and face it on our front foot. If it helps, we can try to minimise the importance of what scares us: dismiss it as a fringe concern, or exaggerate its ridiculous inconsistencies, as Quibblers and Jokesters would. If that still does nothing for us, then it is time to channel our best Hothead and dredge up the courage to face it head-on.

Expecting judgement and failure

More than most, we feel at the mercy of the world around us – a world that contains far more problems than opportunities. At times, it seems as if we are treading a precarious, exhausting path through our lives, like carting a basket of Fabergé eggs through a minefield. Being ourselves, doing anything, even merely being alive, always carries a risk of opening us up to attack, from the flanks, from the rear, from up ahead. This may lead us to face the world skittishly, spinning like a top, trying to keep our anxious gaze on every angle of approach.

We can internalise the idea that everything we do, say, and think, is carried out under the unseen watchful eyes of myriad nameless judges. Then, every action becomes a performance, every choice a test, with critics eyeing us over their half-moon spectacles, waiting to pounce. We go from careful to cautious, self-controlling, and self-evaluating, becoming our own harshest censors. Social research has examined various aspects of the 'surveillance society' that lead us to fear – but also submit to, and take part in – 'disciplinary' observation, from education to medical check-ups to counter-terror.³ The architecture of centralised top-down guarding and monitoring (the 'panopticon'). Distributed networks of (often digital) exchange and reporting that hold us accountable through data about who we are and what we do. The 'synoptic' mass media that encourage us to see and value people behaving in various 'ideal-ised' ways. Mechanisms of exposing our lives to the view of those around us – to whose intrusions we Worrywarts are especially sensitive.

All of these prey on another of our underlying fears: a 'fear of missing out' on some part of ourselves, who we could be, what we could do, and of being excluded or passed over if we do not live up to expectations. The pressure this puts on us to be *better* and do *more* may often clash directly with our deeply ingrained caution. We are torn between pushing further, harder, and pulling back – driven by a raw instinct to advance, or just simply maintain our lot in life. It is the conflict faced by the young translation scholar Robin Swift in *Babel*, torn between the austere acceptance of the Royal Institute of Translation and the growing call to rebellion – the latter embraced far more enthusiastically by the charismatic Ramy Mirza (Keen Bean) and moral Victoire Desgraves (Agoniser). Here, our fear vitalises us, making us taut as bowstrings. The whole uncertain tableau of success and failure stretches out before us. So we inch ahead, each tiptoed step a leap of faith, even finding a perverse normality in our perpetual agitation.

That we live on the edge of our seats is a source of confusion to thinker-types like Revellers or Happy Campers, who struggle to grasp why we cannot settle into a steadier emotional rhythm. It is because, deep down, we suspect that the world cannot be trusted to be a regular, stable, predictable place – no matter how thorough the maps we collect to navigate it. So even if we find we have nothing to worry about, even if the instructions others give us seem to be working, we can start to crave uncertainty just so we can give ourselves something to try to control. But the more we let that tendency run rampant, the less we can simply take our wins when we have them. We could take a leaf out of the Cool Cats' books here, and learn to gently guide our fear to the periphery of our thinking, so we can carve out a space for our inner peace.

The unpleasant alternative is that we may simply let ourselves become addicted to our anxiety. But that can come at a terrible cost. Our motors turn so violently when nothing bad is actually happening that when it does, we may spin right out of control. When there is nothing outside to rattle the foundations of our reality, we may start to shake the beams and pillars ourselves, invent problems and convince ourselves we need to fix them. Like the ambitious ballerina Nina Sayers in *Black Swan*, struggling to withstand the twin pressures of her director Thomas Leroy's stern scrutiny and lascivious advances – if we do not keep our panicky perfectionism safely within its guardrails, it can run us right off the tracks.

While I was working as a lecturer, I ended up in a slightly wearing 'battle of comparisons' with one of my colleagues. I had been hired before her, and we taught very different subjects. But I soon realised that, for better or worse, she was using me as a kind of 'reference point'. Which of our courses had more students signed up for – hers or mine? Who was spending more time on lecture prep? Who had published more articles? At first, these comparisons were easy enough to ignore – chalk them up to the institutional pressures of being an early career academic. But then they started to get pettier, more surreal. Who had the principal said hello to? Whose social media posts were getting more likes and shares? Which of us had spent more time that week reading, playing music, or down the gym?

It got to the point where I hesitated to do or say anything in front of her, just to escape another round of scrutiny. In the end, I cracked. Why was she doing this? 'I want to know whether I'm doing well or not.' But there were lots of ways of doing things well – and we were two totally different people! 'I find it reassuring.' Really? Even things that had nothing to do with our jobs? 'I need to know if there's something I'm missing.' And what would she do when she found it? 'Well, I'm sure there'll be something else to aim for.' More flaws that need fixing? 'Why, what else have you noticed?'

If we become so convinced that we live in a world where every corner is filled with fears, we will eventually find it has become wholly uninhabitable. We are beset with shadows, and we always will be, no matter what we do – so our best bet is to find ourselves a little hermit-cave to turtle up in. In the end, something has to give. If we live our lives highly strung, we put ourselves at risk of coming unstrung entirely. Like Ofelia in *Pan's Labyrinth*, hiding from the destructions of Francoist Spain in a fairytale underworld, we go into denial and fully enter a world of self-created make-believe to avoid acknowledging our traumatic reality.

Consumed by overthinking

Of course, there is a time to stand up to the world, and a time to turn and run away. But as we strain to draw back from every threat, we should keep tabs on which way our fight or flight (or faint, fawn, freeze, and so on) decisions go. We need to be judicious, else we may find ourselves tipping the balance towards giving up every time. That may very well keep us safe – but the more we choose to cave and run, the more we risk abandoning key parts of what makes us ourselves. We cannot keep doing that in the long run. We have to know that there is a baseline we will defend, or we will forget and forgo who we are entirely.

If we become lost in the turmoil of our inner conflict, we can enter into a passive, will-less state of mind – less participants than observers in the narrative of our own lives. If this happens, we may very quickly become susceptible to forces jostling to assert their authority over us, especially ones purporting to be on 'our' side of the defensive perimeter. They might offer to take all of our stressful decisions out of our hands, promise to enforce the law, restore order, take back control – put the genie of total possibility safely back in its bottle. As appealing as these might sound to us, especially in the moments when the cold shiver of fear runs right through us, we cannot lose our autonomy of thought or action – we must not let ourselves be shocked into submission.

The problem is that as Worrywarts, our minds are prone to both thrashing about blindly and cramping up into futility – both of which make it hard for us to think. Philosophical and psychological research has shown that different forms of fear, including anxiety and worry, profoundly erode our cognitive agility and flexibility.[4] Fear raises mental barriers we need to overcome before we can effectively take charge and adjust our approach. It hangs like a vapour in the backs of our minds, seeping into our synapses, and it takes hefty flexing and warming up to crank them into working order.

Our instinctive detachment lets us clarify what our threats are in the first place. Sometimes, we simply need to pull back from the world to take stock – just as in *Life of Pi*, it takes being shipwrecked and cast adrift with only a tiger for company for the shy zookeeper's son Pi Patel to face his anxieties and recentre himself on what gives him real meaning. Distance helps us analyse our potential threats and put them all (literally) into proper perspective. When we draw back, we buy ourselves precious space and time – a chance to unshield our eyes, uncover our ears, and come out of our brace position. We take the opportunity of our retreat into isolation to carry out a full inventory check. It is one of our unique assets that we can grasp the enormous range of options from success to failure and everything in between. But we need those moments of withdrawal to move from conjecture and speculation about what might be there to a grave and sober assessment of what actually is.

However, if this provokes our indecisiveness, it can risk making a bad situation worse. I was out at a gig with a group of friends, when one of them began to complain of acute pain lancing through her stomach. Suddenly, she collapsed, doubled over, crying in agony. We carried her into the foyer and rang the emergency services. Her boyfriend was beside himself. He flapped helplessly, staring at us as the emergency responder fired questions at him. Date of birth? '1993– no, 1991.' Any relevant medical history? 'I don't think so? I don't know.' Are you next of kin? 'Well, I'm her boyf—, I mean, partn—, I, probably not?' What medicines is she taking? 'Does paracetamol count?' The paramedics were not impressed.

At A&E he hung back as we bargained with the doctors to have our friend treated straightaway. Eventually, once she was safely in a hospital bed on an IV drip, he turned to us. 'You go on home; I'll stay here and look after her.' All right, we would go and bring some essentials from their flat. 'But you can't do that, I should be the one doing that!' OK, so was he staying or going? Again, he looked wildly at us, paralysed. A kindly nurse steered him towards a chair and handed us our friend's keys. When we came back, he was exactly where we had left him. Had he slept? 'No, I stayed up all night!' Why? 'In case she needed anything.' If she had, could the doctors not have dealt with it? 'I'm not sure.'

If we want to be charitable to ourselves in these moments, it is a sign of how alone we feel that we try to take on every task ourselves. Rather than taking baby steps, looking for allies to support us along the way, we dither and quail at how overwhelmingly bad everything is – we unleash our own inner C-3PO, frantically calculating the astronomical odds of failure as chaos reigns around us. And if anyone calls us out on our inaction, we can go abruptly from skulking twitchily in the back to throwing ourselves headlong into the breach. Instead of doing this, we need to train ourselves to ask for help sooner. Specifically, we must get better at identifying people we can trust within the 'generic mass' we are primed to be so suspicious about.

As we brood, we may second-guess everything we think we know and believe – even if just to make sure. It is virtually a ritual we put ourselves through. Our selves and our life plans are being called into question? Well, then let us question them *harder*, so we know they can stand the test! We apply to ourselves the strictest diagnoses and the most exacting treatments. Our risk assessments go well beyond the threats in question. We may pull out all the stops, upset the whole applecart, take everything apart to inspect it. That we do so is a sign of quite how hooked we can become on our own anxiety.

But not every threat is a threat of cataclysmic proportions. Some are pretty minor. So we have to put some healthy limits on our wholesale dismantling-and-reconstruction act. It may be useful up to a point – changing tactics when they stop working, trying a new angle to tackle a complex problem. But it can become a dogmatic intellectual safety blanket too. Above all, we must stop our fears from inflating to the level of phobias. Our anxieties about drowning, or falling from high up, help keep us safe from injury. A bit of nerves before entering a packed room full of new people, or getting up on stage to address a crowd, is entirely to be expected. But our lives may get seriously derailed if we are cripplingly afraid to ever go near water, or climb to any height, or interact with the people around us.

Doomsday prepping

One way to make ourselves less vulnerable to the predations of the world is to set our sights a little lower. Expectations management is the flipside of our risk management. If we bring what we think will happen more towards the middle of the bell curve of possibility, then there is a smaller chance that we will be caught unawares. This is, at heart, 'plan B' contingency thinking. It is thinking for a crisis, for when things are not going smoothly, for the 'state of exception'. For all our tendency towards paranoia and phobic superstitions, we also have a deeply pragmatic streak. As a result, we are the true planners of the thinker-type family – like Cool Cats, but with a more pronounced sense of urgency. Or rather, we are *over*planners. We overprepare until there is no terrain we have not combed over.

If we are going to try to establish some semblance of control over our situation, then we have to start by getting our house in order. We speak the language of systems and schedules, itineraries and inventories better than anyone else. It is simply what we learn to do when there are so many variables to consider. Our investors expect returns – so we need to make sure we live and breathe every last item in our fund portfolio, until we see them in our sleep. Our partner, our young children, our ageing parents are all depending on us to bring in enough money at the end of the month – so we had better be firmly on top of every penny coming in and out of our account.

Planning is how we steer a world of limitless possibility into tramlines that align with our aims. Yet research has shown that planning to excess can turn from a useful strategy for managing fear into a debilitating crutch that prevents us from actually addressing it.[5] Planning may satisfy our need for predictability. It gives us something tangible to do that lies in our power to start and finish. It also helps us feel that we are well-prepared to face anything, leaving as little as possible to chance. But this is also one way we tread water while we hesitate. It feels like we are doing something when we plan, and up to a point, we are making our choices better. Beyond that point, however, we are just procrastinating. Planning becomes an unhelpful avoidance strategy if by reducing our fear to a 'planning problem' we are simply denying the reality of our situation. A relationship that has run its course, rather than one that can be saved through better logistics. A project that needs to get done now, not reframed into oblivion. A public health crisis that we can only do so much to shield ourselves from.

In that case, compartmentalising everything into our plan only delays the moment of truth where we have to confront our fears. It reroutes precious cognitive effort towards something that only gives us the illusion of being useful. So rather than submerging ourselves into our best-laid plans, and our tried-and-tested methods, we need to keep checking ourselves. What purpose do they serve? Are they delivering the goods? Should we rethink how we do things? Or throw caution to the wind a bit, and just *get on with it*? We can learn from Hotheads how to find our courage, from Keen Beans how to discover the thrill of the fight, and from Cool Cats and Quibblers how to reduce our problems into easily solvable challenges. In all cases, we learn to see averting disaster as lying eminently within our power. Not everything worrisome becomes a catastrophe – in fact, most of our concerns never grow to be that bad at all. So the risk we incur by facing them rather than turning tail is fairly small. With that in mind, we become able to take baby steps, one after another, to stride on in the direction we wish to head.

The worth of careful reticence

Being a Worrywart comes with a pervasive sensation that there are formless shadows lurking just out of sight, poised to close in on us. Thinking like this does bring us some unambiguous advantages. No other thinker-type is more resolutely minded to put safety first. Few of them have as profound a sense of our own limitations in the face of a vast and often confusing reality, or a higher appreciation for what we *can* control. Among our most positive characteristics is our capacity for self-examination. We make ourselves into our own main project, and keep our focus on that project at all times. We are prepared to shut out the world outside and give ourselves the space to engage in deep, systematic thought. As a result, we are rewarded with a well-grounded understanding of how we want to fit into the bigger picture, and no shortage of plans for how to get there.

These are skills we can easily bring to other thinker-types too. Perhaps most obviously, we take things extremely seriously. There is no danger that we will minimise or trivialise anything about the world – as Revellers and Happy Campers are prone to do out of lusty enthusiasm. We are good at taking advice at the right time, especially when the going gets tough, and we are generally less inclined to rely on our own semi-filtered impressions than Cool Cats or Quibblers. We have a fairly accurate sense of when causes are lost, and when they are still promising enough to keep fighting for – something for Agonisers and Keen Beans to take on board in their endless quests to 'connect'.

Of course, the Worrywart mindset also comes with some penalties attached. As we have seen, we struggle to deal with unexpected events and departures from normality, which give us pause or make us freeze up. This inclination to stop in our tracks severely inhibits our ability to (re)act quickly and decisively. At worst, we give up before things have even really begun. Our bar for catastrophe and incipient failure is among the lowest in the thinker-type family, partly because our speculations tend to run away with themselves. We face the challenges the world throws our way as isolationists – inclined to try and rescue ourselves unaided, blinding ourselves to sources of help and support. But if that fails, we can flip quickly and easily into putting ourselves wholly into other people's hands.

To mitigate the negative outcomes from these tendencies, we can pick up a few tricks from other thinker-types. Key to this is finding ways to let light into our situation – which Happy Campers and Revellers certainly offer us, while Agonisers can show us how to convert our concerns about the world into efforts to change it. We need to grow less sensitive and more confident in our own abilities to meet what the world throws at us, like Cool Cats or Keen Beans. Above all, we should channel our intellects into problem-*solving* rather than merely problem-*finding* – which takes us more into the domain of Hotheads or Jokesters.

Ultimately, the world is an infinite maze of – sometimes malevolent – possibility, and simply being dropped into it, and left to fall or fly, can often feel to us like a tremendous burden to bear. Retreating like porcupines, spines bristling, paws stomping, we are always tempted to scuttle off under the nearest rocky ledge. We know how to make things work when all seems set against us – how to push on even when our world is falling into patchwork disarray. Yet if we live our lives as one endless endurance test, we may become permanently trapped in a world of shadows. If we never stop feeling abandoned, if we are constantly on watch for who is watching us, we live our lives entirely through negation. We are so concerned with being lost that we end up losing what makes us *us*. Certainly, society benefits a lot from the resilience this gives us, but it cannot have us always retreating, looking over our shoulder. Otherwise, we will never start moving forward and looking ahead.

CHAPTER 9

Quibbler

Some people see perfection as a journey, not just a destination. I once had a senior colleague who was notoriously hard to satisfy. Every piece of work that crossed her desk came back a sea of red ink. In any presentation, her languid hand would always appear at the back of the room, followed by a barrage of probing questions. Once, our team was preparing a particularly high-stakes client briefing. She had been quieter than usual, listening to the rest of us batting ideas around, swiftly drawing them up into a draft. Just as we thought it was ready to go, she chimed in. 'I don't think this is what we want to be saying.' But we had all just agreed on it? She pointed at the document. '*This* doesn't work here. We've not discussed *that* at all. There's not enough *here*. And what we say *there* only raises more questions.'

Devastatingly, she had a valid point. One of our team shrugged. 'I think it's fine?' My colleague pursed her lips. I leaned forward. We could move this here, and add more on that there? 'I'm not fully sold.' We could keep the dialogue going? 'I'll put some time in your diary.' Cue one of the longest meetings of my life, tenaciously debating, tweaking, eking out revisions. Eventually, we sent it off. The client was delighted. 'Persuasive. Rigorous. Just what we wanted.' My colleague was sceptical. 'I think we could have done better.'

This style of thinking we can call the *Quibbler*. What are the integral features of our thinking if we fall into this mindset? We might be deeply, grindingly critical in our encounters with the world. We tend not to let things go, consistently finding new ways they could be fixed or improved. We always ask that extra question and make it clear whenever we disapprove of the answer. We may have a low bar for getting bored, shutting off, and turning away. Or perhaps we cannot handle being around anybody or anything we find offensive, and protect ourselves by keeping them firmly at arm's length.

This mindset veers between listlessly disengaging from the world and abruptly disparaging it (see fig. 9.1). We Quibblers are fairly **disgusted**, backed up by a cluster of six personality traits – **emotional**, **introverted**, **disagreeable**, **conscientious**, **closed**, and **honest–humble**. Unlike other emotions, disgust aligns fairly decisively with these traits, while their opposite traits line up just as clearly with the desire that drives the Reveller's thinking (as we shall see in the next chapter). This, in turn, sets the Quibbler slightly apart from other thinker-types, as it has fewer emotional overlaps that might allow it to find common ground with them at the margins.

Quibblers' disgust combines with this mixture of personality traits to give us a mental outlook marked by reluctant resistance. Above all, our emotionality and disagreeableness underscore how averse we are to being taken by surprise by something we dislike. If this happens, it can put us in a profoundly foul mood, and we find ourselves wanting to fiercely push the source of it far away, out of sight and out of mind. Helpfully, our introversion and closedness make it easier for us to disengage and focus on ourselves, keeping what we hold dear out of reach of the world outside. As we do so, our conscientiousness and honesty–humility let us build a haven far from others' prying eyes. They make us determined to investigate and achieve exactly how we want our lives to be, and give us the sheer bloody-minded staying-power to stick at it, come what may.[1]

QUIBBLER

We Quibblers take our facts about the world more or less as they come, though it only takes a few of them, from a couple of choice places, for our objections to start whirring into gear — whether they are old news or hot off the press. We are downbeat about what we learn, and we have little truck with grand ideas to change it, entrenching stubbornly around what was already there before. The experiences that provoke our dislike and disdain can make us question and overhaul our sense of the world, sometimes by pushing back hard against the received wisdom of those around us. The arguments we use to ground our views are sometimes logical, but often rely on a few tried-and-tested shortcuts — and we are fairly loath to take other people's opinions into account.

	Fig. 9.1: The Quibbler		
	Personality traits		
Mental Outlook	Emotional	▭	Emotionally stable
	Conscientious	▭	Careless
	Honest–humble	▭	Biased–superior
	Open to experience	▭	Closed to experience
	Extroverted	▭	Introverted
	Agreeable	▭	Disagreeable
	Emotions		
	Disgusted	▭	Desiring
	Happy (joyful)	▭	Sad
	Fearful (anxious)	▭	Eager (seeking)
	Angry	▭	Calm

	Information		
Mental Picture	Personality-congruent	▮▯▯▯▯▯▯▯▯▯	Emotion-congruent
	Selective	▮▯▯▯▯▯▯▯▯▯	Indiscriminate
	Positive	▯▯▯▯▮▯▯▯▯▯	Negative
	Fast	▯▯▯▯▮▯▯▯▯▯	Slow
	New ▯▯▯▯▯ Previous ▯▯▯▯▯ Long-unused		
	High	▯▯▯▯▯▯▮▯▯▯	Low
	Diverse	▯▯▯▯▯▮▯▯▯▯	Limited
	Predispositions		
	Emotion-congruent	▮▯▯▯▯▯▯▯▯▯	Reasoning-congruent
	Revise/revisit	▯▯▮▯▯▯▯▯▯▯	Defend/maintain
	Conservative/reactionary	▯▯▮▯▯▯▯▯▯▯	Progressive/radical
	New	▯▯▯▮▯▯▯▯▯▯	Previous
	Compliant	▯▯▯▯▯▯▯▮▯▯	Defiant
	Pro	▯▯▯▯▯▯▯▮▯▯	Con
Formulating Thoughts	**Reasoning**		
	Heuristic	▯▯▮▯▯▯▯▯▯▯	Non-heuristic
	Rational	▯▯▯▯▮▯▯▯▯▯	Irrational
	Reasonable	▯▯▯▯▯▮▯▯▯▯	Unreasonable

Becoming a Quibbler

The sensation that lies at the core of how we Quibblers engage with our surroundings is a powerful, involuntary repulsion in every fibre of our being – as though reality itself is inexorably pushing us away, making us fall back. Our sulky, rancorous mood comes from a place of deep and fretful misgiving about the world. Something is rotten in it, and we simply do not know how deep the rot goes. So the only thing we can sensibly do is presume that the disease could spread anywhere. That is why we try to put as much distance between ourselves and what sickens us as we can: we want to avoid the risk of any sort of contamination, physical or spiritual. We want to be left to our own devices, sovereigns of our own domain, and we will not rest until we find an unblemished state of hermetic seclusion.

Every 'disgusting' experience we make lingers and compounds in our minds, gradually instilling in us a sense of deep disenchantment. Even as we quit the field, hardening our hearts, part of us feels really let down. Fundamentally, every one of us anticipates that the world around us will broadly follow a certain semblance of order, intelligible at least to some degree. For us Quibblers in particular, that gets dialled up to an expectation that it ought to live up to a certain aesthetic or moral standard. If it does not, we feel it as a breach of trust, as if reality itself has deceived us. In this vein, research suggests that 'disgusting' experiences serve to alienate us from the world, defiling the 'purity' of what we were assuming we would find within it.[2] We can feel contaminated and degraded – especially if we have experienced highly stigmatised behaviour, such as ecocide, violence, or exploitation. It was all going so well, we thought it was OK, but no – turns out it is *not* fine; actually, it is rather awful.

But even as we turn on our heels and flee, our minds often cannot help dwelling on our experiences, returning in appalled fascination to what caused our visceral reaction. This is a legacy of our earliest years of education and nurture, where our aversion to unpleasant sights, smells, sounds, and so on, is often leveraged as a teaching tool to warn us off criminal, taboo, or simply unsanitary behaviours. But the connection between these experiences and how we Quibblers self-develop is quite unique. For most thinker-types, self-discovery and lesson-learning go hand in hand, one informing the other. Yet Quibblers self-develop not so much *in light* of our experiences, but *in spite* of them. Our discontent and disappointment whenever something repulses us never quite goes away. Our disgust causes a permanent rupture between how we form our authentic selves and how we navigate our surroundings. It ensures that there are some aspects of what we come across in the course of our experiences that we will never be tempted to emulate.

For us to adopt the Quibbler mindset, we need to be confronted, again and again, with circumstances that leave us consistently less than satisfied. Our wants and preferences have to be routinely pushed aside – to the point that we begin to suspect that reality is just not what we were hoping for. This can be fairly low key, if our friends and family ride roughshod over our privacy, our career and study plans, or our ideas for what do with our free time, leaving us wanting or underwhelmed. Or the wider world can hit us with intense blasts of things – new costs, laws, technologies – that run directly counter to our tastes. This can all give us the sense that there is something missing, or simply wrong, and convince us that there ought to be something else, something more.

There are also many walks of life that may simply require us to grit our teeth, steel ourselves, and dissociate in our minds and bodies in order to deal with situations that downright repel us. Perhaps we encounter the grimmer sides of the world through social work, gruesome police investigations, or regularly diagnosing various unpleasant medical conditions – in each case, explicitly contrasted with a 'failed' standard around what a 'healthy' person or society should be like. Or perhaps a sizeable share of our day just goes on cleaning up the mess our nearest and dearest leave scattered around our households, sullying our immaculate home-making. The more we do it, the easier we find it to wall ourselves off, desensitise ourselves to give our minds a break.

When this becomes more than an occasional sensation, if we find ourselves spending a great deal of time and effort grappling with the world in its various flawed states, then a blanket sense of aversion can start to permanently colour our thinking. With little respite from these confrontations, we are routinely denied the opportunity to fully look away, and we rarely reach a point of genuine satisfaction. Instead, we are consumed by tasks and swamped by evidence that keeps reinforcing our disenchantment. This can come in many forms, such as reminders from our doctor, sensational adverts, government messaging, or media coverage that trades on keeping up a drip-drip of unpleasantness. Any ongoing negativity along these lines, which hauls our attention back to what we find off-putting again and again, crowding out any space to cover the existence of possible alternatives, can convince us that there is nothing positive to report, so that repulsion becomes second nature to us.

This gradually cultivates in us a form of hypersensitivity and hypervigilance. We keep looking out into the world, but we learn to look for things wrong with it – because that is what we actually expect to find, instead of any aesthetic or moral ideal. All the same, we hold onto the sense that true perfection is still 'out there'. Even if what we are facing right now is rotten, we can still trace a path towards something pristine. We will just have to be the ones to find this remedy – by ourselves, if need be. Like the anti-heroic vigilante Rorschach in *Watchmen*, we insist that the evil that makes the world a 'dark place' must be exposed and rooted out wherever it is found, even if that leads us into conflict with those around us.

Withdrawal and its perils

At its core, our ability to sever ties with what offends us is a sign of considerable strength. It takes great willpower to sequester ourselves from the world. Disgust forces us to adjust ourselves to the idea that the world is (even) worse than the image we had of it. With great effort, we disengage from what we find too unpleasant to deal with, and fortify ourselves in crestfallen isolation – promising ourselves to ensure that nothing ever perturbs us like that again. Notably, our displeasure is not at ourselves for failing to keep these experiences at bay – since we believe *we* are doing everything right – but at the world for putting us in a position of seeking sanctuary from them.

The danger is that our disconnection from the world can turn into outright opposition. At root, our avoidant spiral can be prompted by smaller inconveniences as well as bigger challenges to our worldview. Maybe we are the only ones in our family group chat who cannot stomach its brand of humour. Perhaps we are continually put out by our neighbours' noisy 4 a.m. raves, or the jumble of used plates and dirty clothes our flatmates live among. If that becomes our dominant experience, it will not take long for us to become the resident spoilsport. Forced into a cold corner, we embrace the cold – squatting like Diogenes the Cynic in our *pithos* barrel, casting aspersions on those around us. If the world wants us to fly solo, then that is what we will do. We put ourselves at the centre of our preoccupations, taking ourselves off to work on our own aims and aspirations.

We seize upon our singleness and turn it into singularity. Retreating into ourselves unveils a whole new landscape of self-discovery. We tend to cleave to the view that what makes us distinct also lets us carve out our own special path – although this can engender in us a particular kind of snobbery, where we place great value on exclusivity. Perhaps we pay 50 per cent extra for our rail ticket so we do not have to be in 'cattle class' with the 'riffraff'. Or maybe we shop in bougier supermarkets if we possibly can, eschewing the lower-grade budget options even if that means swallowing a hefty mark-up.

All the same, we rarely appear ostentatious to others. We may briefly flaunt what we have – but instinctively, we want to lock our treasures in a safe within a castle behind a moat and a portcullis, where we can be free to amass our possessions without the inconvenience of others holding us accountable. Left unchecked, this tendency can make us egocentric, and even turn us into callous misanthropes. We may become convinced that taking part in the world at all will eventually require us to dissolve ourselves in it entirely, so we opt out in a bid to cling onto what we hold dear.

If we do retreat into our corners, we Quibblers are prone to getting painfully stuck there. I remember reconnecting with a former schoolmate after many years. Dispiritingly, he had not quite made the grades for his university place – instead, he had followed a scattered series of volunteering roles from Malawi to Mexico. When I met him, he was between jobs, filling his time with painting, writing poetry, and doing yoga in his parents' basement. 'Universities aren't where *real* thinking happens.' Where else then? Businesses? 'Nah, that's for suckers.' Blogs and podcasts? 'Grifters.' Art collectives? 'Full of fakes.' So where? 'You've got to find the authenticity *in yourself*.'

So: be more like him, in other words? Had he found anyone who was on board with that? His face darkened. A long diatribe followed. Clearly, he had met some people who thought the same way – and, just as clearly, they were at the forefront of his mind, living there rent free. At first, he had thought they were the right sort. Then, one after another, they betrayed him. Said the wrong thing, sold out, let him down in some baroque way. Could it be that they were just getting on with their lives? Was what he read as their scheming malevolence actually something more mundane? No, he was adamant: they had had it in for him.

If we withdraw like this, we may grow deadened towards our surroundings. Whether it dispirits us or not, the world beyond our hermetic chamber keeps turning. The more attention we pay ourselves, the less we focus on what is happening around us. We risk stifling our empathy until it becomes apathy, dissociating not just from what disgusts us, but from everything. We may even succumb to the same self-destructive nihilism as the young army officer Grigory Pechorin in *A Hero of Our Time*. Sharply reflective yet self-centred and manipulative towards those around him, he ultimately becomes bored with every experience and relationship he pursues – which saps his life of meaning and sets him on the path to wasting his considerable potential.

In the pursuit of self-comfort and self-worth, we may overcompensate. We aim for completeness behind our barricades, trying to reach the apex of pleasure just by ourselves. The little perfections of our home décor, a showroom with not a glass or magazine out of place. Our larder stocked with our favourite foods, and not a crumb more. Every ideal we craft wholly for ourselves, without anybody else weighing in.

It is certainly valuable for us to work out who we really are and what really makes us tick. But if we never do anything else, we may struggle to forge meaningful bonds and connections beyond our little realm – and we will find it harder to come across anything that sits quite right with us. We need to realise that everything we do, day after day, depends on quiet networks of help and collective effort – from the support of our families and friends to public services and infrastructure. That does not stop us being self-reliant and finding our fulfilment within ourselves. But it does mean that, if we vacate the world too far, we risk dooming ourselves to vacancy in our own lives too.

From holding back to lashing out

One reason we Quibblers segregate ourselves from the world is that we have an extraordinarily well-developed, keenly discerning emotional sensibility. Like Yuri Zhivago, we are torn between feeling intense pangs – of high ideals and passionate connection, and of the darkness that threatens them both. No surprise, then, that we put up protective barriers: we need to stave off overload. But our emotional defence also takes the form of emotional attack. We deplore the awfulness we meet in the world, so we fight fire with fire, venom with vitriol. All the more so if we tie this awfulness to particular kinds of people who are significantly different from us and 'ours'.

One of the most important purposes of disgust is to safeguard cohesion within 'our group'. Our moral and political leaders, families, and faith communities do this by fostering a solidarity of examplehood among 'the elect', the 'in-group' we should strive to be part of. Psychology and social theory emphasise that one of the most effective ways of doing this is to paint a distasteful picture of 'out-groups' and 'othered' individuals who embody what we should *not* be like.[3] It becomes much easier to give full expression to our dislike when there is someone or something we can focus on – and judging them becomes a lot simpler if there is some aspect of them we see as immoral or 'impure'. Our social training tells us that if we just look hard enough, we will eventually find the cancer, the interloper, the intruding sickness. That message makes us averse to having anything to do with anyone outside what is 'ours'.

This kind of moralised disgust, drummed into us over time, motivates us to avoid transgressing norms, and shun and expel anyone who does from our social circles. But effective though this is, we should not go too far in our judgemental rejection of those who fall short of our standards. We may end up drawing the borders around who and what is 'ours' so tightly that we grow averse to having anything to do with anyone but our closest people – which effectively means putting ourselves into a sort of social quarantine. Or we may take a much more confrontational approach to asserting our personal boundaries, which we need to keep a tight rein on to avoid sliding down the helter-skelter into outright bigotry and prejudice. We may be delicate flowers, but we have thorns too. Certainly, we still back away if we can, but we are also prone to beating a fighting retreat.

How disgust manifests in our thinking evolves as the object it attaches to recedes out of our immediate experience. At first, our acute sensibility gives us a quick, brittle temper. In the heat of the moment, this can make us decidedly touchy – especially towards those who will insist on touching us, like Keen Beans and Revellers with their incessant inquisitiveness. Over time, as we self-focus and self-heal, our scarred sensibilities settle into a tense, bilious, existential cynicism. We have had quite enough of our noxious experience the first time round to expose ourselves to another one like it again – so we put in place whatever rules and sanctions we can to remove that risk as far as possible.

In this way, we can put all the world on trial, presuming guilty until proven innocent. In our fraught, nauseated state of mind, it is not hard for us to find reasons to confirm our scepticism. We summon the energy for periodic bursts of inquisition and judgement. A salutary reminder that yes, things are still just as toxic and vile as we remember – so keep steering clear! But we are not really trying to change things, partly because we are convinced that they are beyond redemption. We merely want to castigate or punish them for being that way.

This can go in several different directions. One is that our crabby suspicion leaves us too flustered and diffident to engage properly with anyone or anything. We recoil from one encounter to the next. We cannot seem to settle down, and we become increasingly vocal with every new complaint. No amount of compensation can fix the saga of our delayed flight, our subpar hotel. No apology note can ever be artful enough to make up for our friend's drunken stupidity – we are done with them, however much grovelling they do.

Yet we can only keep a lid on our agitation for so long. After all, we are prickly customers. If we are struck enough times, at some point we will strike back. That is when the dam can suddenly burst, when emotional defence becomes attack, and we hit back with the force of an allergic reaction. Usually, nobody sees it coming, since we keep ourselves buried until the last moment. Cobra-like, we maintain the element of surprise right up until we strike. And then we call in the air raid, launch the dawn assault, unleash the hounds without a moment's hesitation. Sometimes we even astonish ourselves. In the blink of an eye, we explode out of our torpor. And once lit, our fire is hard to control – and still harder to put out.

But we can also go the exact opposite direction. Barricading ourselves away puts ever more hurdles in the path of us playing an active part in the world. We may skitter listlessly from one experience to the next, only ever opening ourselves up reluctantly. We are emotional, profoundly so, but also emotionally uncommunicative and unavailable. If we become convinced that it is fruitless to put any effort in, we revert to a kind of stand-offish autopilot. We give our partners the silent treatment; we phone it in to the job we cannot stand anymore, call in sick just to avoid seeing our colleagues. If we can, we ignore the emotional difficulties of the situations in which we find ourselves. If we cannot, we feebly let them pass us by. Better we go through our lives inertly swaddled in cotton wool, or so we may decide, than run the risk of getting involved.

And yet, we cannot escape the world, however hard we try. Instead, we turn so strongly inwards, and so far away, that we make ourselves irrelevant to it – if we are so disinclined to engage with anything around us, we may end up completely incapacitated. We should claim the opportunities the world offers us, not deny them to ourselves out of hand. 'The crowd' might bring us chaos, grime, disruption – but if we reject it, we only let ourselves become entirely lost to it, and lost within it. We cannot allow the insulating fortifications we build for ourselves to become an isolating cage. We want to be solitary, but if we take that too far, all we achieve is solitary confinement.

The inner dilemmas of aversion

This is a fairly extreme form for our withdrawal to take. What we Quibblers are more likely to do if someone or something repulses us is a bit more unusual, even paradoxical. Behind closed doors, as we lick our wounds, our minds begin to race. All the energy we keep for ourselves, we suddenly pour into thinking, turning what disgusts us over and over in our minds, teasing out every exquisite iota of disapproval. We think it to pieces, as a proxy for the destruction we cannot wreak on it in person. And for those who share our critical disposition but make the mistake of turning it on what we value, we can trump their cynicism to devastating effect. That is what fashion editor Miranda Priestly does in

The Devil Wears Prada, when her intern Andy Sachs sniggers at the minute differences between two choices of accessorising belt.

However, this is also often how we turn our isolation from a burden into a blessing. We treat it as an opportunity to gain some proper perspective on what offends us. We keep not just a safe distance, but a critical, objective distance too. Our detachment is analgesic, allowing us to cope with the costs of carrying out necessary but unappealing everyday work. At the same time, it lets us carve out an analytical space of our own. As studies of cynicism among employees and voters indicate, criticism does not necessarily take the form of nuanced philosophical critique.[4] Rather, our distrust of those who set the tone in our organisations – business executives, government elites, others we see as outside 'our' immediate cohort of co-equals – stops us automatically and reflexively buying into the arguments they deploy. We may not have arguments of our own to offer instead, or be invested enough to make the effort. Instead, our cynical disinterest helps us exercise a healthy degree of judicious pushback against our superiors' messaging. Ours is not the Cool Cats' well-intentioned, empathetic disinterest, but sceptical apathy closer to the Jokesters' carefully calculated remove.

For our own authenticity, we look inward, positively, defensively; to our surroundings, we look outward, negatively, aggressively. Our remarkably fertile imagination helps us bridge this chasm: it can summon all manner of abominations, but it can also emancipate us from our distasteful world. We want to create an exemplary intellectual and physical space, a utopian sanctuary of harmony preserved from the dystopia outside. That also means we are determined to make ourselves a person worthy of inhabiting this space. Not a stray thought or wasted gesture, not a crease or wrinkle in sight. Clarity starts at home, until we consummate our ideal.

By pursuing our self-realisation away from the world rather than within it, we think at a level of complexity that not all other thinker-types share. Among them, Jokesters echo most closely the hermetic divide we create between our thoughts and our surroundings. Of course, keeping up this dual-track thinking puts our mindsets under enormous pressure. If we are honest with ourselves, we would prefer not to have to think about the world at all.

Yet, reluctantly, we accept that we must give both tracks of thinking their due. So we dutifully push our minds back out beyond our protective ramparts. We force them to confront what disgusts us beyond mere condemnation, to determine what it is about the world we can rescue. Like TV's Dr Gregory House, even at our most curmudgeonly, even when we unleash our exasperation at our patients' bizarre ailments, we still do what we can to intervene, to understand and treat the world in line with our ideals. Even if we still end up withdrawing, at least we owe ourselves a full picture of what exactly we are withdrawing from. We are systematic in our criticism and our judgement – we hold the world to a high standard, to see what passes muster.

One of my academic friends had a mentor along these lines. Trouble brewed right from their first meeting. He stared at her impassively as she set out what she hoped to achieve. When she finished, he tilted his head and grimaced. 'And what's the value of all this?' New material? New approach? New insights? 'I don't see this getting any traction.' She was flummoxed. If he disliked her project, why had he hired her? 'This is your chance to go back to the drawing board.' How? 'That's for you to work out.' Disappointed, my friend left and set about rewriting her research plan. Try as she might, she could get no guidance out of her mentor. 'We'll speak again when you're ready.'

In due course, it was time for her to present at her departmental seminar. To her shock, when she finished speaking, her mentor intervened. 'Obviously, it's been something of a struggle for her. She'll have a better idea what she's doing next time.' Another faculty member raised his hand. Was she not supposed to be working on . . . ? We were expecting to hear about . . . ? Precisely what my friend had wanted to do in the first place! In no time at all, she switched to work with him instead. Several years, several jobs and institutions later, she came back to give a professorial lecture on her research. Her first mentor was sat with his colleagues in the front row. 'I *still* don't see what makes this all worthwhile.'

As mentorship goes, little short of a nightmare! But from our Quibbler perspective, that kind of thinking makes a certain amount of sense. When we confront the world, we are caught between two contradictory tendencies. One is flat-out refusal. Once we commit to severing ties, we can be very bull-headed about restoring them again. We would rather simply block them out. We feel this most clearly in our personal lives. We broke up with our ex for a reason; we were right to fall out with our friend. Why should we invite them back in? It would take some pretty careful negotiation to get back to being on good terms.

The other tendency is morbid curiosity. Deep down, we are finely attuned to what is going on – particularly if it is odd or unfamiliar. In fact, that is what piques our engagement the most. More ghastly tales to recount, scandals to savour, villains we can roundly condemn. We work out where to turn our attention partly by letting ourselves be put off by everything else. We expose our senses to novelty and variety in its most repellent forms to help us determine what we are actually attracted to.

Why do we feel so strongly about keeping the things we reject at arm's length? Partly because doing anything else feels like a climbdown from our unassailable position of strength. It feels like we are forgiving them – a forgiveness they do not deserve. We would help ourselves a lot if we learn to let things go from time to time. Be more Cool Cat, take things more dispassionately in our stride. Nobody is asking us to change our minds – just put what displeases us out of them.

Powered by our objections

When we Quibblers retire inwards and devote our mental energies to working out our aims, we do so in a spirit of defiance. We hold our ideal of perfection front and centre in our minds – like a personal mantra, a rule for life, or a psychological tattoo that shapes our every interaction. We let the world know that we are judging it by *our* standards, and we do not hesitate to mark it down if it refuses to share our judgement. Unlike other thinker-types, we develop and assert ourselves as a sort of revenge, burying the world in our accomplishments. We are a little bit Lisbeth Salander (*The Girl with the Dragon Tattoo*), turning our worst experiences into a personal mission for justice and order.

Our disgust galvanises us to think and act with a relentless urgency that few can match. But we should not have to see our self-development as retribution against what is happening around us. We cannot just triangulate the positives by doing the opposite of whatever we see as the negatives about our situation. That may be a start, but it only gets us halfway towards a new way of doing things. The more autonomous thinker-types – Cool Cats, Jokesters – remind us that we are quite capable of working on ourselves regardless of what else is going on. Meanwhile, the more gregarious ones – like Agonisers and Keen Beans – can impress on us that our surroundings might be quite useful for realising our plans.

This aside, however, our cold resentment keeps us focused, centred, alert. A perverse conscience stops us growing lazy, careless, or too comfortable. It reminds us why we plot and plan, calculate and speculate, work hard for our achievements. The world will not help us, nor leave us alone. All we have to rely on, in the end, is ourselves. Our resentment can turn 'us *away from* the world' into 'us *against* the world'. Eventually, one has to win and the other lose. If we feel let down by the world, we become willing to let it down in response. If even our prickly eruptions are no good, then we need to make our stand one for the ages. Let fire rip through us unchecked, go for an all-out internecine assault.

This is ultimately the provocation we Quibblers pose to other thinker-types: if things do not go the way you want, what are you going to do about it? Are you going to stand up for yourself? And how far are you willing to go? It is the provocation the Marquise de Merteuil presents in *Dangerous Liaisons*, deploying her considerable intellect to carefully stage-manage how society perceives her – and use every scrap of power she can muster to destroy those who have wronged her.

Psychological studies suggest that disgust makes us far more severe in our judgements if we are convinced that we are in the right.[5] We see any violations of social conventions not just as different ways of doing things, but as transgressions that deserve a firm response. We rigidly reject things in other people that give us 'the ick' – from minor infractions and slights to what we read as inherent character flaws. The more sensitive to disgust we are, the more extreme our moral view of our negative experiences becomes. We then leave no room for manoeuvre, and no space for nuance: they are *just* inherently wrong.

The danger when we strike back at these transgressions is that we find the most waspish ways to punish the world for offending us. We become our monsters' monster. This is our point of no return, and we need to be very sure before we cross this particular Rubicon. Is it really worth it? Once we go down this path, hurling ourselves into open conflict, there is nowhere left for us to go. We turn our adversaries into enemies, unleashing our forces as hard on them as we can. Once done, it cannot be undone. If we push back against the world so violently, sacrificing our self-control, there is no more room for us to withdraw.

It goes without saying that most people will not take kindly to this. The more empathetic thinker-types might make a last-ditch effort to convince us that there is another way – that there are subtler methods to get what we want than declaring total war. But even those efforts have their limits, and soon quail under the ferocity of our assault. By becoming the same as whoever or whatever we condemn, we open ourselves up to condemnation too. So it had better work, and we had better be prepared to face the consequences. If we are going to fire our cannon, we must make sure it is made of sterner stuff than glass.

The purist's place in society

Being a Quibbler can feel like standing at the margins of a barren landscape, surveying its mires and its wilderness in search of a passable way through. There are several ways this mindset works extremely well for us. We have a highly developed sense of our ideals, won through long and careful (self-)observation, and we hold the world to exacting standards of what is good, right, and true. We value our personal boundaries as a hermetic seal around the inner sanctum where we try to realise our 'best life'. And we are extremely good at identifying the full roster of problems in whatever we happen to confront, mercilessly squeezing out every last detail and imagining a better alternative. All in all, we are not easily derailed by pain or unpleasantness, and we are better-versed than most in shutting out these experiences and forging ahead with our lives.

We have much to teach other thinker-types in this regard. Our most fundamental message is that ideals do not just come about by themselves, as Happy Campers and Revellers seem to think, but must be worked for, to dispel the ever-present shadow of corruption. We insist that none of us have to 'go with the flow' of everything we encounter, and that often we should specifically reject it and carve out our own path — a key lesson to help Cool Cats and Keen Beans get less caught up in minor details. It is entirely valid for us to focus on ourselves and leave the world to its own devices. This can help Agonisers dial back how sensitive they are to others' situations, and Hotheads put a brake on how instinctively they turn what they feel into how they respond.

But our mindset can also work against us in several ways. We may struggle to get comfortable anywhere, with anyone or anything, or find the peace of mind for genuine long-range creativity. By pushing the world away if it does not meet our standards, we risk becoming ineffectual bystanders. Yet we can also be gluttons for punishment — even though we are repulsed by what we see, we can never quite bring ourselves to turn our backs to it completely. Ironically, this may only worsen the situation, since raising criticisms by themselves is no guarantee of any future transformation. That would require us to be a shade less thorny, to roll up our sleeves and engage with the world proactively instead.

We need to handle moments when our expectations are frustrated without immediately turning inwards, away from the world — channelling Agonisers' and Keen Beans' determination to investigate what else is out there. We must learn how to forge our own well-crafted, idiosyncratic path without losing the ability to relate to other people — letting them 'do their thing', as Happy Campers and Revellers do effortlessly, while we do ours. And if we must part ways with them, we should arrest the slide from disagreement to open conflict, venting our dissatisfaction without lashing out — soberly, as Cool Cats would, or defused with some Jokester comic relief.

It is a wearing, grinding task to act as society's Doubting Thomases – but someone has to do it. Prowling distrustfully like lynxes through the undergrowth, eyes and ears sharp, fastidiously grooming themselves and pawing filth out of their dens. We dig into the tiniest details, assume nothing, and take nobody at face value. But if we spend all our time hacking away at what other people get wrong, we never get round to putting forward what we find right. That we set the world high standards is not a bad thing – though it loses its sheen if we reduce ourselves to little more than pernickety bean-counters. If all we do is dispose of other people's waste, we waste ourselves and waste away. Society needs us to do our best deconstruction now and then. Yet, if we puncture everything we lay our eyes on, nothing will ever get off the ground.

CHAPTER 10

Reveller

We all need people who are willing to open their hearts to us. A few Christmases ago, the first after my mother passed, I mentioned to some friends that I was at a loss for how to spend the holiday. Maybe abroad? Maybe go out? A few days later they messaged me. 'We've got a better idea. Why don't you come to ours? We can do everything you'd have done at home-home!' Did they not mind me crashing their plans? 'This year, your plans are our plans.' Were they aware of the industrial quantities of glühwein and stollen that would require? 'Oh, we know! We're ready.'

Christmas Eve rolled around. As I entered their flat, my senses tingled with recognition. Scents of baked salmon and roast goose drifting from their kitchen. Their living room a sea of red and green and gold, glinting in the candlelight. A pile of presents nestling under a majestic tree. And, incredibly, a gaggle of friends – some of mine, some of theirs – all beaming at me from out of the warm glow. I was bowled over. How had they managed it? They waved away my question and pulled me over to the head of the table. Dinner, carols around the tree, games into the small hours. Home away from home-home. 'It's the Christmas you *should* have had.' But how did they know? 'We're your family too, remember?'

This final mindset is best described as the *Reveller*. What are its hallmarks – and ours, if we join the Reveller party? Perhaps we get tunnel vision about the things we like and fantasise away their flaws. We never hesitate to spoil ourselves and the people dearest to us. That penchant for finding ways to 'glow up' and zhoosh up our lives, where there is no such thing as 'enough is enough'. We live for putting on a show, craving the turned heads and craned necks. And maybe we are inveterate romantics, falling head-over-heels again and again, always going back for more.

Ours is a mindset of rose-tinted indulgence, easily and invariably enthralled whenever we encounter pure beauty (see fig. 10.1). We feel a fair amount of **desire**, supported by a blend of six personality traits – **emotionally stable**, **extroverted**, **agreeable**, **careless**, **open**, and **biased–superior**. Desire, like disgust, significantly favours some traits more than others. That is why these two emotions fit completely and exclusively within one thinker-type each – and, like the Quibbler, sets the Reveller slightly apart from the rest of the family.

Based on how desire interacts with these personality traits, the Reveller demeanour is one of attentive attachment. At its heart, agreeableness and emotional stability together push us to want close relationships of all kinds, and make us secure enough in ourselves to pursue them from a place of trust. The way we respond to the pull of connection also benefits enormously from our extroversion and bias–superiority. These put us firmly in the driving seat of determining precisely what we want from each relationship, and parlaying our all-embracing positivity into a whole network of different intimacies. All of this is undergirded by our carelessness and openness, which prevent us from getting too tightly wedded to any of our wants and needs, or ruining our pleasure by dissecting our liaisons too far – and help us simply move on when they have served their purpose.[1]

We Revellers pick up as many details as we can about what is happening around us, though we are often picky about our sources, and torn between what we have previously found out and what we are discovering right this moment. We delight in what we learn about the situations we are in, consistently adding new layers of experimentation and tolerance. Generally, that means finding ways to align our thinking with the prevailing 'mood of the room', though we stand our ground pretty resolutely once we settle into our own views. Our reflections are sometimes systematic, sometimes less so; there are moments where we internalise other people's arguments, and others where we ignore them. We tend to attach our opinions to a few rules of thumb, apart from occasional bursts when we insist on thinking things through in full.

	Fig. 10.1: The Reveller		
MENTAL OUTLOOK	Personality traits		
	Agreeable		Disagreeable
	Open to experience		Closed to experience
	Extroverted		Introverted
	Conscientious		Careless
	Honest–humble		Biased–superior
	Emotional		Emotionally stable
	Emotions		
	Happy (joyful)		Sad
	Fearful (anxious)		Eager (seeking)
	Angry		Calm
	Disgusted		Desiring

	Information		
MENTAL PICTURE	Personality-congruent	▮▮▮▮▮▮▮▮▮	Emotion-congruent
	Selective	▮▯▮▮▮▮▮▮▮	Indiscriminate
	High	▮▯▮▮▮▮▮▮▮	Low
	New ▮▮▮▯ Previous ▮▮▮▮ Long-unused		
	Positive	▮▮▮▮▯▮▮▮▮	Negative
	Fast	▮▮▮▮▯▮▮▮▮	Slow
	Diverse	▮▮▮▮▮▮▯▮▮	Limited
	Predispositions		
	Emotion-congruent	▮▮▮▮▮▮▮▮▮	Reasoning-congruent
	Pro	▮▯▮▮▮▮▮▮▮	Con
	Compliant	▮▮▯▮▮▮▮▮▮	Defiant
	New	▮▮▮▮▯▮▮▮▮	Previous
	Revise/revisit	▮▮▮▮▮▮▮▯▮	Defend/maintain
	Conservative/reactionary	▮▮▮▮▮▮▮▯▮	Progressive/radical
FORMULATING THOUGHTS	Reasoning		
	Heuristic	▮▮▮▯▮▮▮▮▮	Non-heuristic
	Reasonable	▮▮▮▮▯▮▮▮▮	Unreasonable
	Rational	▮▮▮▮▮▯▮▮▮	Irrational

Becoming a Reveller

More than any other thinker-type, we Revellers are creatures of the heart. We approach the world with a burning, slightly pole-axing prickle of attraction, a surging leap that starts in our stomach and catches high up in our chest. It is an involuntary feeling of resolve, of triumphant wonder, which takes away our self-consciousness and calls us to embrace the certainty of letting it take control. As we move through our surroundings, one encounter after another carries an aura of enticing importance that draws us tantalisingly in. They exert a pull on us, which acts as a kind of 'trailer' for what they have to offer us. In turn, these pulls make us feel adventurous, emboldened, cheeky as well as crafty – equal parts coquettish and spellbinding. We trust ourselves, as if endowed with superhuman strengths that only these encounters can unlock, senses only they can awaken. So we turn to pursue them, roaming freely and single-mindedly to explore the world in search of more.

The social experiences that instil this mindset in us are ones that portray the world as an endless, interlocking series of standing invitations. Throughout our lives, we are presented with emotionally loaded investments of all kinds that offer us their own hints of the sublime. Dating apps that claim they will find us 'the one', stock options that might make us millionaires, novelty tricks and self-help guides that assure us they will 'hack' our lives. They require our commitment – of effort and energy, time, capital outlay – and in return, they promise to satisfy our pent-up yearning and keep giving us *more*. This promise also plays a huge part in our self-discovery, especially during our earliest years of childhood and schooling. At first, whether we like poetry or pottery, pick German or geography, nerd out on Pokémon or *Magic: The Gathering*, is because we are pleasurably drawn towards them. But whether we stick with any of these things depends on how far they live up to their promise, and let us tangibly feel the payoffs of partaking in them. How well they give us the gratification we expect decides whether we keep coming back for more.

The stronger our attraction to something, the more deeply we become absorbed and engrossed in it. Over time, our sense of self, of what we aim for in life, can become steadily swallowed up by the objects of our fixation – they become an increasingly large part of who we are. Studies of our self-consciousness from philosophy to addiction theory, from consumer research to sex therapy, emphasise how much weight all of us place on our desires in the way we construct our identities.[2] Revellers, however, follow that path further than anyone else, and take this self-identification with our wants to a whole new level. We may start to see everything we do, every new piece of knowledge we acquire and skill we pick up, as part of a long, possibly lifelong, preparation to put ourselves and our efforts more at the disposal of what we desire.

We sign up for psychology classes because the person we fancy is also taking them. We hang out in a certain bar because that is where they go. We dye our hair and wear our cutest top in the hope they notice. We change our lives in fairly harmless ways all the time. But our desires can also easily drag us down the road to self-abnegation. We might pull all-nighters and sleep in the office in service of our obsessions and passion-projects, cut out mealtimes and snack at our desks, bail on family, friends, and even our relationships. We may devote every scrap of endurance and perseverance we have to our single-minded goals. And even as they expand their presence in our lives, becoming a more and more defining part of us, that may never be big enough – we may still want more.

Every time we answer the call of what attracts us, and follow where it pulls us, we feel released from our inner tension. In due course, we come to associate pursuing what we love with a feeling of being 'at home' – in comfortable spaces that offer us a lifetime's worth of opportunities to explore and near-infinite permission to explore them. Institutions of all stripes try to encourage this feeling and (re)create these spaces by promising us satisfaction in exchange for our commitment to them. Fundamentally, they acknowledge that any external 'must' they might impose needs a powerful internal 'want' supporting it. We do what they expect of us only partly because the laws and rules demand it, but also because we consciously choose to do it. Instead of putting checks and obstacles in our path, these authorities highlight the attractions of 'living up to' our expected roles. Extra credit, work perks, bonuses, and rewards are all designed to show us the broad possibilities that lie open to us within them. Their goal is to turn our internal 'want' into a 'need' that motivates and spurs us on – especially when the going gets tough and the sublime recedes from view.

The constant pulls like this from every direction, influences that spur our wants, create a tug-of-war inside us between a smörgåsbord of desires, all of which we want to explore. The result is that we can be quite changeable in which attractions we perceive and pursue from moment to moment. We experience desire at many different levels, and we have a wide range of appetites to sate. Urgent cravings for cookies and cocktails. Wistful longings for faraway places and romantic walks. Our often-voracious sex drive. Everyone has these to some extent, but we Revellers stand out for how explicitly we own these appetites and wants. Others might question their desires, repress them, expect the world not to pay them any heed. We, however, take up space for ourselves and our wants, and expect that they will be satisfied. Like the pampered Mia Wallace in *Pulp Fiction*, we may greedily demand that all our desires are met all the time – and cajole whoever is around us into ensuring that they are. But far more likely is that we reserve the right to be spontaneous, to demand this one moment, that the next, the other the one after.

The tyranny of magnetism

For Revellers, the world is a source of endless stimulation. Heady glamour and primal lust, ethereal elegance and seductive temptation. It bewitches us with its wiles, and we try to project the same pull right back into it. We want to catch everyone's attention and lure them in. Our craving for closeness is intensely personal and mesmerisingly sensual, often rooted in a deep physical spur of arousal (sexual as well as non-sexual). We desire, and desire to be desired; we exude a self-confident poise and charisma that radiates out from us like a summoning beacon.

As we learn to love and be loved, in platonic and romantic ways, we also learn to compress the distance between us and those around us. We internalise the rules of reciprocity: we draw others in by going out to approach them, gain their attention by making ourselves vulnerable *and* taking the lead. This sensation of being pulled towards others can make us quite forceful in how we engage with them. We rarely hesitate to assert ourselves, pursuing whomever or whatever attracts us, deciding – even if only temporarily – that we cannot do without them. That stunning backless velvet dress. Those dazzling gold earrings. The Louis Vuitton to tuck under one arm, the gorgeous date to hang on the other. We see them, we cannot bear to be apart from them – the mere fact they are not yet ours means we have already been starved of them for too long.

We may be fortunate enough that if we have to have something, then we will find a way to get it. Perhaps we just need to throw money at the situation, since everyone and everything has a price. This is the approach of the gum-chewing Violet Beauregarde and the bratty Veruca Salt in *Charlie and the Chocolate Factory*, in their attempts to 'win' ownership of Willy Wonka's chocolate empire. One uses her brash competitiveness to try to outshine the other 'golden ticket' children; the other relies on the persuasive force of her father's money. Of course, both ultimately prove less successful than the unassuming sincerity of Charlie Bucket.

We are unapologetic go-getters, and we stop at nothing to reach what we desire. Organisational psychology has identified several ways that desire underpins our entrepreneurial drive.[3] Core to this is our yearning for independence and self-efficacy – to wrest control of our material 'lot', achieve growth, expansion, better performance, social change. At the same time, psychoanalytic research suggests that we want to secure these rewards by struggling for them from a position of material lack. Getting our payoffs only brings us so far: part of what makes them pleasurable for us is the proactive process of working for them.

What is paramount is that we get what we feel should be coming to us. Where dogged persistence will not do, we may turn to other, less scrupulous means. Showing we want something *hard* can turn into an endurance test for us and for those around us. It is this expression of supreme will that fascinates Nick Carraway about the ever-optimistic Jay Gatsby, who uses the vast proceeds from his bootlegging empire to fund endless over-the-top parties at his home in West Egg, convinced that this is the way to attract the attention of his former lover Daisy Buchanan. At our best, our desire teaches us to be tenacious. Yet, at our worst, that same tendency means we may not always know when to stop. We cannot let reaching out turn into pestering or steamrolling other people's willingness to play along. If we keep battering away, increasingly grandiose and larger-than-life, we will just put people off. Nobody owes us their attention or their consent.

One of my postdoctoral cohort once took me to a party at her new university. No sooner had we arrived than I ran into a former tutor – a brilliant international relations scholar with an unerring ability to concoct projects and magic up bright ideas. 'I'm glad we've run into each other. I've got something to ask you. Would you excuse us?' Briskly, he steered me to a table and started talking business. A new research centre, lots to explore, keen to have me involved. I thanked him for thinking of me and promised to stay in touch. When I rejoined my colleague, she was full of questions. 'What did he want?' I told her about the invitation. 'Oh, I'd love to do something like that too. Will you mention me to him?' Sure, I could put them in touch.

Months went by. Occasional news about the centre, little progress. Undeterred, my colleague brought it up again and again, every week, even every few days. 'Did you email him? Give him my name?' Before, we had talked about everything from dating to travel to weekend plans. Now, the only topic was the centre. Eventually, I connected them. Almost instantly, my colleague's messages dried up. A year later, at the centre launch, there she was, glued to my old tutor's side. I went over to say hi. Loudly, she turned to introduce me to him. I looked at her nonplussed. What was that about? I already knew him, I had been the one to introduce her. 'Oh, did you? I don't remember.'

The more obstinately and unwaveringly we chase our desires and push our ambitions to the fore, the likelier it is that we rub other thinker-types up the wrong way. Agonisers and Quibblers may easily be hurt or affronted if we ride roughshod over them in pursuit of our goals – while even equally single-minded Hotheads or Jokesters will react poorly if we trample over their ambitions.

No matter how slyly we try to hide it, our determination to captivate all comers can quickly flip over into narcissistic egoism.

The spectrum of our affection

Of course, this is an extreme case of the Reveller mindset. However inexorably we experience the pull of desire, we generally do not go charging in hell for leather without a moment's thought. After all, desires come in many forms, and we are usually able to manage them and keep them strictly in proportion. There are plenty of people out there we do *not* love, fantasise about, or favour, whom we do not have to make 'ours'. We are simply OK with them. We like them, perhaps even appreciate them – but we save our really intense desire for people who are truly special to us.

Fundamentally, our default stance towards the world is relaxed, accepting, and shrewdly tolerant. Social research underlines the importance of desire as the social glue that holds together communities and groups.[4] Approaching, building bridges, and establishing solidarity with the people we interact with – in our friendship groups and neighbourhoods, at work, in wider society –

relies on aligning with each other's wants and sources of satisfaction. This means finding ways to meet each other where we are at, and reaching empathetically beyond our individual expectations in search of shared projects. This is especially crucial while our relationships are still forming – as recent hires, fresh pupils, or new partners – as we learn the ropes and figure one another out. As a highly active emotion, desire is far more powerful than passive natural affiliation or recognition in oiling the wheels of social interaction, especially between people with very different experiences of the world. We Revellers know, as much by trial and error as by any great intuition, how to hit the sweet spot of even temper that lets us present as personable and easy-going.

Perhaps the most important forms that attraction can take are friendly affection and mutual regard. We sense a pull towards other people based on an essential affinity between us and them – they make us feel good in a way that lets everything else seem brighter, lighter, and more colourful. We can get a rush when we meet someone and realise we have something in common. We rejoice in already knowing and understanding them a little bit, in a slightly unique way. Over time, we learn that this opens up new pathways for our relationship: frank conversations, knowing looks, private jokes. A route into their inner life, permission to bypass the boundaries they put up towards everyone else. An intimacy only we and they enjoy. That rapport softens into a more generic humane goodwill towards people we have less in common with. We may still feel a considerate sensitivity towards them. Let them have their rights! Let them go where they please, marry who they want, speak free. But we do not extend to them the same tenderness we invest in the people, objects, or situations that we consider 'ours'.

We are also capable of turning the emotional dial right down. Our desire is not the same as Gloomsters' sadness, Hotheads' anger, or Worrywarts' fear – each of which tends to surge up and overwhelm them with little warning, only to just as suddenly recede. It may be similarly pronounced and all-consuming, but it generally comes over us more like a steady sea-change. We feel as intensely as they do without losing control – a rare talent among the thinker-type family.

What we have here is interest. Pretty much any passing crush, distraction, or sudden whimsy can captivate us, since we are primed to yearn for them. But we need to ensure that we stay focused for long enough to keep us concentrating, doing our tasks, learning our roles, and fulfilling our social expectations. We need to train ourselves to control our attention so we are not pulled around at random – something Cool Cats and Quibblers can both help us with.

Meanwhile, at the opposite end from gentle affection lies the wholesale emotional submission that desire constantly gestures us towards. We do not really know why certain people or things appeal to us, give us tingles or flushes or make us catch our breath. We might cobble together an explanation, but ultimately, we have to admit there is an ineffable mystery at the end of every rainbow. However, if we answer their appeal with total compliance, we risk falling prey to slavish personal dedication – as in cult fanbases for charismatic evangelists, eccentric film directors, and global pop icons, or the strictures of the latest fad diets or edgy new countercultures. Our love for the rituals and values we put our faith in may grow into fundamentalist attachment, our thinking and behaviour ossify into dogma.

When we love someone or something this intensely, we are giving them a place of astounding priority in our minds – at times even over ourselves. It is the most essential form of altruism, born out of an understanding of solidarity that sees everyone we extend it to as irrevocably a part of us and 'our own'. We no longer just coexist, we coextend, our boundaries blending into one another's seamlessly. The danger is that we may become so infatuated that we change ourselves to fit them. It is not even that we choose their interest over ours, but that we may no longer see our interest as existing independent of theirs. This feeling of self-dissolution in the other is easy to give an epic, operatic gloss – like the tragically steadfast devotion of the geisha Cio-Cio-San in *Madame Butterfly*. In place of such self-sacrifice, we need to carve out a way to stand by 'our people' – offer them help and support, adulation and loyalty – without dissolving into them entirely. Once that kind of desire has taken control, our mindsets can become wholly subordinated to its unpredictable whims.

The dilemmas of (in)constant attraction

One of our strongest characteristics as Revellers is that we are highly attuned to what is happening around us. For us, the act of paying attention itself is deeply meaningful, because that is precisely how we first express our yearning. The force of that underlying prickle of attraction, and the pull it exerts on us, is specifically to steer our senses in its direction rather than any other. Whether or not we feel this pull is the prelude to deciding whether or not we make whoever or whatever it came from 'ours'.

Which wants we prioritise at any moment can shift, fluidly and abruptly. A grad school friend once messaged me out of the blue to ask my advice. 'I feel it's time for a career pivot. I've got offers, but I'm just so torn between different routes my life could take. Can we meet?' He suggested a time and place. I found him draped in the corner of a cocktail bar, dark leather furnishings, rose gold *objets*, mood lighting. A book in Tamil lay on the table, and a Moleskine notebook with various calligraphic transcriptions. His way of transporting himself back to South Asia, he told me. 'Those vibrant colours!' Was that where he wanted to go? 'Oh no, no!' He wafted away my prompting airily.

His choices, it turned out, were far more prosaic. Law school in the US, a lectureship in Belgium, political consulting in New Zealand. I was surprised. None of these seemed especially like him. What happened to the transcendental philosophy he had always lived and breathed? 'Oh, I still love that too! And I'll keep doing it alongside!' How would he have time? Why not just throw himself fully into *one* of these new careers? 'I just can't bring myself to choose!' Well, lucky to have so many options. He looked at me hazily. 'Do you think . . . I should say yes to them all?' Definitely not. His face faded, and he stared past me. 'Oh. Well, thanks anyway . . .'

For better or worse, we may carry an air of wilful inconstancy. We boomerang in and out of friendship groups. We take up lovers and partners and then drop them again, ricocheting from short-term relationship to casual hookup to one-night stand. This can utterly exasperate other people, who see our freewheeling hedonism as either fundamentally immature or devoid of any moral decorum.

To an extent, they have a point: yes, we do see our commitments as malleable, always liable to revision, never so strong that they permanently box us into a corner. But this undersells the role changeability plays in how we normally engage with the world. We let our thinking be oriented from moment to moment by what attracts us – lifelong Don Quixotes tilting at one windmill after another. Of course, we can hold our gaze on our long-term interests – our Dulcinea del Toboso remains always in our mind's eye. But we see no reason why that should get in the way of answering other inclinations as and when they present themselves. Otherwise, we would simply latch onto the first few things that happen to draw us in and never engage with anything else ever again.

Instead, our entire sense of who we are and what we want emerges cumulatively, through our journey from one interest to the next. It is not irresponsibility but heedful observation and forethought that makes us embrace the fact that our emotional attachments will grow, shrink, and evolve over time. If we are dedicated to them, we are fully dedicated. Once we extend our compassion and love towards somebody or something else – friends and partners, comrades and collaborators – our commitment to them becomes extremely hard to dislodge from the outside. We only move on from them if *we* decide they no longer meet our wants and needs, if we stop being willing to extend the boundaries of what is 'ours' to include them. While we are in, we stay in – until we decide it is time to get out.

It is not hard to see why our craving for connection can appear superficial, opportunistic, even insincere. Yet that is a drastic misunderstanding of our mindset. It is precisely because we are so alert to the appeals of the world that we recognise the many ways it can be desirable – however fleeting that desirability may be. We have seen enough school crushes, forbidden infatuations, and Hinge dates come and go that we are inclined to wait a little before we take the step from attraction to commitment. Making them 'ours', making ourselves vulnerable to them, is a far more momentous decision than just having a bit of a taste to sate our fleeting desire. So our dilemma is how we can pursue a little bit of attachment and involvement without falling head-over-heels, without becoming overattached and overinvolved.

This misunderstanding means we get blamed anytime our connections become messy or chaotic, or whenever we appear to be neglecting those around us. But for us, the feeling of neglect lies the other way around. Because we can so easily see the appeal of things, we feel severely remiss if we do not give them the proper time of day. Our overriding experience is that opportunities vanish as swiftly as they appear. So we should seize the moment, strike while the iron is hot, or we risk missing out on something incredible. One-time offer, take it or leave it! Grab it now, only while stocks last! That is the inkling we are responding to in these moments. But it is not an inkling most other people share. So if we are going to jump at these chances, we also need to remember that we may come to be judged by our litany of broken friendships, failed relationships, abandoned hobbies, or departed jobs.

Catching our social butterflies

We Revellers assiduously seek out not just social connection but social contact. For us, wanting somebody or something is an intensely sensory experience. Flirtatious brushes and glances with our lover. Gentle cuddles, passionate embraces, kisses that feel as if time is standing still. All of them are rocket fuel for us. The same too for the little considerations and thoughtful gestures from family and friends – cards, flowers, station pick-ups. What makes these so powerful is that they go in both directions. Having someone actively give us their attention is a far stronger way of feeding our appetite than merely passively letting us attend to them.

We want to form connections with others because we sense that there is something about them to admire and esteem, and that part of being contented in ourselves – living a life worthy of admiration and esteem in its own right – is enhancing ourselves through association with them. There is probably something to like or even love about whoever or whatever we come across. If we are going to judge them at all, we should do so benevolently, proportionately, giving them their due. We should let them show us how they can enhance our lives. And we can achieve this best by intertwining ourselves with them, locked in a mutual embrace.

This is where the passion in our mindset comes into its own. When we are passionate about someone or something, all our senses thrum and whirr. Like Agonisers, Happy Campers, and Keen Beans, we are highly dynamic and energetic: we find the surging leap of attraction profoundly invigorating, and we throw ourselves into every opportunity we get to feel it. We go to networking drinks and social nights. We introduce ourselves to everyone, give them our cards, get their numbers. This can often require us to put in a large amount of effort. Going out, putting ourselves out there, stretching out to discover the mystical delights of the unknown is often a (highly) active choice – which means we need to build up considerable reserves of social capacity to resource it.

Social research suggests that we can work up this level of energy for a vast range of desirable objects – erotic lust and longing, consumer goods, or our 'personal relationship' to the divine, to name just a few.[5] Our fantasies are lively, affirming, and creative. Our upward spiral is nourished even further if we find new ways to access what we are after. And our desire is infectious: the more we feel our passion satisfied, the more we try to meet other people's desires in turn. If we feel loved, kindly treated, and endowed with gifts, we 'pay it forward' to help those around us feel the same. All our social relationships feed off this cyclical emotional contagion, from vibrant friendship groups to high-performance corporate organisations.

Yet desire always remains a risky gambit. We Revellers are proud and purposeful, conscious of striking a balance between surrendering to its will-o'-the-wisp and managing how far we let it impact our thinking. This is what unites the initial impulsive passion that Count Alexei Vronsky shows to Anna Karenina with his later coolness and superficiality – which steers her further and further towards Agoniser-ish frustration and insecurity. Difficult though this may be, we are better equipped to keep our affective balance than, for instance, Gloomsters or Hotheads, who are liable to plunge headlong into their emotions. Our greater emotional self-possession generally prevents us from following their lead. It gives us evasive manoeuvres that help us dodge the majority of such affective takeovers, and keep our feelings on just the right amount of leash.

All the same, a strong element of trust always stays part of the picture. Building our sense of meaning and purpose on sensual, aesthetic attraction can make us a hostage to fortune. Taken too far, it may leave us with gaps in our knowledge of the world because the material was not quite sexy or snazzy enough to capture our interest. Our mindset gambles on enchantment to distinguish true from false, right from wrong, 'ours' from 'not ours'. But we can never quite know whether our ability to grow fond of something, or someone, is in fact just a fond delusion.

To persevere in our mindset, we Revellers must deliberately ignore the times when our attempts to reach out failed, when our expectations turned out to be naïve mistakes. We have to channel our best Emma Bovary, sustaining our dreams of glamour and romance even as the harsh realities of our life push us ever closer to ruin and destruction. Perhaps we really do live a charmed life in our own little land of milk and honey, where our needs are always met, our demands never refused, our overtures never rebuffed. But even the wealthiest, most privileged people have to hear the word 'no' now and again. In a way, every encounter requires us to take a leap of faith – because even though we generally assume the best of people, we truthfully have no idea how they will respond until they do. All we can go on is whether our desires remain sated or unsated, when all is said and done.

Eking out every last morsel of hedonistic pleasure and self-gratification is a mental calculus of refreshing simplicity, which cuts through the Gordian knots that other thinker-types tie and twist and (over)think themselves into. At the end of the day, did we get what we wanted and avoid what we did not? Did we find pleasure and avoid pain? This simple assessment is why we are convinced we have no choice but to see all our attractions as fleeting inclinations. We can only control how we feel up to a point; beyond that, we just cannot help what we find appealing, who we think is hot, what we like doing. But what we can control is what we do about it. We can let ourselves fall for someone or keep them firmly in the 'friend zone', make them part of our 'chosen family' or leave them as a casual acquaintance. We owe it to ourselves not to pin our dreams blindly on any single object of our focus – or we risk burdening it with a certainty and expectation of permanence we simply have no good reason to expect.

The right time to get transfixed

Being a Reveller gives us the feeling of stepping into a giant shimmering vortex, bathed in a sultry light, drawn willingly into its floating embrace. Our mindset comes with several major upsides. It encourages us to let go of our hang-ups and trust in our instincts. We are acutely aware that the world is pregnant with possibility: we sense how much we gain if we engage with it and how much we lose if we do not. This instils in us a firm conviction that whatever it is we want, we (only) have to go out and get it. Our fondest boast is that we are securely in control of our emotional state, marshalling and deploying all its different shades. And in that vein, we have a rare ability to find exactly the right wavelengths to relate to other people.

Much of our mindset is valuable as gold dust to other thinker-types. We celebrate the delights of being in touch and in tune with the world around us. We recognise that we can decide when to open or close our boundaries – a useful antidote to Hotheads' rage and Worrywarts' anxieties when theirs are crossed. We also understand the value of positive fellow-feeling, assuming the best of other people, and deferring judgement about them – rather than expecting them to earn our approval, as Jokesters and Quibblers do. And we grasp that how we feel about others and how they feel about us is ultimately a game, with wins and losses along the way, but always more rounds to come – in contrast to Cool Cats' earnestness and Gloomsters' resignation.

Yet there are some warning signs we should not overlook. We are not quite as in control as we presume: we may recognise our desires very precisely, but we do not always understand why we feel them. There is a 'pinball effect' in how our sense of self emerges — accumulating the various things, people, and situations we are drawn to — which means that we bounce between external factors, rather than being self-motivated. As a result, we risk overdoing things, persisting too far, and being overly forward because we expect others to reciprocate. Likewise, we risk sowing confusion, as our willingness to 'refine' how we feel means other people may never quite be sure where they stand with us. In both cases, we struggle to accept emotional outcomes that are not to a large extent on our terms — especially when other people either give back less or more to us than we are prepared to give them.

We can overcome these pitfalls by drawing on the collected wisdom of the thinker-type family. We can discover how to take up space for what we want without coming across as entitled by looking across at the Quibblers' perfectionism or Worrywarts' efforts to carve out their 'safe zone'. We can train ourselves to incorporate other people's concerns without abandoning our own by learning from Cool Cats' and Happy Campers' benign, live-and-let-live contentment. And if our overtures fail to yield any new connections, we can better reconcile ourselves to an indifferent world by appropriating Gloomsters' ready acceptance, mixed with Jokesters' self-assurance.

At its best, we can enjoy a luxurious, almost paradisical existence. Like dolphins with their ostentatiously frolicsome displays, courting and cavorting, capable of enduring bonds and transient encounters — yet stopping at nothing to sate their quest for pleasure. We buy what the world is selling, opening our minds to whatever we have not yet explored. Yet the more we devote our existence to the untrammelled pursuit of earthly delights, the more we may sacrifice our sense of overall direction. We know what we like and how to go after it, an incredible skill to boast in an uncertain world. But we can satisfy that far better than simply letting ourselves be seduced by every immediate appeal. It is all very well for us to let go, but we must not let ourselves go in the process – or we may let ourselves down. Our gift is to accept and exploit to the fullest what the world has to offer, though not so much that we take our eyes off the horizon and stop trying to see what lies beyond.

Conclusion

So there we have it, the ten members of the thinker-type family. Now let us imagine we are following them on an excursion. The Keen Bean is bounding on ahead, sticking their head in windows and down passageways, lifting things up off the ground to inspect them. The Worrywart is picking their way gingerly after them, wincing fussily, trying to coax them back to the group. The Happy Camper is ambling along with a vague smile, whistling under their breath, stifling a laugh as they nearly trip over something the Keen Bean has dropped. The Jokester is just behind, head turned to smirk at something, elbowing the Happy Camper and leaning in to share a wry remark.

The Gloomster trudges after them, hands in pockets, staring unseeingly at the floor. The Agoniser guides them along with a consoling hand on their arm, eyes fixed earnestly on their face, trying to catch the others' attention. Following them, the Reveller is revolving slowly on the spot with their arms outstretched, eyes dreamily shut, inhaling deeply, letting it all sink in. The Quibbler skirts past them with a pointed sigh, rolling their eyes, muttering a curse under their breath. And bringing up the rear, the Cool Cat is pacing along with impassive, measured steps, wearing an expression of blankly placid indulgence – tugged this way and that by a Hothead trying to shake off their hand, glowering stroppily at everything around them.

Quite the family portrait! Almost hard to imagine them all in the same place, rather than splitting off and going their own separate ways. At the very least, they will all be getting very different things out of their outing. If we asked them, we would probably get ten different stories about what it was like. For some, home time could not come soon enough. For others, the day could have lasted forever. Just think what they must be like at weddings, on family film night, or on a summer getaway. Imagine them trying to decide where to rent a flat, or send their children to school, or even ordering a meal at a restaurant! Goodness knows however they manage to get by.

But they do manage all the same. Like all families, they have their agreements and disagreements, their fallings-out and their makings-up, their partings of ways and their comings back together again. What this all comes down to is that each thinker-type has its own special way of getting along – or, if we are honest, sometimes *not* getting along – with every single one of the others. Some of them can have extraordinary heart-to-hearts. We look forward to seeing some of them every time we are all together. With others, we can barely stand to be in the same room, and we have to steel ourselves to get through family gatherings or team meetings whenever they are around. Sometimes, we find a way of seeing eye to eye, despite (or maybe even because of) having almost nothing in common. With others, even though they are so close that we might as well be carbon copies, we cannot help cringing at the awkward, gushy, or embarrassing stuff they come out with.

As with all families, it takes every member to make up the set. In just the same way, if we look at society as a whole, we can find any number of people who could play the part of these ten types. If any one or more of the thinker-types were missing, the family dynamic of how we think would look painfully lopsided. Without

CONCLUSION

the two happy thinker-types, the family would be too plaintive; without the sad ones, too ribald. Without the angry one, it would be too anodyne; without its calm mirror, too awash with emotion all round. And so on and so forth around the whole wheel.

Now – ultimately, inevitably – we come to the all-important question. We have met all the ten thinker-types in quite some detail, and we have discovered their various unique mindsets. Bit by bit, we have got to grips with their mental outlooks, had a glimpse of their mental pictures, and started to think our way into their reflections. We now have a sense of the kinds of social roles and experiences that foster different thinker-types within us. So where do we think we fall?

For now, I want to pass this question to you – because, at its heart, this book is about letting you explore the different sides of how we think. What I hope we have discovered together is what it is like to inhabit the various thinker-types. What it is like to move from our most fundamental, visceral, physiological reactions to the world around us through different layers of instinct and intuition all the way up to the most complex parts of our thought processes.

As you read about one thinker-type or another, did you find yourself thinking 'huh, that sounds familiar' or 'hmm, not sure about this one'? Or perhaps 'oh, hang on, maybe'? Or 'yes, exactly!' or even 'gosh, did not know I came across like that'? Do you know which one you want to hang your hat on? Or are you still a bit on the fence, torn between two or three or maybe even more types?

I am sure you have also been asking yourself whether these thinker-types sound like people you know, or perhaps who you would want to know. Who do you think you would get along with best and worst? Who would you want as lovers, flatmates, bosses, and co-workers? Who would you want to lead the country? Who would you trust to operate on you or look after your elderly relatives? Who do you want to give you life advice or teach your children? Have you got someone in mind for every member of the thinker-type family?

Over to you, to make of this book whatever you want to make of it. I hope you find it useful. I hope it makes you happy and sad, I hope it angers you and calms you down, I hope it makes you eager as well as fearful, I hope it disgusts you and fills you with desire. I hope it makes you conscious, right in your core, of every single shade of the wonderful, incredible, deep layers of thinking we are all capable of. I hope it illuminates for you the mindsets you are familiar with, and especially the ones you are not. Let each one take hold of you. Notice what it feels like to embody it, in your stomach, in your chest, in your heart, in your head. Take note – literally, if you like! – of what it is doing to your thinking. What colours the world takes on. What stands out about it, good and bad. What straight or convoluted avenues your mind wanders down. That is how *you* think, right now. Own it, acknowledge it, accept or transform it. Make it yours.

Epilogue

This book is, in effect, a hypothesis. It does something that has not really been tried before in a systematic way. The point of a lot of social research is to look 'under the bonnet' of the things we deal with in our everyday lives – to shine a light on what is *really* going on, on how they *actually* work. The fruits of this mission have led us in fascinating new directions. In many cases, they have broken exciting new ground in helping us better understand ourselves. Hundreds of thousands of scholars, writers, teachers and students, technicians and inventors, patrons and publicists have worked on bettering our grasp of society over the centuries. Individually and in clusters, they have discovered new avenues for themselves and their successors to explore. In the process, the enterprise of social research as a whole has succumbed to a vast degree of specialisation. Many disciplines and fields of social enquiry have emerged, which in turn are subdivided into many narrower areas of research. Each of them is rigorously committed to focusing on its own little corner, paring away all the extraneous details that get in the way of looking at *that* specific bit of society, and *that bit only*.

There is nothing wrong with that, of course. The smaller or more narrowly defined the object we focus on, and the longer we give ourselves to focus on it, the more likely it is that our exposure to it will build up into valuable experience – and from there into unparalleled expertise. The problem is that, having picked which corner to head into and busy themselves with, social researchers on the whole do not generally take the time to retread their steps and look back at the room as a whole. Social research has become very good at presenting us with myriad little shiny mosaic-pieces, each of which tells its own fragmentary story about the human condition. But it tends to leave all these mosaic-pieces in a disaggregated jumble on the floor, rather than compositing them into a full picture. Social research should not just be about breaking things into shards. Where it can really add value, where it comes into its own, is when it joins all these shards up again with a unifying seam – a golden thread of narrative interpretation that makes what it has *de*constructed make *re*constructed sense.

How We Think is a project precisely in this vein. It brings together the large and disparate social research literature that has examined how *some* elements of how we think and why we do so relate to *other* elements. A sizeable volume of research articles has tested the correlations, alignments, and other connections between, for instance, personality and emotions, personality and predispositions, emotions and predispositions, personality and reasoning, and emotions and reasoning. It has also explored how particular personality traits, emotions, predispositions, reasoning styles and so on are treated and emphasised by certain professions. Yet, aside from occasional literature reviews, which still often remain quite discipline-specific, there has been very limited effort to pull all of these separate associations and insights together again into a single coherent analysis.

But *How We Think* aspires to a lot more than just to act as an up-to-date compendium of thinking-related social research. It also sets out to provide an intuitive framework to help anyone who wants to better understand how our social experiences shape our thinking to navigate what is ultimately a vast and at times overwhelming body of insights. Ideally, it aims to allow us to inhabit as far as possible the different 'states of mind' that social research on aggregate has revealed. To recognise and better understand ourselves and others, and perhaps even galvanise and feed back into further social research.

That is a pretty ambitious aim for just one book. Given what is at stake here, meshing together our understandings of how our minds work and how society influences us, it might be helpful to shine a light on some of my working. This means taking something of an intellectual grand tour far and wide through different fields and categories of social enquiry.

I deliberately focused on telling the story of *what it is like to be* each of the thinker-types in the earlier chapters, without a cumbersome penumbra of footnotes to offer buttressing support. But in light of that, it is only fair that I now do some bonnet-lifting of my own, and point out the main moving parts that drive my analysis, at least in outline. We can think of this as an introductory overview to some extremely rich and varied scholarly discussions – ones that, above all, are still very much ongoing!

One of the major challenges of the kind of syncretic approach I am using is that it is not always possible to incorporate everything equally and evenly. The reason is quite straightforward: social researchers do not always agree with each other. What some of them say about how we think is not always entirely compatible with what others say. Sometimes, they may be diametrically opposed, even logically contradictory. Sometimes, they simply 'talk past' each other.

These differences might be macro-level disputes about the value or priority of different ways of tackling particular objects of study. Qualitative versus quantitative. Theoretical versus empirical. Deep-level versus surface-level. Or they might be more micro-level debates about how to gather and present evidence. What criteria of assessment to use. How to choose a representative population sample. How to ensure validity across contexts and cultures. Or what terminology best captures what we are trying to say. In either case, these differences can have a profound effect on the conclusions that researchers come to. Navigating that is partly about making informed analytical choices. Not every mosaic-piece will fit neatly and seamlessly alongside every other.

The philosophy and science of how we think

Out of the many competing currents of social research on the theme of how we think, a number have proven relatively robust to how our understanding of ourselves and our minds has evolved over time. From them, models have emerged to represent different aspects of our mental structures and processes. As we have seen over the course of this book, there are five main elements within how we think. Each of them is the subject of scholarly discussions that stretch back decades, if not further.

First, we have personality, which defines our long-term mental structures. Right from the get-go, this confronts us with one of the most significant analytical choices we can make. Do we prefer to see personality as divided into *types* – distinct qualitative categories based on certain personality profiles? Or should we rather look at it in terms of *traits* – which break down these categories into quantifiable patterns or tendencies? Personality types have certainly made better inroads into the public mind. We can think of the 'type A–type B' classification, the Myers–Briggs Type Indicator and Keirsey Temperament Sorter, the 'psychopath test', and the Enneagram model, which have found their way into everything from dating profiles to recruitment criteria.[1] Type-based analysis might also seem like an easier reach for a book that seeks to explain our inner lives in terms of 'thinker-*types*'. But even as these typologies have become better known and have risen in popularity, they have come in for severe criticism in academic research for their lack of scientific rigour and robustness, including far more variation in individual results than a truly accurate model should permit. As much as they might appeal to our intuitions about what we and others are like, they do not hold up well in the white heat of experimental scrutiny.

Instead, personality researchers have found far better evidence to support the existence of core personality traits, foundational building blocks or anchor-points for how we think. Here too there is an analytical choice to be made. Social research has not quite settled on a single definitive roster of what these traits are, nor how to tell them apart from each other. Small but significant clusters of scholars have carved out a space for models focusing on excellence or decency,[2] as well as the long-running evolving psychometric assessment criteria of the Minnesota Multiphasic Personality Inventory (MMPI).[3] But by far the best-established model is one that uses the 'Big Five' traits: *openness to experience* (sometimes a little judgementally called *intellect* or *culture*), *conscientiousness* (or *dependability*), *extroversion* (or *surgency*), *agreeableness* (or *pleasantness*), and *emotional stability* (or, again quite judgementally, *neuroticism*).[4] This 'five-factor' or 'OCEAN' model has been used for the overwhelming majority of personality studies in academic psychology. However, in the last two decades, a revised 'six-factor' or 'HEXACO' version has gained increasing support, which subtly tweaks the definition of the 'Big Five' and adds a separate trait of *honesty–humility* to give a 'Big Six'.[5] Other multi-factor models have been put forward, such as the 'alternative five'.[6] There is also an ongoing debate about how well all of the 'OCEAN/HEXACO' factors replicate across experimental samples or cultural contexts – and limited agreement on what the 'opposite terms' that describe 'low scores' for each of these traits should be.[7] But whether in five- or six-trait format, this model has proven a rich and reliable source of insight for personality research, so I have opted to use it to underpin the 'thinker-types' here, adding my own terminology for the opposites of each of the six factors.

Next, we have emotions, which mark our shorter- or longer-term reactions to our experiences, from sentiments and impressions up to moods and temperaments. The thinker-types I have outlined in this book are probably the closest thing we have in modern social research to an emotional or emotion-led thinking typology. The main questions that preoccupy emotion research are what the building blocks are that underpin our emotional range, and how they relate to each other. The primary issue here is not so much that different researchers have put forward vastly different sets of emotions to explain how we feel. There is relatively strong consensus on a handful of core emotions, which appear in some form in more or less any emotion model: happiness, sadness, anger, fear, and disgust.[8] It is when we try to look beyond this 'core' group that major differences and disagreements start to appear.[9] Some models treat anxiety as its own separate emotion, while others subsume it into fear.[10] Some treat pride as a form of happiness, and guilt or shame as forms of sadness, while others keep them all separate.[11] Some expand the list considerably, adding a range of culturally wide-ranging emotions including admiration, amusement, anticipation, awe, calmness, care, confusion, entrancement, interest, lust, nostalgia, relief, satisfaction, surprise, and trust.[12] Several offer ways of combining these emotions into 'tree-structured' clusters, with a small list of primary core emotions, plus secondary and tertiary versions.[13] A few even start to combine these building blocks into more complex emotions, though the consensus for these is even weaker. These include emotions such as contempt (disgust plus anger), love (happiness plus trust), optimism (anticipation plus happiness), remorse (sadness plus disgust), or submission (trust plus fear).[14]

A large factor in the disagreements between emotion researchers is the intuitively appealing idea that emotions work as opposing pairs, with respective tendencies to have a 'positive' and 'negative' affective reaction to world events.[15] Perhaps the most obvious such pairing is happiness–sadness. But beyond that, there is no clear path to working out how exactly the other core emotions should be paired up, or which one of them is the 'positive' and which the 'negative'. Disgust as a clear negative generally gets paired with trust as a positive, although the lack of consensus around trust leaves the weighting in this pairing quite skewed and possibly incomplete. Fear as a similarly clear negative often gets paired with either anger or anticipation as positives.[16] Yet the idea of anger as anything other than a strongly negative emotion raises methodological questions (as well as more than a few eyebrows), which has led rival models to suggest an alternative pairing with positive calm.[17] Meanwhile, anticipation is also often put together with negative surprise, though since neither is fully accepted as a core emotion the pairing as a whole ends up fairly analytically weak.[18]

Ultimately, the latest 'state of play' is best expressed by a model called the 'hourglass of emotions'. This uses insights from sentiment analysis in the world of AI and computer science to settle on four 'positive–negative' pairings, each of which has low, medium, and high levels of intensity: joy–sadness ('introspection'), calmness–anger ('temper'), eagerness–fear ('sensitivity'), and pleasantness–disgust ('attitude').[19] Substitute desire for pleasantness, add seeking to eagerness, and retain happiness as the synonym for 'joy', and we arrive at the emotions I use for this analysis.

With these in hand – the 'Big Five/Six' and the 'hourglass of emotions' – we have the ingredients to put together our mental outlooks, the perspectives or vantage points for our thinking. This is where the first batch of associations and correlations come in: the ones that group clusters of personality traits based on how often they are found to co-occur in people, and those that connect the incidence of certain traits in people to the prevalence of certain emotions in how they think.[20] Both of these are the subject of well-contained but highly active areas of psychological research. These are being added to and revised on a very regular basis – although a fairly clear consensus for both kinds of connections has already begun to emerge. What precisely these connections are should be relatively evident from how I have constructed the mental outlooks for each of the ten thinker-types, so I will not rehash them at length here.

Instead, I will confine myself to just two important points to note. First, social research has found ways of connecting happiness and sadness to more or less the full gamut of personality traits at both ends of the trait spectrums. In some ways, this fits our intuitions of how important both of these emotions are to all of our thinking from day to day, and how versatile our experience of each of them can be. I have addressed this by giving each of them two thinker-types – Happy Camper and Jokester for happiness, Gloomster and Agoniser for sadness – to reflect the internal clusters of personality traits. Second, I have consciously chosen to lead with emotions as the dominant characteristic of each mental outlook. Partly because the personality-led equivalent would take us too close to the oversupply of personality typologies above. But also because how we experience thinking 'in the moment' is far more guided by emotion than personality. Among other things, this makes it easier to describe *what it is like* to think like each of the thinker-types in a more vivid and differentiated way.

So much for the mental outlooks I have given the ten thinker-types. Now, what about their mental pictures and reasoning? We can start with the information we acquire and experiences we make ourselves as we move through the world. Here, there are no great methodological disputes as severe as the ones for personality and emotions. The general view in social research has coalesced around seeing information as fundamentally sense-data we gain from stimuli in our surroundings. These are either the result of our direct physical contact and interactions with the people and objects around us, or indirectly prompted by 'cues' that represent what happens outside our immediate space of experience.[21] Where some modest disagreement arises is about how active or passive we are in gaining information from these stimuli. Some accounts emphasise the decisive role of our attention and awareness, which can be caught by people and things (passive) but which we can also direct (active). Others stress the 'scripts' we follow to glean the information we want to get in a selective way – how we receive it (passive), accept it (active), and sample it (active) when we form opinions about the world. Still others look at the 'valences' that can be embedded into information – the positive or negative 'spin' that comes in tow with it when we get it (passive), which we cannot always untangle from it (active) as we take it all in.[22]

This last one takes us neatly onto the predispositions that we use as a kind of lens to interpret our information, or the norms for how we should do so. The choice we have to make here is less about which of several competing models we are going to use. Rather, it is more about how to bridge areas of social research that talk about what are in the end very similar and closely related things in utterly divergent ways, using totally unrelated terms. Interpreting information is ultimately a matter of coming to judgements about it. What is right or wrong, what is true or untrue, and so on. These take the form of either epistemological claims about what is 'the case', or evaluative claims about what status something has according to some criterion of estimation.[23]

Social research that lies at the more philosophical end of the spectrum tends to understand these judgements in terms of values – longer-term foundational beliefs that link to the abstract concepts and ideas we use to understand the world. Meanwhile, survey research and opinion polling typically looks at them in terms of attitudes – organised groups of beliefs that foster intuitive, lasting orientations towards specific objects (happenings, people, things, and so on), which underpin our opinions about them.[24] Values and attitudes are clearly related, though the precise relationship between them is still a live issue. Abstract and concrete, general and specific, inward and outward, implicit and explicit, permanent or momentary – all of these have been raised as possible ways of delineating between them.

Where a lot of these distinctions in how we look at information and predispositions come into their own is when we try to square off the effects that personality and emotions have on how we acquire information, and how we impose predispositions on it. This is where the next batch of associations that this book relies on comes into view. Social research has mapped the correlations between personality traits and predispositions, including how closely we conform to our existing predispositions when we form opinions, and our tendencies towards progressive and conservative values. It has also done the same for the relationships between personality traits and information, including our levels of attention and awareness.[25] Similar work has tested the link between particular emotions and predispositions, such as how inclined we are to stick with or reconsider our current convictions. And it has explored the connections between emotions and information, including again our attentiveness, whether we rely on older or newer information, and how likely we are to accept or resist social stimuli and cues.[26] Again, I will let the thinker-types show exactly which way all these various effects go. My main observation is that the ways that personality traits and emotions affect how we use information and predispositions in our thinking can either exacerbate and reinforce each other, or have more of a mitigating impact. This is where a lot of the subtlety in characterising how the various thinker-types think originally stems from.

The way I have chosen to put this set of connections here is to try to explain how our mental outlooks shape the mental pictures we form of what is happening around us. The idea is that we do not generally keep our information and predispositions in separate mental silos but instead fuse them into more or less coherent mental depictions of the world. This takes us to the parts of social research concerned with theories of public opinion.[27] Perhaps the most powerful legacy these theories have bequeathed us is the insight that, as much as we might think that we are thinking about the world as it is, what we are actually doing is thinking about the world as we represent it to ourselves. We live, and act, and even think within a very specific environment. Yet how we get information about it and the predispositions we carry inside us ready to spring to judgement have an interfering, mediating effect on how we think about our environment. Our mental pictures are actually a kind of 'pseudo-environment', a version of the world over which we have already handed down a basic verdict. Where we already affirm or deny, praise or censure what we are aware of being the case within it.[28] Given the many connections between our mental outlooks and our mental pictures, the conclusion we can draw is that what we are like deep down, mixed with how we happen to be feeling, has a major impact on what we think the world looks like.

Finally, we have the styles of reasoning we use to think about these mental pictures, the thinking practices that give us our sophisticated reflections about the world. Again, the main choice here is one of bridging two parallel schools of thought in social research about how we make sense of what all the other prior ingredients of our thinking are telling us. How we deliberate, how we form arguments, how we process our verdicts on the world into fully 'thought-out' opinions. The first, generally from the philosophical tradition, explores the role of rationality.[29] The way we streamline and systematise how we gather information and apply our predispositions to it, the way we use stepwise logic to refine how effectively we turn our mental pictures into complex intellectual positions. Here, the main areas of contention are how thinly or thickly the idea of rationality ought to be defined. Is it just a matter of finding better inputs for our thinking and being efficient in our reflections?[30] Or should we be imposing more stringent conditions around coherence, rules of inference, high or low use of information, or the quality of our argued outcomes for an opinion to 'count' as rational?[31] In turn, some of these debates flow over into the question of reasonableness, which addresses how far we are willing to take other people's views into account when we formulate our opinions.[32] This is a smaller topic in social research, and somewhat orthogonal to the main discussions around rationality. But the two become united by a few extended discussions about how far rational and reasonable ways of thinking are aligned with each other, and how far they are in irredeemable conflict.

The second school of thought, which owes its origins above all to behavioural economics, looks at the role of heuristics, the 'rules of thumb' and mental shortcuts that allow us to cut some corners compared to the rigorous reasoning implied by full rationality.[33] If using systematic logic to capture everything in our mental pictures and work it through into our opinions is 'thinking slow' – high-effort, steady, time-consuming – then heuristics can be seen as 'thinking fast' – less demanding, tolerably accurate, and easy to get through. There has been something of an explosion of social research on heuristics since the idea was introduced, with new and improved understandings of the rules of thumb we use in our everyday lives emerging constantly.[34] Anchoring and adjustment, how we use defined starting points to inform later opinion shifts. Availability, how easily information comes to mind. Contagion, treating information as good or bad by association. Familiarity, preferring already-known predispositions and information to new ones. Peak-end, favouring the most intense or most recent information when shaping our mental pictures. Similarity, how close information is to our mental 'prototypes', and many others. Despite this ever-expanding variety of heuristics, the essential feature they have in common is that they offer an explicit alternative to rational thinking that we can all access. This has prompted further debate about how far heuristics should be seen as cognitive biases – an inhibited version of 'good' rational thinking. In parallel, it has also encouraged discussion on whether the two not only sit comfortably alongside each other but actually support one another in crucial ways.[35]

As before, there is plenty of evidence that whether we think rationally or irrationally, reasonably or unreasonably, heuristically or non-heuristically, is linked to both our personality traits and our emotions. Addressing this final cornerstone of the ten thinker-types lets us integrate the last series of correlations that psychological research has explored. The effect of personality traits on how much weight we give reason in our thinking, the effect of 'positive' and 'negative' emotions on whether we opt for more heuristic or systematic processing, and many others.[36] As with our mental pictures, the exact constellation of traits and emotions that go into each mental outlook can similarly exacerbate or mitigate each other's individual effects on how we reason our way towards the opinions we have about the world. It is these subtle combinations that give each thinker-type its inimitable and distinctive thinking style. Or, to put it another way, it is the effect that our mental outlooks have on our reasoning that is perhaps the most directly visible way we bring how we think to bear on the world around us.

The theory of how society shapes our minds

Social research into the different components of how we think has given us the tools we need to reconstitute all these myriad cross-cutting associations, correlations, and links into something closer to a recognisable set of descriptive profiles. But to round these profiles out fully into social characters, we need to look at explanations for why we end up adopting or playing one of these characters – or perhaps a couple of them – more than the others. On the face of it, any of us could end up thinking like any of them. There is nothing inherent to our nature or our biology that is stopping us from exhibiting or experiencing any of these personality traits, emotions, ways of gaining information, predispositions, or styles of reasoning, and exploring the avenues of thinking that come with them. Yet that does not explain why some of them seem to be more like us, more familiar, more relatable than others. As crude as it is, we can think about this in terms of 'means'. Our minds supply us with the basic 'means of thinking', and the ability to use them. So what decides which of them we end up reaching for, which of them we deploy, which of them end up in demand?

If there is nothing inside us to explain this, then we need to look to outside factors. It is pretty much the bread-and-butter for social research to look at how our surroundings influence what we are like, including how we think. There is growing evidence to suggest that even the most fundamental elements of how we think are susceptible to change thanks to our social experiences during our lifetimes.[37] Different branches of social research put this in different terms. Communal norms, context, ideology, material conditions, opinion-climates, prevailing culture, reference groups, and other more or less tangible causes. Though all of these have subtly different meanings and emphases, what they have in common is that they see what we are like as fundamentally responding to how we live. The way social enquiry tends to understand this is tied to action, and the circumstances of action: what we do, how, when, where, and in relation to whom. If we think about action in terms of a series of duties and tasks, which we carry out through specific routines, on certain schedules, in particular places, and alongside a fairly constant set of peers, then how we live boils down to the occupations we have.[38] Some economistic strands of social research restrict the label of 'occupation' exclusively to formal professional employment, above all contractual, salaried wage-labour.[39] But we can also interpret 'occupation' more broadly, more akin to 'preoccupation', in the vein of 'what occupies us', or 'what we spend our time and effort doing'. To avoid putting too much weight on the world of work, and too little on what we do outside it, I have opted for the broader approach.

Viewed in these terms, there are plenty of social occupations we hold during our lives, either at the same time or in rapid succession. To take only a few, we can be an artist, athlete, civil servant, contractor, defendant, grandchild, juror, manager, nurse, officer, parent, patient, pupil, shopper, tutor, voter, worker, and much more besides. The question social research is then faced with is how we go from a situation where (some of) these occupations take up more and more space in our daily lives, to a situation where they become more and more an inherent part of who we are. Important to us, integral to our lives, a major source of our identity. The answer lies in the particular expectations each of these occupations has for what we should do, how, when, where, and in relation to whom, and how it gets us to live up to them. If we hold a certain occupation, it gives us a certain perspective, or point of view, onto the world from which we look at it.[40] It gives us certain dispositions, or frames of mind, that give us the inclination to regard the world and behave in specific ways.[41] Norms that bind and regulate our behaviour to be 'good' or 'right' as the occasion demands.[42] Practices that aggregate our 'good' and 'right' behaviour into repeated and easily memorised patterns, pursuits, or routines.[43] Structures, cohesive arrangements and frameworks built out of selected parts of the world around us.[44] And systems, organic institutions or networks that guide how our patterned practices interact with our framing structures.[45]

Sociological research especially has come to bracket these various expectations together under the term '*habitus*'.[46] Quite how general or specific these *habitus* are is a subject of lively disagreement. Some strands of research see them as applying at the level of large groups of people, such as countries, industry sectors, or socioeconomic classes. Others are inclined to get a little more granular and refine them down to the level of individual jobs.[47] I lean towards the latter end of the scale. The sheer level of complexity and specialisation that society has reached means that people who reside in the same country, work in the same industry, or exist in the same class stratum can have very different experiences of life on a daily basis. It is rarely grand narratives or sweeping gestures that guide us in the moment. Instead, it is much more contingent, localised, even parochial expectations about how to deal with what lies in front of us that affect us. This is especially true of how we think. The expectations attached to our social occupations do not just affect our general actions, they also carefully circumscribe the thinking we do – need to do, are required to do – as part of performing these roles day to day. They give us intellectual vantage points from which to view the world, lenses that colour and clarify our view, primers that tell us how to think 'right' or 'well', scripts of instructions for us to follow when we think, design plans of models and schematic parameters to 'house' our thinking, and simulations to illustrate the approaches and methods we should use when we think.[48] All of these together determine how we deploy the five elements that go into our thinking. They do so based on the duties and tasks, the routines, schedules, places, and peers we are expected to use them for.

The crucial question for how these occupational expectations shape who we are is how we come to take them on and make them our own. Social research has offered up many different terms to capture this process, all of which focus on different parts of a common theme: how we as individuals grapple with, and reconcile ourselves to, what our surroundings are putting on us. Some traditions frame this in terms of how we internalise these expectations, making ourselves responsible for making sure that we abide by them. Others prefer to look at how we identify with and 'subjectivise' our occupations and what they want from us, to do with taking ownership of the role they have foisted upon us. Still more talk about how society's institutions 'interpellate' us with these expectations, seeing our occupations as 'calling' us to act in certain ways, and us as answering these 'calls'.[49] Ultimately, all of these are part and parcel of how our occupations socialise us. Quite literally, how they turn us into the kinds of people that our 'parts' of society as a whole expect, need, and require us to be. How through 'mimetic' imitation of other people around us, we pick up how we should act and think. How through repetition, day after day, we get used to acting and thinking that way. And how through a multitude of complementary, interlocking processes, we are kept acting and thinking that way. Through money, management, rewards and sanctions, publications, rituals, nurture and treatment, qualifications and training, and many more.[50]

What this leaves us with, as people who have many occupations, is a whole range of competing versions of what we should be like. Not all of them will always align neatly, or even fit together particularly well at all. Sometimes they may clash so viciously that we find ourselves torn between them, trying (and possibly failing) to keep the various aspects of our lives fully satisfied. This may seem like a daunting situation for us to be in. But there are several strands of social research that see this as more of an opportunity. That we can, or must, choose between different occupations' expectations can help us be more amenable to some, and resistant to others. To ride out any tensions between who they expect us to be and who we actually are. To find ways through the moments when these expectations leave us adrift, unable to deal with what the world presents us with. To receive alternative ideas for how to act and think from elsewhere in society. And to take a step back and process when these expectations are being pushed on us, rather than simply following them blindly and immediately.[51]

What these all point towards is how important it is to recognise the hybridity that lies at the heart of how we act and how we think.[52] The multifaceted way in which we create our own specific blend of influences from the different parts of our lives to craft our identity, which make us uniquely who we are. It is this hybridity that explains why we will have affinities with certain thinker-types that are similar in some ways and different in others compared to those of our friends, our family, our work colleagues and classmates, fellow team members, neighbours, and so on. In ways we might expect, and ones that may have never occurred to us before. And it is hybridity that explains how the building blocks of the ten thinker-types can be combined into a potentially infinite variety of different answers to the essential question of 'how we think'.

EPILOGUE

Ten thinker-types – for now

That brings to a close our whistlestop tour of the insights on which this book rests. If we want to put it in these terms, it is an outline sketch of the theoretical model I have used to develop and devise everything we have read here. Of course, there is a lot more we could say about every part of 'how we think' and 'how society shapes our minds'. These are vast topics that researchers across the world have wrestled with for centuries. From the classical arguments of Hippocrates and Galen, al-Rāzī and Ibn Sīnā, Charaka and Suśruta, to the scattered army of neuroscientists, opinion researchers, philosophers, psychologists, and sociologists addressing them today. It is only really possible to give a carefully curated taster of them all here. To lay out a series of doors we can choose to walk through, leads we may follow into their respective corners of social enquiry. At the same time, what we know about these themes, how we understand and interpret and measure them, is still very much a work in progress. And it will almost certainly remain as such for a long time to come.

This is not a bad thing by any means. Just because we have not quite got to the bottom of something does not mean that what we have learned so far is not worth mentioning. Science, the arts, the humanities, and everything in between would be remarkably taciturn professions if everyone involved in them always waited until they had completely and definitely 'finished off' a topic before daring to offer any comments on it. When researchers write articles and books, posts and reports, hold lectures, give papers, deliver presentations, or sit down for interviews, they are very rarely saying that 'their work here is done'. Even if they were, it would not be difficult to find others in their fields more than ready to disagree with them, often vehemently. Rather, in all these cases, researchers are giving the rest of us, in their direct audiences and beyond, a progress update.

That is how we should see this book too. As a milestone marker of where we have got to in understanding how we think and why we do so.

Where we land, then, is that we live in a world where who we are in society – and specifically what we do in society – regularly and routinely exposes us to certain experiences. Over time, we come to associate these experiences more and more with certain emotions. Whenever these emotions awaken within us, they unlock certain sides of our personalities, making them more and more pronounced. Together, these increasingly push us to find out about the world, judge it, and reflect on it in certain ways more than the others available to us. All of this may be more or less transparent to ourselves and to the people around us. But we undoubtedly detect its effects in whether, how, and how far we agree or disagree with how others see, feel, and think about the world.

We can find similar patterns of thinking in people spread across very different walks of life. In our classrooms and offices, in our student dorms and hospital wards, our bars and living rooms, our temples and parliaments. At the same time, we can feel the contrary pulls towards different patterns of thinking vying for primacy within our own hearts and heads. We can follow these pulls where they try to lead us, we can try to balance them, we can strain against them in the opposite direction – but they will keep being there all the same. To live in society is to be shaped by it. That is true of our bodies, the living plasticine that can be modelled and moulded into almost any shape. It is just as true of our minds.

Acknowledgements

How We Think has been the work of many years, of several months, and of a handful of weeks. It began as my doctoral research at the University of Oxford, and covered a period that spanned my move from the sprawling half-quads and deer parks of Magdalen College to the otherworldly time-capsule of All Souls College. The months of converting the project from a thesis, first to a proposal, then to the opening stages of a manuscript were spread across periods of sporadic work during the first two years of the Covid-19 pandemic. These two *années de pelèrinage* took me from central Oxford via a year in neo-Hanseatic comfort near the Norfolk coast and a month in the London Borough of Enfield to a view with a room in the Florence *quartiere* of Campo di Marte, nestled at the foot of the Fiesole hill road. The final sprint, meanwhile, took three periods of near-monastic seclusion. One I underwent in the idyllic haven of a farmstead outside the ancient Tuscan *comune* of Barberino di Mugello. The second came after my return to the island, in a stable conversion near the sleepy outskirts of Wokingham, ensnared in the commuter tendrils of the sprawling metropolis. The last came, perhaps appropriately, after a return to Oxford – this time straddling both the 'town' and the 'gown' sides of its deeply graven divide.

No reckoning could truly capture all the many connections and exchanges that have found their way into *How We Think*, however subtly or indirectly, from chance conversations to prolonged debates, from casual encounters to enduring intimacies. My greatest intellectual and professional debt I owe to my doctoral supervisor Michael Freeden, whose patience and generous support allowed me to cycle through several ways of looking at my chosen topic before settling on the one that eventually took shape as my thesis. As a theorist of ideas and ideologies, I owe a profound debt of thanks to my colleagues at the *Journal of Political Ideologies* and the University of Nottingham, especially Hugo Drochon and Mathew Humphrey. And in my capacity as a think-tanker and 'thought-leader' on education policy and national strategy, I am deeply obliged to my former colleagues from my various professional lives, including Zainab Agha, Philip Bray, Benjamin Clayton, Alex Downing, Andy Forbes, Ann Limb, Steven Lynch, Mike Mavrommatis, Lucy Smith, and Sandy Steele for their interest in my research agenda, and for giving me the latitude to pursue it alongside my day-to-day work.

This book occupied a significant portion of my work as a Max Weber Fellow at the European University Institute, Florence, and I am thankful for the support of my mentors Philipp Genschel, Juho Harkonen, Erik Jones, and Karin Tilmans over the course of my two years there. For exchanges personal and political, pastoral and philosophical, over countless *aperitivos*, Ichnusas, negronis, and *schiacciatas*, I am deeply indebted to my colleagues on the Max Weber Programme and at the Robert Schuman Centre for Advanced Studies. First among these are my *commilitoni* in the office at Villa Schifanoia: Vicky Donnaloja, Vicki Finn (and Pablo Paniagua), Marta Migliorati, Farah Ramzy, and Troy Vettese. To these must be added Télio Cravo, Jessica di

ACKNOWLEDGEMENTS

Cocco, Martina Ferracane, Makoto Fukumoto, Natalia Garbiras-Díaz, Emma Kluge, Eroll Kuhn, Cristiana Lauri, Morshed Mannan, Takuya Onoda, Or Rosenboim, and Francesca Zanasi.

I am truly fortunate to lead a life enriched by a wealth of deep and unique friendships, legacies of shared contexts and experiences scattered across space and time. It would be impossible to do justice to them all, so I will have to restrict myself to naming those of my dearest friends who have shaped most profoundly the thinking that forms the backbone of *How We Think*. As foils and inspirations, as listeners and questioners, as comrades and role-models, and as sources of unconditional love, which I give back to them with interest. They include Claire and Philip Ahlquist, Udit Bhatia, Imogen Clark, Benedict Coleridge, Megan Dent, Puneet Dhaliwal, Maísa Edwards, Sophie Frew, Ian Jordan, Anik Laferrière, Bruno Leipold, Elisabeth Löffler, Sabrina Martin, Robin McGhee, Ruth Minton, David Nicholson Thomas, Elizabeth O'Brien Ingleson, Joanne Paul, Rosie Scott-Griffin, Dhaneesha Senaratne, Will Sheldon, Pascale Siegrist, Ruth Spencer Jolly, Jennifer Warburton, Hugh Wilkinson, and many more.

Finally, this project would never have become possible without the inspirational support, insightful vision, and intuitive wisdom of several brilliant women. First among them is my extraordinary mother Doris Hermann-Ostrowski, whose dedication and love sustained me from the moment I first drew breath. She knew full well what an array of lives we can lead, how many roles we play, and what quirks of circumstance move us from context to context during our time on this earth. She was looking forward to reading *How We Think*, and to translating it into German, and it is a source of insuperable grief to me that now she never will.

Over my years at Oxford and the EUI, I was lucky to benefit from the mentorship of Cécile Fabre, Kalypso Nicolaïdis, and Ann Thomson, and I will always value their counsel in every new enterprise I undertake. As an idea, a project, and a piece of writing, *How We Think* owes its emergence to the genius of Georgina Capel and her team, who first encouraged me to discover my public voice. At Hodder & Stoughton, I have had the unrivalled pleasure of working with Kirty Topiwala, who seized on this project's potential, as well as Anna Baty, Izzy Everington, and Celia Hayley, whose editorial dexterity has taught me invaluable lessons that have revolutionised how I write. Finally, as this project inched towards its crucial closing stages, it has coincided with the start of the most beautiful journey life can offer with मेरी जान Amiya Bhatia. She has witnessed me, buoyed me up with endless grace, and counselled me in my thinking. I am deeply thankful to her, our 'chosen sister' Meghna Jayanth, and both of their extended families for having welcomed me into their hearts.

There are many more who have shaped me, in many ways, loud and quiet. This book has benefited immeasurably from all of their hands, and my gratitude to them is as profound as it is eternal.

Notes

1. Happy Camper

1. See, for instance, Tomas Chamorro-Premuzic, Emily Bennett, and Adrian Furnham, 'The happy personality: Mediational role of trait emotional intelligence', *Personality and Individual Differences* 42(8) (2007), 1633–39; Kristina M. DeNeve and Harris Cooper, 'The happy personality: A meta-analysis of 137 personality traits and subjective well-being', *Psychological Bulletin* 124(2) (1998), 197–229; K.V. Petrides, Ria Pita, and Flora Kokkinaki, 'The location of trait emotional intelligence in personality factor space', *British Journal of Psychology* 98(2) (2007), 273–89; Christopher J. Soto, 'Is Happiness Good for Your Personality? Concurrent and Prospective Relations of the Big Five With Subjective Well-Being', *Journal of Personality* 83(1) (2015), 45–55; Serena Villata, Elena Cabrio, Imène Jraidi, Sahbi Benlamine, Maher Chaouachi, Claude Frasson, and Fabien Gandon, 'Emotions and personality traits in argumentation: An empirical evaluation', *Argument & Computation* 8(1) (2017), 61–87.
2. See, for example, Anna-Maria Isola, Lotta Virrankari, and Heikki Hiilamo, 'On Social and Psychological Consequences of Prolonged Poverty–A Longitudinal Narrative Study From Finland', *Journal of Social and Political Psychology* 9(2) (2021), 654–70; Paul K. Piff and Jake P. Moskowitz, 'Wealth, poverty, and happiness: Social class is differentially associated with positive emotions', *Emotion* 18(6) (2018), 902–5; Mariano Rojas, 'Poverty and people's wellbeing', in Wolfgang Glatzer, Laura Camfield, Valerie Møller, and Mariano Rojas (eds.), *Global Handbook of Quality of Life* (Dordrecht: Springer, 2015), 317–50.
3. See, for instance, Mohammed Aboramadan and Yasir Mansoor Kundi, 'Emotional culture of joy and happiness at work as a facet of wellbeing: a mediation of psychological safety and relational attachment', *Personnel*

Review 52(9) (2023), 2133–52; Timothy A. Judge, Shuxia (Carrie) Zhang, and David R. Glerum, 'Job satisfaction', in Valerie I. Sessa and Nathan A. Bowling (eds.), *Essentials of Job Attitudes and Other Workplace Psychological Constructs* (Abingdon: Routledge, 2020), 207–41; Remy Magnier-Watanabe, Caroline F. Benton, Toru Uchida, and Philippe Orsini, 'Designing jobs to make employees happy? Focus on job satisfaction first', *Social Science Japan Journal* 22(1) (2019), 85–107; Wido G.M. Oerlemans and Arnold B. Bakker, 'Motivating job characteristics and happiness at work: A multilevel perspective', *Journal of Applied Psychology* 103(11) (2018), 1230–41; Cibele Satuf, Samuel Monteiro, Henrique Pereira, Graça Esgalhado, Rosa Marina Afonso, and Manuel Loureiro, 'The protective effect of job satisfaction in health, happiness, well-being and self-esteem', *International Journal of Occupational Safety and Ergonomics* 24(2) (2018), 181–9.

4. For studies on the link between happiness and spending, see Stephanie Gillison and Kristy Reynolds, 'Shopping for yourself versus shopping for someone else', *Journal of Consumer Marketing* 33(4) (2016), 225–34; Thomas Gilovich, Amit Kumar, and Lily Jampol, 'A wonderful life: experiential consumption and the pursuit of happiness', *Journal of Consumer Psychology* 25(1) (2015), 152–65; Ronald Goldsmith, 'The Big Five, happiness, and shopping', *Journal of Retailing and Consumer Services* 31(1) (2016), 52–61.

5. On happiness and social communities, see Max Haller and Markus Hadler, 'How Social Relations and Structures can Produce Happiness and Unhappiness: An International Comparative Analysis', *Social Indicators Research* 75 (2006), 169–216; Ambrose Leung, Cheryl Kier, Tak Fung, Linda Fung, and Robert Sproule, 'Searching for Happiness: The Importance of Social Capital', in Antonella Delle Fave (ed.), *The Exploration of Happiness: Present and Future Perspectives* (Cham: Springer, 2013), 247–67; Allison Ross, Craig A. Talmage, and Mark Searle, 'Toward a Flourishing Neighborhood: the Association of Happiness and Sense of Community', *Applied Research in Quality of Life* 14 (2019), 1333–52; Nancy Ross, 'Health, happiness, and higher levels of social organisation', *Journal of Epidemiology and Community Health* 59 (2005), 614; Maria Spiliotopoulou and Mark Roseland, 'Achieving Community Happiness and Well-Being Through Community Productivity', in Scott Cloutier, Sara El-Sayed, Allison Ross, and Melanie Weaver (eds.), *Linking Sustainability and Happiness: Theoretical and Applied Perspectives* (Cham: Springer, 2021), 7–19.

6. On the effect of early-years socialisation on generosity in later life, see Kirsten H. Blakey, Erin Mason, Mioara Cristea, Nicola McGuigan, and Emily J. E. Messer, 'Does kindness always pay? The influence of recipient affection and generosity on young children's allocation decisions in a resource distribution task', *Current Psychology* 38 (2019), 939–49; Kristen Dunfield, Valerie A. Kuhlmeier, Laura O'Connell, and Elizabeth Kelley,

'Examining the Diversity of Prosocial Behavior: Helping, Sharing, and Comforting in Infancy', *Infancy* 16(3) (2011), 227–47; Tina Malti, Michaela Gummerum, Sophia Ongley, Maria Chaparro, Marta Nola, and Na Young Bae, '"Who is worthy of my generosity?" Recipient characteristics and the development of children's sharing', *International Journal of Behavioral Development* 40(1) (2016), 31–40; Markus Paulus and Chris Moore, 'Producing and understanding prosocial actions in early childhood', *Advances in Child Development and Behavior* 42 (2012), 271–305; by Antonio Tintori, Giulia Ciancimino, Rossella Palomba, Cristiana Clementi, and Loredana Cerbara, 'The Impact of Socialisation on Children's Prosocial Behaviour. A Study on Primary School Students', *International Journal of Environmental Research and Public Health* 18(22) (2021), 12017; Michalinos Zembylas, 'Pedagogies of generosity: Towards a multidimensional understanding that nurtures "critical generosity"', *Education, Citizenship and Social Justice* 20 (2025).

2. Jokester

1. For a selection of studies linking personality traits with, for instance, pleasurable emotions and well-being measures, see Jeromy Anglim, Sharon Horwood, Luke D. Smillie, Rosario J. Marrero, and Joshua K. Wood, 'Predicting Psychological and Subjective Well-Being From Personality: A Meta-Analysis', *Psychological Bulletin* 146(4) (2020), 279–323; Howard Berenbaum, Philip I. Chow, Michelle Schoenleber, and Luis E. Flores, 'Personality and pleasurable emotions', *Personality and Individual Differences* 101 (2016), 400–6; Peter Hills and Michael Argyle, 'Happiness, introversion–extraversion and happy introverts', *Personality and Individual Differences* 30(4) (2001), 595–608; Deepa Tanksale, 'Big Five personality traits: Are they really important for the subjective well-being of Indians?', *International Journal of Psychology* 50(1) (2015), 64–9; Emad Shdaifat, Tamadur Shudayfat, and Amira Alshowkan, 'The relationship between personality traits and happiness: the mediating role of emotional regulation', *BMC Nursing* 23(1) (2024), 327; Arash Ziapour, Alireza Khatony, Faranak Jafari, and Neda Kianipour, 'Correlation of personality traits with happiness among university students', *Journal of Clinical and Diagnostic Research* 12(4) (2018), CC26–9.
2. On humour as a coping mechanism, see Sarah Christopher, 'An introduction to black humour as a coping mechanism for student paramedics', *Journal of Paramedic Practice* 7(12) (2015), 610–17; Zöhre Kaya and Ferdi Yağan, 'The Mediating Role of Psychological Resilience in the Relationship between Coping Humour and Psychological Well-being', *Journal of*

Theoretical Educational Science 15(1) (2022), 146–68; Agnieszka Kruczek and Małgorzata Anna Basińska, 'Humour, stress and coping in adults', *Advances in Psychiatry and Neurology* 27(3) (2018), 181–95; Sari Lenggogeni, Ann Suwaree Ashton, and Noel Scott, 'Humour: coping with travel bans during the COVID-19 pandemic', *International Journal of Culture, Tourism and Hospitality Research* 16(1) (2022), 222–37; Adrián Pérez-Aranda, Jennifer Hofmann, Albert Feliu-Soler, Carmen Ramírez-Maestre, Laura Andrés-Rodríguez, Willibald Ruch, and Juan V. Luciano, 'Laughing away the pain: A narrative review of humour, sense of humour and pain', *European Journal of Pain* 23(2) (2019), 220–33.

3. On the psychology of scarcity, see, for instance, Maria John, Alicia P. Melis, Daniel Read, Federico Rossano, and Michael Tomasello, 'The preference for scarcity: A developmental and comparative perspective', *Psychology and Marketing* 35(8) (2018), 603–15; Kristin Layous, Jaime Kurtz, Joseph Chancellor, and Sonja Lyubomirsky, 'Reframing the ordinary: Imagining time as scarce increases well-being', *Journal of Positive Psychology* 13(3) (2018), 301–8; Michael Lynn, 'The Psychology of Unavailability: Explaining Scarcity and Cost Effects on Value', *Basic and Applied Social Psychology* 13(1) (1992), 3–7; Anuj K. Shah, Eldar Shafir, and Sendhil Mullainathan, 'Scarcity Frames Value', *Psychological Science* 26(4) (2015), 402–12; C.R. Snyder, 'Product Scarcity by Need for Uniqueness Interaction: A Consumer Catch-22 Carousel?', *Basic and Applied Social Psychology* 13(1) (1992), 9–24.

4. On seriousness and play, see, for instance, Steven Connor, *Styles of Seriousness* (Stanford, CA: Stanford University Press, 2023); Wendelin Küpers, 'Interplay(ing) – embodied and relational possibilities of "serious play" at work', *Journal of Organizational Change Management* 30(7) (2017), 993–1014; Catherine Li, Chloe Lau, Lital Yosopov, and Donald H. Saklofske, 'The seriousness of humour: Examining the relationship and pathways between sexist humour and the Dark Tetrad traits', *Current Psychology* 42 (2023), 32030–53; René T. Proyer, 'Playfulness and humor in psychology: An overview and update', *HUMOR* 31(2) (2018), 259–71; René T. Proyer, Nancy Tandler, and Kay Brauer, 'Playfulness and creativity: A selective review', in Sarah R. Luria, John Baer, and James C. Kaufman (eds.), *Creativity and Humor* (New York, NY: Academic Press, 2018), 43–60.

3. Gloomster

1. See, for instance, Kate A. Barford and Luke D. Smillie, 'Openness and other Big Five traits in relation to dispositional mixed emotions', *Personality and Individual Differences* 102 (2016), 118–22; Ryan Donovan, Aoife Johnson, Aine deRoiste, and Ruairi O'Reilly, 'Quantifying the links between

personality sub-traits and the basic emotions', *International Conference on Computational Science and its Applications* (ICCSA 2020), 521–37; Mi-Sook Park, Kyung Hwa Lee, Sunju Sohn, Jin-Sup Eom, and Jin-Hun Sohn, 'Degree of extraversion and physiological responses to physical pain and sadness', *Scandinavian Journal of Psychology* 55(5) (2014), 483–88; Sebastian Schindler and Jan Querengässer, 'Coping with sadness – How personality and emotion regulation strategies differentially predict the experience of induced emotions', *Personality and Individual Differences* 136 (2019), 90–95; Laura J. Speed and Marc Brysbaert, 'Ratings of valence, arousal, happiness, anger, fear, sadness, disgust, and surprise for 24,000 Dutch words', *Behavior Research Methods* 56 (2024), 5023–39.

2. On sadness and withdrawal, see Nico H. Frijda, *The Emotions* (Cambridge: Cambridge University Press, 1986); Richard S. Lazarus, *Emotion and adaptation* (Oxford: Oxford University Press, 1991); Randolph M. Nesse, 'Evolutionary explanations of emotions', *Human Nature* 1 (1990), 261–89; Janice Zeman, Margaret Cameron, and Natalee Price, 'Sadness in youth: Socialization, regulation, and adjustment', in Vanessa LoBue, Koraly Pérez-Edgar, and Kristin A. Buss (eds.), *Handbook of Emotional Development* (Cham: Springer, 2019), 227–56; Janice Zeman and Judy Garber, 'Display rules for anger, sadness, and pain: It depends on who is watching', *Child Development* 67(3) (1996), 957–73.

3. On sadness and self-care, see Renuka Joshi and Sapna Tomar, 'Effect of optimism/pessimism attitude on depression and coping strategies', *Indian Journal of Positive Psychology* 3(4) (2012), 445–47; Maria-Antonia Martorell-Poveda, Angel Martinez-Hernáez, Natalia Carceller-Maicas, and Martin Correa-Urquiza, 'Self-care strategies for emotional distress among young adults in Catalonia: a qualitative study', *International Journal of Mental Health Systems* 9(9) (2015); Lucille Sanzero Eller, Inge Corless, Eli Haugen Bunch, Jeanne Kemppainen, William Holzemer, Kathleen Nokes, Carmen Portillo, and Patrice Nicholas, 'Self-care strategies for depressive symptoms in people with HIV disease', *Journal of Advanced Nursing* 51(2) (2005), 119–30; Holly Sawyer, 'Mindfulness: Strategies to implement targeted self-care', *Journal of Interprofessional Education & Practice* 31 (2023), 100614; Victoria Vaughan Dickson, Margaret M. McCarthy, and Stuart M. Katz, 'How do depressive symptoms influence self-care among an ethnic minority population with heart failure?', *Ethnicity & Disease* 23(1) (2013), 22–28; Helen C. Vidler, 'Women making decisions about self-care and recovering from depression', *Women's Studies International Forum* 28(4) (2005), 289–303.

4. On sadness and depression, see George A. Bonanno, Laura Goorin, and Karin G. Coifman, 'Sadness and grief', in Michael Lewis, Jeannette M. Haviland-Jones, and Lisa Feldman Barrett (eds.), *Handbook of Emotions* (London: Guilford Press, 2008), 797–810; John Bowlby, *Attachment and*

Loss, vol. III – Loss: Sadness and Depression (London: Pimlico, 1998); Allan V. Horwitz and Jerome C. Wakefield, *The Loss of Sadness: How psychiatry transformed normal sorrow into depressive disorder* (Oxford: Oxford University Press, 2007); Sabine Mouchet-Mages and Franck J. Baylé, 'Sadness as an integral part of depression', *Dialogues in Clinical Neuroscience* 10(3) (2008), 321–7; Jerome C. Wakefield and Steeves Demazeux (eds.), *Sadness or Depression? International perspectives on the depression epidemic and its meaning* (Dordrecht: Springer, 2016).

5. See Yoy Bergs, Ondrej Mitas, Bert Smit, and Jeroen Nawijn, 'Anticipatory nostalgia in experience design', *Current Issues in Tourism* 23(22) (2020), 2798–2810; Cristiano Castelfranchi and Maria Micelli, 'Anticipation and emotion', in Roddy Cowie, Catherine Pelachaud, and Paolo Petta (eds.), *Emotion-Oriented Systems* (2011), 483–500; Paul J. Silvia and Jack W. Brehm, 'Exploring alternative deterrents to emotional intensity: Anticipated happiness, distraction, and sadness', *Cognition and Emotion* 15(5) (2010), 575–92.

6. Kaitlyn Creasy, 'On the problem of affective nihilism', *Journal of Nietzsche Studies* 49(1) (2018), 31–51; Nicolette Gable, '"Willful Sadness": American Decadence, gender, and the pleasures and dangers of pessimism', *Journal of Gender Studies* 26(1) (2017), 102–11; Dacher Keltner, Phoebe C. Ellsworth, and Kari Edwards, 'Beyond simple pessimism: Effects of sadness and anger on social perception', *Journal of Personality and Social Psychology* 64(5) (1993), 740–52; Buse Keskindag and Meryem Karaaziz, 'Influence of Depressive Symptoms on Pain Catastrophizing in Healthy Young Adults: The Role of Sadness, Self-criticalness and Pessimism', *Journal of Rational-Emotive and Cognitive-Behaviour Therapy* 37(1) (2019), 1–16; Geert Lovink, *Sad by design: On platform nihilism* (London: Pluto Press, 2019).

4. Agoniser

1. For a series of studies that cover the unique sympathetic forms of sadness, anger, and fear explored here, see, for instance, Kristopher J. Brazil, Anthony A. Volk, and Andrew V. Dane, 'Is empathy linked to prosocial and antisocial traits and behavior? It depends on the form of empathy', *Canadian Journal of Behavioural Science / Revue canadienne des sciences du comportement* 55(1) (2023), 75–80; Liliana Bujor and Maria Nicoleta Turliuc, 'The personality structure in the emotion regulation of sadness and anger', *Personality and Individual Differences* 162 (2020), 109999; Yuan Fang, Yan Dong, and Lanran Fang, 'Honesty-humility and prosocial behavior: The mediating roles of perspective taking and guilt-proneness', *Scandinavian Journal of Psychology* 60(4) (2019), 386–93; Hongyu Fu and Zhonglu Zhang, 'The relationship between Honesty-Humility and malevolent creativity:

Sequential mediation models with prosocial moral emotional traits and prosocial tendencies', *Current Psychology* 43 (2024), 7424–36; Davide Marengo, Kenneth L. David, Gökçe Özkarar Gradwohl, and Christian Montag, 'A meta-analysis on individual differences in primary emotional systems and Big Five personality traits', *Scientific Reports* 11 (2021), 7453; Angelo Panno, Valeria De Cristofaro, Camilla Oliveti, Giuseppe Carrus, and Maria Anna Donati, 'Personality and environmental outcomes: The role of moral anger in channeling climate change action and pro-environmental behavior', *Analyses of Social Issues and Public Policy* 21(1) (2021), 853–73; Vanessa M. Sinclair, Gabriela Topa, and Donald Saklofske, 'Personality correlates of compassion: a cross-cultural analysis', *Mindfulness* 11 (2020), 2423–32; Mary E. Stewart, Klaus P. Ebmeier, and Ian J. Deary, 'Personality correlates of happiness and sadness: EPQ-R and TPQ compared', *Personality and Individual Differences* 38(5) (2005), 1085–96.

2. Joseph P. Forgas, 'Can sadness be good for you?', *Australian Psychologist* 52(1) (2017), 3–13; Melissa M. Karnaze and Linda J. Levine, 'Sadness, the architect of cognitive change', in Heather C. Lench (ed.), *The Function of Emotions: When and why emotions help us* (Cham: Springer, 2018), 45–58; Tim Lomas, 'The quiet virtues of sadness: A selective theoretical and interpretative appreciation of its potential contribution to wellbeing', *New Ideas in Psychology* 49(1) (2018), 18–26; Laura J. Noval, Günter K. Stahl, and Chen-Bo Zhong, 'The Sadder but Nicer Effect: How Incidental Sadness Reduces Morally Questionable Behavior', *Journal of Business Ethics* 194 (2024), 351–68.

3. Eliza Ahmed, Nathan Harris, John Braithwaite, and Valerie Braithwaite, *Shame Management through Reintegration* (Cambridge: Cambridge University Press, 2001); John Braithwaite, *Crime, Shame and Reintegration* (Cambridge: Cambridge University Press, 1989); Miranda Forsyth and Valerie Braithwaite, 'From reintegrative shaming to restorative institutional hybridity', *International Journal of Restorative Justice* 3(1) (2020), 10–22; Kristina Murphy and Nathan Harris, 'Shaming, shame, and recidivism: A test of reintegrative shaming theory in the white-collar crime context', *British Journal of Criminology* 47(6) (2007), 900–17; Lode Walgrave and Ivo Aertsen, 'Reintegrative shaming and restorative justice: Interchangeable, complementary or different?', *European Journal on Criminal Policy and Research* 4(1) (1996), 67–85.

4. On sadness, empathy, and delivering bad news, see Walter F. Baile, 'Giving bad news', *The Oncologist* 20(8) (2015), 852–3; Lesley Fallowfield and Valerie Jenkins, 'Communicating sad, bad, and difficult news in medicine', *Lancet* 363(9405), 312–9; Gregory J. Jurkovich, Becky Pierce, Laura Pananen, and Frederick P. Rivara, 'Giving bad news: the family perspective', *Journal of Trauma and Acute Care Surgery* 48(5) (2000), 865–73; Marianne Schmid

Mast, Annette Kindlimann, and Wolf Langewitz, 'Recipients' perspective on breaking bad news: How you put it really makes a difference', *Patient Education and Counseling* 58(3) (2005), 244–51; Charles J. Schubert and Patricia Chambers, 'Building the skill of delivering bad news', *Clinical Pediatric Emergency Medicine* 6(3) (2005), 165–72; Asta Kristiina Toivonen, Sari Lindblom-Ylänne, Pekka Louhiala, and Eeva Pyörälä, 'Medical students' reflections on emotions concerning breaking bad news', *Patient Education and Counseling* 100(10) (2017), 1903–9.

5. Heather M. Gray, Keiko Ishii, and Nalini Ambady, 'Misery Loves Company: When Sadness Increases the Desire for Social Connectedness', *Personality and Social Psychology Bulletin* 37(11) (2011), 1438–48; Xin Feng, Kate Keenan, Alison E. Hipwell, Angela K. Henneberger, Michal S. Rischall, Jen Butch, Claire Coyne, Debra L. Boeldt, Amanda K. Hintze, and Dara E. Babinski, 'Longitudinal associations between emotion regulation and depression in preadolescent girls: Moderation by the caregiving environment', *Developmental Psychology* 45(3) (2009), 798–808; Sara F. Waters and Ross A. Thompson, 'Children's perceptions of the effectiveness of strategies for regulating anger and sadness', *International Journal of Behavioral Development* 38(2) (2014), 174–81; Zeman, Cameron, and Price, 'Sadness in youth'.

5. Hothead

1. On the occasionally contradictory evidence surrounding anger, see, for instance, Eddie Harmon-Jones, Mikey Xu, Kinga Szymaniak, Thomas F. Denson, Brandon J. Schmeichel, and Cindy Harmon-Jones, 'Humility and anger', *Personality and Individual Differences* 236 (2025), 112980; Lauri A. Jensen-Campbell, Jennifer M. Knack, Amy M. Wadrip, and Shaun D. Campbell, 'Do Big Five personality traits associated with self-control influence the regulation of anger and aggression?', *Journal of Research in Personality* 41(2) (2007), 403–24; Aire Mill, Liisi Kööts-Ausmees, Jüri Allik, and Anu Realo, 'The role of co-occurring emotions and personality traits in anger expression', *Frontiers in Psychology* 9(123) (2018); Christopher R. Pease and Gary J. Lewis, 'Personality links to anger: Evidence for trait interaction and differentiation across expression style', *Personality and Individual Differences* 74 (2015), 159–64; Jesús Sanz, María Paz García-Vera, and Inés Magán, 'Anger and hostility from the perspective of the Big Five personality model', *Scandinavian Journal of Psychology* 51(3) (2010), 262–70.
2. On anger, arrogance, and entitlement, see Nelson Cowan, Eryn J. Adams, Sabrina Bhangal, Mike Corcoran, Reed Decker, Ciera E. Dockter, Abby T. Eubank, Courtney L. Gann, Nathaniel R. Greene, Ashley C. Helle, Namyeon Lee, Anh T. Nguyen, Kyle R. Ripley, John E. Scofield, Melissa

A. Tapia, Katie L. Threlkeld, and Ashley L. Watts, 'Foundations of arrogance: A broad survey and framework for research', *Review of General Psychology* 23(4) (2019), 425–43; Pina Filippello, Neil Harrington, Caterina Buzzai, Luana Sorrenti, and Sebastiano Costa, 'The Relationship Between Frustration Intolerance, Unhealthy Emotions, and Assertive Behaviour in Italian Students', *Journal of Rational-Emotive and Cognitive-Behavior Therapy* 32 (2014), 257–78; Joseph P. Forgas, William D. Crano, and Klaus Fiedler (eds.), *The psychology of populism: Tribal challenges to liberal democracy* (Abingdon: Routledge, 2021); Katie Fracalanza, Naomi Koerner, Sonya S. Deschênes, and Michel J. Dugas, 'Intolerance of Uncertainty Mediates the Relation between Generalized Anxiety Disorder Symptoms and Anger', *Cognitive Behaviour Therapy* 43(2) (2014), 122–32; Neil Harrington, 'Frustration Intolerance Beliefs: Their Relationship with Depression, Anxiety, and Anger, in a Clinical Population', *Cognitive Therapy and Research* 30 (2006), 699–709.

3. On anger and closed-mindedness, see Jennifer S. Lerner, Julie H. Goldberg, and Philip E. Tetlock, 'Sober Second Thought: The Effects of Accountability, Anger, and Authoritarianism on Attributions of Responsibility', *Personality and Social Psychology Bulletin* 24(6) (1998), 563–74; Keltner, Ellsworth, and Edwards, 'Beyond simple pessimism'; Wesley G. Moons and Diane M. Mackie, 'Thinking straight while seeing red: The influence of anger on information processing', *Personality and Social Psychology Bulletin* 33(5) (2007), 706–20; Elizabeth Suhay and Cengiz Erisen, 'The role of anger in the biased assimilation of political information', *Political Psychology* 39(4) (2018), 793–810; Douglas Yacek, 'Should anger be encouraged in the classroom? Political education, closed-mindedness, and civic epiphany', *Educational Theory* 69(4) (2019), 421–37.

4. On anger and fundamentalism, see John Thomas Alderdice, 'Sacred Values: Psychological and Anthropological Perspectives on Fairness, Fundamentalism, and Terrorism', *Annals of the New York Academy of Sciences* 1167(1) (2009), 158–73; Michael B. Salzman, 'Globalization, religious fundamentalism and the need for meaning', *International Journal of Intercultural Relations* 32(4) (2008), 318–27; William A. Stahl, 'One-dimensional rage: the social epistemology of the new atheism and fundamentalism', in Lori G. Beaman (ed.), *Religion and Canadian Society: Contexts, Identities, and Strategies* (Toronto, ON: Canadian Scholars' Press Inc., 2012), 249–59; Charles B. Strozier, David M. Ternan, James W. Jones, and Katharine A. Boyd (eds.), *The Fundamentalist Mindset: Psychological Perspectives on Religion, Violence, and History* (Oxford: Oxford University Press, 2010); Wilson Vincent, Dominic J. Parrott, and John L. Peterson, 'Effects of traditional gender role norms and religious fundamentalism on self-identified heterosexual men's attitudes, anger, and aggression toward gay men and lesbians',

Psychology of Men and Masculinity 12(4) (2011), 383–400; Michalinos Zembylas, 'Engaging Emotional Fundamentalism in the University Classroom: Pedagogical and Ethical Dilemmas', *British Journal of Educational Studies* 72(4) (2024), 483–500.

5. For a selection of readings on these terms, see Seyla Benhabib, *The Rights of Others: Aliens, Residents, and Citizens* (Cambridge: Cambridge University Press, 2004); Aryeh Botwinick, 'Same/other versus friend/enemy: Levinas contra Schmitt', in Jens Meierhenrich and Oliver Simons (eds.), *The Oxford Handbook of Carl Schmitt* (Oxford: Oxford University Press, 2016), 338–66; William Connolly, *Identity\Difference: Democratic Negotiations of Political Paradox* (Ithaca, NY: Cornell University Press, 1991); Chantal Mouffe, *On the Political* (London: Routledge, 2005).

6. Cool Cat

1. For a wide range of studies starting to explore the role of calmness, see, for instance, Aileen Fischer, Martin Voracek, and Ulrich S. Tran, 'Semantic and sentiment similarities contribute to construct overlaps between mindfulness, Big Five, emotion regulation, and mental health', *Personality and Individual Differences* 210 (2023), 112241; Jeremy M. Hamm, Carsten Wrosch, Meaghan A. Barlow, and Ute Kunzmann, 'A tale of two emotions: The diverging salience and health consequences of calmness and excitement in old age', *Psychology and Aging* 36(5) (2021), 626–41; Marja Kokkonen and Lea Pulkkinen, 'Examination of the paths between personality, current mood, its evaluation, and emotion regulation', *European Journal of Personality* 15(2) (2001), 83–104; Malgorzata Sobol-Kwapinska, 'Calm down — It's only neuroticism. Time perspectives as moderators and mediators of the relationship between neuroticism and well-being', *Personality and Individual Differences* 94 (2016), 64–71; Jessie Sun, Scott Barry Kaufman, and Luke D. Smillie, 'Unique associations between Big Five personality aspects and multiple dimensions of well-being', *Journal of Personality* 86(2) (2018), 158–72; Jodi K. Whitaker and Brad J. Bushman, '"Remain Calm. Be Kind." Effects of Relaxing Video Games on Aggressive and Prosocial Behavior', *Social Psychology and Personality Science* 3(1) (2011), 88–92.

2. On calm and openness, see Patrik Grahn, Johan Ottosson, and Kerstin Uvnäs-Moberg, 'The Oxytocinergic System as a Mediator of Anti-stress and Instorative Effects Induced by Nature: The Calm and Connection Theory', *Frontiers in Psychology* 12 (2021); Christian G. Jensen, Jon Lansner, Anders Petersen, Signe A. Vangkilde, Signe P. Ringkøbing, Vibe G. Frokjaer, Dea Adamsen, Gitte M. Knudsen, John W. Denninger, and Steen

G. Hasselbalch, 'Open and Calm – A randomized controlled trial evaluating a public stress reduction program in Denmark', *BMC Public Health* 15(1245) (2015); Da Jiang, Helen H. Fung, Tamara Sims, Jeanne L. Tsai, and Fan Zhang, 'Limited time perspective increases the value of calm', *Emotion* 16(1) (2016), 52–62; Michele Kane, 'Creating a culture of calm: Mindfulness unfolding in the classroom', *Gifted Education International* 34(2) (2018), 162–72.

3. On calm and peace, see Tim Lomas, Pablo Diego-Rosell, Koichiro Shiba, Priscilla Standridge, Matthew T. Lee, and Alden Yuanhong Lai, 'The world prefers a calm life, but not everyone gets to have one: global trends in valuing and experiencing calmness in the Gallup World Poll', *Journal of Positive Psychology* 19(6) (2023), 1023–36; Richard D. Parry, 'Pleasure, Pain, Calm, and the Philosophical Life', in Daniel Bloom, Laurence Bloom, and Miriam Byrd (eds.), *Knowing and Being in Ancient Philosophy* (Basingstoke: Palgrave Macmillan, 2022), 205–19; Frédéric Ramel, *Benevolence in International Relations: A Political Essay* (Bristol: Bristol University Press, 2025); Yiheng Xi, Li Zhou, and Dong Guo, 'The power of calmness in times of the COVID-19 pandemic: The different roles of peace of mind and career calling in enhancing work engagement—A mediation analysis based on social support', *Frontiers of Psychology* 14 (2023).

4. On calmness, job performance, and productivity, see Neetu Choudhary, M. Muzamil Naqshbandi, P.J. Philip, and Rajender Kumar, 'Employee job performance: The interplay of leaders' emotion management ability and employee perception of job characteristics', *Journal of Management Development* 36(8) (2017), 1087–98; Crystal I.C. Chien Farh, Myeong-Gu Seo, and Paul E. Tesluk, 'Emotional intelligence, teamwork effectiveness, and job performance: The moderating role of job context', *Journal of Applied Psychology* 97(4) (2012), 890–900; Joyce Hogan and Brent Holland, 'Using theory to evaluate personality and job-performance relations: A socioanalytic perspective', *Journal of Applied Psychology* 88(1) (2003), 100–12; Ernest H. O'Boyle Jr., Ronald H. Humphrey, Jeffrey M. Pollack, Thomas H. Hawver, and Paul A. Story, 'The relation between emotional intelligence and job performance: A meta-analysis', *Journal of Organizational Behavior* 32(5) (2011), 788–818; Kelsey A. Richels, Eric Anthony Day, Ashley G. Jorgensen, and Jonathan T. Huck, 'Keeping Calm and Carrying On: Relating Affect Spin and Pulse to Complex Skill Acquisition and Adaptive Performance', *Frontiers in Psychology* 11(2020); S. Rothmann and E.P. Coetzer, 'The big five personality dimensions and job performance', *SA Journal of Industrial Psychology* 29(1) (2003), 68–74.

5. Amanda M. Acevedo, Kate A. Leger, Brooke N. Jenkins, and Sarah D. Pressman, 'Keep calm or get excited? Examining the effects of different types of positive affect on responses to acute pain', *Journal of Positive*

Psychology 17(3) (2020), 409–18; Lena Azbel-Jackson, Laurie T. Butler, Judi A. Ellis, and Carien M. van Reekum, 'Stay calm! Regulating emotional responses by implementation intentions: Assessing the impact on physiological and subjective arousal', *Cognition and Emotion* 30(6) (2015), 1107–21; Norman Farb, Jennifer Daubenmier, Cynthia J. Price, Tim Gard, Catherine Kerr, Barnaby D. Dunn, Anne Carolyn Klein, Martin P. Paulus, and Wolf E. Mehling, 'Interoception, contemplative practice, and health', *Frontiers in Psychology* 6 (2015); Aleksandra M. Herman, Hugo D. Critchley, and Theodora Duka, 'The role of emotions and physiological arousal in modulating impulsive behaviour', *Biological Psychology* 133 (2018), 30–43; Elsa Mastico, 'Keep Calm and Carry On: Mood Effects on Emotion Regulation Strategies', *Symposium of University Research and Creative Expression (SOURCE)* (2020), 112; Dan Rea, 'Maximizing the Motivated Mind for Emergent Giftedness', *Roeper Review* 23(3) (2001), 157–64.

7. Keen Bean

1. On the link between personality and various subsidiary facets of eagerness, see, for instance, Anton Aluja, Óscar García, and Luís F. García, 'Relationships among extraversion, openness to experience, and sensation seeking', *Personality and Individual Differences* 35(3) (2003), 671–80; Liisi Ausmees, Maie Talts, Jüri Allik, Uku Vainik, Timo T. Sikka, Tiit Nikopensius, Tõnu Esko, and Anu Realo, 'Taking risks to feel excitement: Detailed personality profile and genetic associations', *European Journal of Personality* 36(6) (2021), 965–90; Jessica Berner, Ana Luiza Dallora, Bruna Palm, Johan Sanmartin Berglund, and Peter Anderberg, 'Five-factor model, technology enthusiasm and technology anxiety', *Digital Health* (2023), 9; Reinout E. de Vries, Kilian W. Wawoe, and Djurre Holtrop, 'What is engagement? Proactivity as the missing link in the HEXACO model of personality', *Journal of Personality* 84(2) (2016), 178–93; Meera Komarraju and Steven J. Karau, 'The relationship between the big five personality traits and academic motivation', *Personality and Individual Differences* 39(3) (2005), 557–67; Marengo et al., 'A meta-analysis on individual differences'; Wanshuang Zhang, Lujia He, Yuzhou Chen, and Xumei Gao, 'The relationship between Big Five personality traits and fear of missing out: A meta-analysis', *Personality and Individual Differences* 230 (2024), 112788.
2. On eagerness and acquisition, see Eduardo B. Andrade, Terrance Odean, and Shengle Lin, 'Bubbling with excitement: An experiment', *Review of Finance* 20(2) (2016), 447–66; Xiaoyan Luo, Xing (Stella) Liu, and Lisa C. Wan, 'Excited or calm? Effects of endorsers' emotions on tourists' impulsive buying', *Journal of Travel Research* 64(1) (2025), 35–50; Anna S. Mattila and

Jochen Wirtz, 'The role of store environmental stimulation and social factors on impulse purchasing', *Journal of Services Marketing* 22(7) (2008), 562–7; Sabine Moeller and Kristina Wittkowski, 'The burdens of ownership: reasons for preferring renting', *Managing Service Quality: An International Journal* 20(2) (2010), 176–91; Michel Tuan Pham and Jennifer J. Sun, 'On the Experience and Engineering of Consumer Pride, Consumer Excitement, and Consumer Relaxation in the Marketplace', *Journal of Retailing* 96(1) (2020), 101–27; Suzanne B. Shu and Joann Peck, 'Psychological ownership and affective reaction: Emotional attachment process variables and the endowment effect', *Journal of Consumer Psychology* 21(4) (2011), 439–52; Bas Verplanken and Astrid Herabadi, 'Individual differences in impulse buying tendency: feeling and no thinking', *European Journal of Personality* 15(S1) (2001), S71–S83.

3. On toxic positivity, see Barbara Ehrenreich, *Bright-Sided: How the Relentless Promotion of Positive Thinking Has Undermined America* (New York, NY: Metropolitan Books, 2009); Anishka Jain, Rameshbabu Tamarana, Uvashree Santosh, and Ritik Singh, 'Relationship between Dominating Personalities and Toxic Positivity: Mediating Roles of Intrapersonal and Interpersonal Control', *Journal of the Indian Academy of Applied Psychology* 50(1) (2024), 186–95; Louis Laberge-Côté, 'Resilience Training in Dance: On Toxic Positivity, Attentional Focus, and Playful Discomfort', *International Journal of Arts Education* 18(1) (2022), 17–34; Hannah G. Shipp and Katherine C. Hall, 'Analyzing the concept of toxic positivity for nursing: A dimensional analysis approach', *Journal of Advanced Nursing* 80(8) (2024), 3146–57.

4. On play and playfulness, see David J. Abramis, 'Play in work: Childish hedonism or adult enthusiasm?', *American Behavioral Scientist* 33(3) (1990), 353–73; Yulia Golland, Boaz M. Ben-David, Mara Mather, and Shoshi Keisari, 'Playful brains: a possible neurobiological pathway to cognitive health in aging', *Frontiers in Neuroscience* (2025); Gwen Gordon, 'Well played: The origins and future of playfulness', *American Journal of Play* 6(2) (2014), 234–66; Marjaana Kangas and Signe Siklander, 'Editorial: Playfulness, games, and playful learning to promote good', *Frontiers in Education* 8 (2023); Leland Masek, 'Identifying Playfulness: An Empirical Study on How Adults Recognize and Define Playfulness Across Culture', *Games and Culture* (2024); Rob Tieben, Janienke Sturm, Tilde Bekker, and Ben Schouten, 'Playful persuasion: Designing for ambient playful interactions in public spaces', *Journal of Ambient Intelligence and Smart Environments* 6(4) (2014), 341–57.

5. On eagerness, belonging, and self-expression, see Julie Fitzmaurice, 'Incorporating consumers' motivations into the theory of reasoned action', *Psychology and Marketing* 22(11) (2005), 911–29; Axel Honneth, *The Struggle for Recognition: The moral grammar of social conflicts* (Cambridge: Polity, 1995

[1992]); Jingyi Lu, Hebing Duan, Xiaofei Xie, 'Eagerness and Optimistically Biased Metaperception: The More Eager to Learn Others' Evaluations, the Higher the Estimation of Others' Evaluations', *Frontiers in Psychology* 9 (2018); John P. McClure and James M. Brown, 'Belonging at work', *Human Resource Development International* 11(1) (2008), 3–17; Simon Moss, Damian Ritossa, and Simon Ngu, 'The Effect of Follower Regulatory Focus and Extraversion on Leadership Behavior', *Journal of Individual Differences* 27(2) (2006), 93–107; Bojan Obrenovic, Jianguo Du, Danijela Godinić, and Diana Tsoy, 'Personality trait of conscientiousness impact on tacit knowledge sharing: the mediating effect of eagerness and subjective norm', *Journal of Knowledge Management* 26(5) (2022), 1124–63.

8. Worrywart

1. On how personality relates to the various forms of fear and anxiety, see, for instance, Michael C. Ashton, Kibeom Lee, Beth A. Visser, and Julie A. Pozzebon, 'Phobic tendency within the five-factor and HEXACO models of personality structure', *Journal of Research in Personality* 42(3) (2008), 734–46; David A. Ellis and Kayleigh J. Renouf, 'Predicting fear of crime: personality outperforms prior victimisation', *Journal of Forensic Psychiatry and Psychology* 29(3) (2018), 403–18; Hayley K. Jach and Luke D. Smillie, 'To fear or fly to the unknown: Tolerance for ambiguity and Big Five personality traits', *Journal of Research in Personality* 79 (2019), 67–78; Crenguța Mihaela Macovei, Ștefania Bumbuc, and Fabiana Martinescu-Bădălan, 'The role of personality traits in mediating the relation between fear of negative evaluation and social interaction anxiety', *Frontiers in Psychology* 14 (2023), 1268052; Marengo et al., 'A meta-analysis on individual differences'; Speed and Brysbaert, 'Ratings of valence'.
2. On the cultural theory of haunting and spectres, see Merlin Coverley, *Hauntology: Ghosts of Futures Past* (London: Oldcastle Books, 2021); Jacques Derrida, *Specters of Marx: The State of the Debt, the Work of Mourning and the New International* (Abingdon: Routledge, 1994 [1993]); Mark Fisher, *The Weird and the Eerie* (London: Watkins Media, 2016); Jacques Lacan, *Écrits* (New York, NY: W. W. Norton & Co., 2006 [1966]); Slavoj Žižek, *The Sublime Object of Ideology* (London: Verso, 1989).
3. On fear and surveillance, see Maša Galič, Tjerk Timan, and Bert-Jaap Koops, 'Bentham, Deleuze and Beyond: An Overview of Surveillance Theories from the Panopticon to Participation', *Philosophy & Technology* 30(1) (2017), 9–37; Rebecca A. Goldstein, 'Who Needs the Government to Police Us When We Can Do It Ourselves? The New Panopticon in Teaching', *Cultural Studies ↔ Critical Methodologies* 4(3) (2004), 320–28; Ella Hafermalz, 'Out of

the Panopticon and into Exile: Visibility and control in distributed new culture organizations', *Organization Studies* 42(5) (2021), 697–717; Aurélie Leclercq-Vandelannoitte, 'The panopticon, an emblematic concept in management and organization studies: Heaven or hell?', *International Journal of Management Reviews* 25(1) (2023), 52–74; Thomas Mathiesen, 'The viewer society: Michel Foucault's "Panopticon" revisited', *Theoretical Criminology* 1(2) (1997), 215–34; Elizabeth Stoycheff, Juan Liu, Kai Xu, and Kunto Wibowo, 'Privacy and the Panopticon: Online mass surveillance's deterrence and chilling effects', *New Media & Society* 21(3) (2019), 602–19.

4. On the cognitive effects of fear, see Quy Nguyen Huy, 'How contrasting emotions can enhance strategic agility', in Neal M. Ashkanasy and Cary L. Cooper (eds.), *Research Companion to Emotion in Organizations* (Cheltenham: Edward Elgar, 2008), 546–60; Jonathan K. Lee and Susan M. Orsillo, 'Investigating cognitive flexibility as a potential mechanism of mindfulness in Generalized Anxiety Disorder', *Journal of Behavior Therapy and Experimental Psychiatry* 45(1) (2014), 208–16; Junchol Park and Bita Moghaddam, 'Impact of anxiety on prefrontal cortex encoding of cognitive flexibility', *Neuroscience* 345 (2017), 193–202; Paul Slovic, 'What's fear got to do with it? It's affect we need to worry about', *Missouri Law Review* 69 (2004), 971–90; Lorraine Stomski and Kelly Jensen, 'Building learning agility through psychological safety', in Veronica Schmidt Harvey and Kenneth P. De Meuse (eds.), *The Age of Agility: Building learning agile leaders and organizations* (Oxford: Oxford University Press, 2021), 365–81; Bjørn Yngve Tollefsen, 'The rule of fear: political thinking in the age of terror', in Lee Baxter and Paula Brăescu (eds.), *Fear within melting boundaries* (Amsterdam: Brill, 2020) 139–47.

5. On fear, anxiety, and planning, see Sarah J. Ahmed and C. Dominik Güss, 'An Analysis of Writer's Block: Causes and Solutions', *Creativity Research Journal* 34(3) (2022), 339–54; Laren R. Conklin, Todd J. Farchione, and Steven Dufour, 'The Unified Protocol for Anxiety Disorders', in David H. Barlow and Todd J. Farchione (eds.), *Applications of the Unified Protocol for Transdiagnostic Treatment of Emotional Disorders* (Oxford: Oxford University Press, 2018), 38–52; Patrick Gosselin, Camille Castonguay, Marika Goyette, Rosemarie Lambert, Mallorie Brisson, Philippe Landreville, and Sébastien Grenier, 'Anxiety among older adults during the COVID-19 pandemic', *Journal of Anxiety Disorders* 92 (2022), 102633; Gabrielle Marcotte-Beaumier, Bailee L. Malivoire, Naomi Koerner, and Melina M. Ovanessian, 'The Role of Overt and Covert Avoidance Strategies in Generalized Anxiety Disorder Symptoms and Fear of Emotion', *Journal of Psychopathology and Behavioral Assessment* 44 (2022), 344–52; Erin M. Sahlstein, 'Making Plans: Praxis Strategies for Negotiating Uncertainty–Certainty in Long-Distance Relationships', *Western Journal of Communication* 70(2) (2006), 147–65.

9. Quibbler

1. On the links between disgust and different personality models, see, for instance, Donovan et al., 'Quantifying the links'; Barry A. Druschel and Martin F. Sherman, 'Disgust sensitivity as a function of the Big Five and gender', *Personality and Individual Differences* 26(4) (1999), 739–48; Annika K. Karinen, Joshua M. Tybur, and Reinout E. de Vries, 'The disgust traits: Self–other agreement in pathogen, sexual, and moral disgust sensitivity and their independence from HEXACO personality', *Emotion* 23(1) (2023), 75–86; Speed and Brysbaert, 'Ratings of valence'; Anne J. Standish, Jacob A. Benfield, Michael J. Bernstein, and Sarah Tragesser, 'Characteristics of Borderline Personality Disorder and Disgust Sensitivity', *Psychological Record* 64(4) (2014), 869–77; Joshua M. Tybur and Reinout E. de Vries, 'Disgust sensitivity and the HEXACO model of personality', *Personality and Individual Differences* 55(6) (2013), 660–65.

2. On alienation and disenchantment, see Seray Akça and Faruk Gençöz, 'The Experience of Disgust in Women Exposed to Domestic Violence in Turkey', *Journal of Interpersonal Violence* 37(15–16) (2022), NP14538–NP14563; Daniel Dwyer, 'The logic of disenchantment: A phenomenological approach', in Pol Vandevelde and Sebastian Luft (eds.), *Epistemology, Archaeology, Ethics: Current Investigations of Husserl's Corpus* (London: Continuum, 2010), 53–65; Susan Miller, *Disgust: The Gatekeeper Emotion* (Abingdon: Routledge, 2013); Steven Seidman, 'Defilement and disgust: Theorizing the other', *American Journal of Cultural Sociology* 1(1) (2013), 3–25; Luke Treglown and Adrian Furnham, 'Employee Disenchantment: The Development of a New Construct and Measure', *Psychology* 13(10) (2022), 1517–38; Leila Michelle Vaziri, 'Alienation, Abjection, and Disgust: Encountering the Capitalocene in Contemporary Eco-Drama', *Journal of Contemporary Drama in English* 10(1) (2022), 231–46.

3. On bigotry and hate, see Kathryn Abrams, ' "Fighting fire with fire": Rethinking the role of disgust in hate crimes', *California Law Review* 90 (2002), 1423–64; Stephen Eric Bronner, *The Bigot: Why prejudice persists* (New Haven, CT: Yale University Press, 2014); Maayan Katzir, Matan Hoffmann, and Nira Liberman, 'Disgust as an essentialist emotion that signals nonviolent outgrouping with potentially low social costs', *Emotion* 19(5) (2019), 841–62; Eliot R. Smith and Diane M. Mackie, 'Aggression, hatred, and other emotions', in John F. Dovidio, Peter Glick, and Laurie A. Rudman (eds.), *On the Nature of Prejudice: Fifty Years after Allport* (Oxford: Blackwell, 2005), 361–76; Kathleen Taylor, 'Disgust is a factor in extreme prejudice', *British Journal of Social Psychology* 46(3) (2007), 597–617; Niza Yanay, *The Ideology of Hatred: The psychic power of discourse* (New York, NY: Fordham University Press, 2013).

4. On disgust, cynicism, and scepticism, see Rebecca Abraham, 'Organizational cynicism: Bases and consequences', *Genetic, Social, and General Psychology Monographs* 126(3) (2000), 269–92; Lynne M. Andersson, 'Employee Cynicism: An Examination Using a Contract Violation Framework', *Human Relations* 49(11) (1996), 1395–1418; Michael S. Cole, Heike Bruch, and Bernd Vogel, 'Emotion as mediators of the relations between perceived supervisor support and psychological hardiness on employee cynicism', *Journal of Organizational Behavior* 27(4) (2006), 463–84; Natalie Ferres and Julia Connell, 'Emotional intelligence in leaders: an antidote for cynicism towards change?', *Strategic Change* 13(2) (2004), 61–71; Peggy Schyns, 'The Young and Cynical: Measurement, Characteristics and Consequences of Political Cynicism among Dutch Youth', *Politics, Culture, and Socialization* 5(2) (2015), 7–8; Dale C. Spencer, Rosemary Ricciardelli, Dale Ballucci, and Kevin Walby, 'Cynicism, dirty work, and policing sex crimes', *Policing: An International Journal* 43(1) (2020), 151–65.

5. On disgust and moral judgement, see Hanah A. Chapman and Adam K. Anderson, 'Trait physical disgust is related to moral judgments outside of the purity domain', *Emotion* 14(2) (2014), 341–8; Brian Collisson, Eliana Saunders, and Chloe Yin, 'The ick: Disgust sensitivity, narcissism, and perfectionism in mate choice thresholds', *Personality and Individual Differences* 238 (2025), 113086; Denise Dellarosa Cummins and Robert C. Cummins, 'Emotion and deliberative reasoning in moral judgment', *Frontiers in Psychology* 3 (2012), 328; Laura Moretti and Giuseppe di Pellegrino, 'Disgust selectively modulates reciprocal fairness in economic interactions', *Emotion* 10(2) (2010), 169–80; Bunmi O. Olatunji, Bieke David, and Bethany G. Ciesielski, 'Who am I to judge? Self-disgust predicts less punishment of severe transgressions', *Emotion* 12(1) (2012), 169–73; Simone Schnall, Jonathan Haidt, Gerald L. Clore, and Alexander H. Jordan, 'Disgust as embodied moral judgment', *Personality and Social Psychology Bulletin* 34(8) (2008), 1096–1109; Thalia Wheatley and Jonathan Haidt, 'Hypnotic disgust makes moral judgments more severe', *Psychological Science* 16(10) (2005), 780–84.

10. Reveller

1. On the intersections of desire and personality, see, for instance, Gorkan Ahmetoglu, Viren Swami, and Tomas Chamorro-Premuzic, 'The relationship between dimensions of love, personality, and relationship length', *Archives of Sexual Behavior* 39 (2010), 1181–90; Eva Asselmann and Julie Specht, 'Taking the ups and downs at the rollercoaster of love: Associations between major life events in the domain of romantic relationships and the

Big Five personality traits', *Developmental Psychology* 56(9) (2020), 1803–16; Reinout E. de Vries, Jeroen Pronk, Tjeert Olthof, and Frits A. Goossens, 'Getting along And/Or Getting Ahead: Differential Hexaco Personality Correlates of Likeability and Popularity among Adolescents', *European Journal of Personality* 34(2) (2020), 245–61; Uwe Hartmann, Kristina Heiser, Claudia Rüffer-Hesse, and Gabriele Kloth, 'Female sexual desire disorders: subtypes, classification, personality factors and new directions for treatment', *World Journal of Urology* 20 (2002), 79–88; Mirnader Miri, Mohammad Ali Besharat, Masoud Asadi, and Shima Shahyad, 'The relationship between dimensions of personality and sexual desire in females and males', *Procedia – Social and Behavioral Sciences* 15 (2011), 823–7; David P. Schmitt and Todd K. Shackelford, 'Big Five traits related to short-term mating: From personality to promiscuity across 46 nations', *Evolutionary Psychology* 6(2) (2008); Alan B. Shafer, 'The Big Five and sexuality trait terms as predictors of relationships and sex', *Journal of Research in Personality* 35(3) (2001), 313–38; T. Joel Wade and Jamie Vanartsdalen, 'The Big-5 and the perceived effectiveness of love acts', *Human Ethology Bulletin* 28(2) (2013), 3–12.

2. On desire, identity, and self, see Lucy Bailey, 'Control and desire: The issue of identity in popular discourses of addiction', *Addiction Research & Theory* 13(6) (2005), 535–43; Russell W. Belk, Güliz Ger, and Søren Askegaard, 'The missing streetcar named desire', in Cynthia Huffman, David Glen Mick, and S. Ratneshwar (eds.), *The Why of Consumption: Contemporary Perspectives on Consumer Motives, Goals, and Desires* (Abingdon: Routledge, 2000), 98–119; Anthony F. Bogaert and Lori A. Brotto, 'Object of desire self-consciousness theory', *Journal of Sex & Marital Therapy* 40(4) (2014), 323–38; Scott Jenkins, 'Hegel's concept of desire', *Journal of the History of Philosophy* 47(1) (2009), 103–30; Teodros Kiros, *Self-Construction and the Formation of Human Values: Truth, Language, and Desire* (Westport, CT: Praeger Publishers, 2001).

3. On desire and entrepreneurship, see Susan J. Ashford and Stewart J. Black, 'Proactivity during organizational entry: The role of desire for control', *Journal of Applied Psychology* 81(2) (1996), 199–214; Willie T. Chinyamurindi and Herring Shava, 'The influence of economic motivation, desire for independence and self-efficacy on willingness to become an entrepreneur', *The Southern African Journal of Entrepreneurship and Small Business Management* 11(1) (2019); Michaela Driver, 'Never social and entrepreneurial enough? Exploring the identity work of social entrepreneurs from a psychoanalytic perspective', *Organization* 24(6) (2017), 715–36; Doris Fay and Sabine Sonnentag, 'A Look Back to Move Ahead: New Directions for Research on Proactive Performance and Other Discretionary Work Behaviours', *Applied Psychology* 59(1) (2010), 1–20; Daniel Hjorth, 'Public entrepreneurship: desiring social change, creating sociality', *Entrepreneurship & Regional*

Development 25(1–2) (2013), 34–51; Chandra S. Mishra and Ramona K. Zachary, 'The Theory of Entrepreneurship', *Entrepreneurship Research Journal* 5(4) (2015), 251–68; Kan Ouyang, Bonnie Hayden Cheng, Wing Lam, and Sharon K. Parker, 'Enjoy your evening, be proactive tomorrow: How off-job experiences shape daily proactivity', *Journal of Applied Psychology* 104(8) (2019), 1003–19; Sharon K. Parker, Ying Wang, and Jenny Liao, 'When Is Proactivity Wise? A Review of Factors That Influence the Individual Outcomes of Proactive Behavior', *Annual Review of Organizational Psychology and Organizational Behavior* 6 (2019), 221–48.

4. On desire and group formation, see James Arvanitakis, 'Staging *Maralinga* and looking for community (or why we must desire community before we can find it)', *Research in Drama Education: The Journal of Applied Theatre and Performance* 13(3) (2008), 295–306; Jeremy Brent, 'The desire for community: Illusion, confusion, and paradox', *Community Development Journal* 39(3) (2004), 213–23; Michelle Drouin and Lesa Rae Vartanian, 'Students' feelings of and desire for sense of community in face-to-face and online courses', *Quarterly Review of Distance Education* 11(3) (2010), 147–59; Jonathan Haidt, 'The positive emotion of elevation', *Prevention & Treatment* 3(1) (2000); Paul W. Ludwig, *Eros & Polis: Desire and community in Greek political theory* (Cambridge: Cambridge University Press, 2002); Özerk Yavuz, Adem Karahoca, and Dilek Karahoca, 'A data mining approach for desire and intention to participate in virtual communities', *International Journal of Electrical and Computer Engineering* 9(5) (2019), 3714–9; Iris Marion Young, 'The Ideal of Community and the Politics of Difference', in Linda J. Nicholson (ed.), *Feminism/Postmodernism* (Abingdon: Routledge, 1989), 300–23.

5. On energy and passion, see Russell W. Belk, Güliz Ger, and Søren Askegaard, 'The fire of desire: A multisited inquiry into consumer passion', *Journal of Consumer Research* 30(3) (2003), 326–51; Russell W. Belk, Henri Weijo, and Robert V. Kozinets, 'Enchantment and perpetual desire: Theorizing disenchanted enchantment and technology adoption', *Marketing Theory* 21(1) (2020), 25–52; Julie J. Exline and Joshua A. Wilt, 'Not just love and safety, but excitement, energy, fun, and passion: relational predictors of gratitude to God and desires to "pay it forward"', *Journal of Positive Psychology* 19(1) (2024), 107–20; Petra Kipfelsberger and Heike Bruch, 'Increasing energy and performance through customer passion: An organizational level study', *Emotions and the Organizational Fabric (Research on Emotion in Organizations, vol. 10)* (Leeds: Emerald Publishing, 2014), 49–78; Robert V. Kozinets, Anthony Patterson, and Rachel Ashman, 'Networks of desire: How technology increases our passion to consume', *Journal of Consumer Research* 43(5) (2017), 659–82; Bonnie A. Nardi, 'Objects of desire: Power and passion in collaborative activity', *Mind, Culture, and Activity* 12(1) (2005), 37–51.

Epilogue

1. Meyer Friedman, *Type A Behavior: Its Diagnosis and Treatment* (Plenum Press, 1996); Meyer Friedman and Ray Rosenman, 'Association of specific overt behaviour pattern with blood and cardiovascular findings', *Journal of the American Medical Association*, 169(12) (1959), 1286–96; David Keirsey and Marilyn Bates, *Please Understand Me: Character and Temperament Types* (Prometheus Nemesis Book Co, 1984); Isabel Briggs Myers, *Gifts Differing: Understanding Personality Type* (Davies-Black Publishing, 1995 [1980]); Don Richard Riso and Russ Hudson, *Understanding the Enneagram: the practical guide to personality types* (Houghton Mifflin, 2000).
2. Gregory John Boyle, 'Critique of Five-Factor Model (FFM)', in Gregory John Boyle, Gerald Matthews, and Donald H. Saklofske (eds.), *The SAGE Handbook of Personality Theory and Assessment: Vol.1 – Personality Theories and Models* (Sage, 2008); Stephen R. Briggs, 'The optimal level of measurement for personality constructs', in David M. Buss and Nancy Cantor (eds.), *Personality Psychology: Recent trends and emerging directions* (Springer, 1989); Oliver P. John, 'Towards a taxonomy of personality descriptors', in David M. Buss and Nancy Cantor (eds.), *Personality Psychology: Recent trends and emerging directions* (Springer, 1989); Hanoch Livneh and Cheryl Livneh, 'The five-factor model of personality: Is evidence for its cross-media premature?', *Personality and Individual Differences* 10(1) (1989), 75–80; John W. Santrock, *A Topical Approach to Life-Span Development* (McGraw-Hill, 2005); Niels G. Waller and Yossef S. Ben-Porath, 'Is it time for clinical psychology to embrace the five-factor model of personality?', *American Psychologist* 42(9) (1987), 887–9.
3. Yossef S. Ben-Porath and Auke Tellegen, *Minnesota Multiphasic Personality Inventory-3* (University of Minnesota Press, 2020); B.C. Schiele, Abe B. Baker, and Starke R. Hathaway, 'The Minnesota multiphasic personality inventory', *Journal-Lancet* 63 (1943), 292–7; Auke Tellegen, Yossef S. Ben-Porath, John L. McNulty, Paul A. Arbisi, John R. Graham, and B. Kaemmer, *The MMPI-2 Restructured Clinical Scales: Development, validation, and interpretation* (University of Minnesota Press, 2003).
4. H.E.P. Cattell, 'The original big five: A historical perspective', *European Review of Applied Psychology* 46(1) (1996), 5–14; James J. Conley, 'Longitudinal stability of personality traits: A multitrait-multimethod-multioccasion analysis', *Journal of Personality and Social Psychology* 49(5) (1985), pp.1266–82; Paul T. Costa and Robert R. McCrae, *The NEO Personality Manual* (Psychological Assessment Resources, 1985); Lewis R. Goldberg, 'The structure of phenotypic personality traits', *American Psychologist* 48(1) (1993), 26–34; Robert R. McCrae and Oliver P. John, 'An introduction to the five-factor model and its applications', *Journal of Personality* 60(2) (1992),

175–215; Robert R. McCrae, Paul T. Costa, and Thomas A. Martin, 'The NEO–PI–3: A More Readable Revised NEO Personality Inventory', *Journal of Personality Assessment* 84(3) (2005), 261–70.

5. Michael C. Ashton, *Individual Differences and Personality* (Academic Press, 2017); Michael C. Ashton and Kibeom Lee, 'Empirical, Theoretical, and Practical Advantages of the HEXACO Model of Personality Structure', *Personality and Social Psychology Review* 11(2) (2007), 150–66; Michael C. Ashton and Kibeom Lee, 'The HEXACO Model of Personality Structure and the Importance of the H Factor', *Social and Personality Psychology Compass* 2(5) (2008), 1952–62; Kibeom Lee and Michael C. Ashton, 'Psychometric Properties of the HEXACO Personality Inventory', *Multivariate Behavioral Research* 39(2) (2004), 329–58.

6. Marvin Zuckerman, 'Zuckerman–Kuhlman Personality Questionnaire (ZKPQ): an alternative five-factorial model', in Boele De Raad and Marco Perugini (eds.), *Big Five Assessment* (Hogrefe & Huber, 2002), 377–96; Marvin Zuckerman and C. Robert Cloninger, 'Relationships between Cloninger's, Zuckerman's, and Eysenck's dimensions of personality', *Personality and Individual Differences* 21(2) (1996), 283–5.

7. Anton Aluja, Óscar García, and Luís F. García, 'Replicability of the three, four and five Zuckerman's personality super-factors: exploratory and confirmatory factor analysis of the EPQ-RS, ZKPQ and NEO-PI-R', *Personality and Individual Differences* 36(5) (2004), 1093–1108; Peter Becker, 'Beyond the Big Five', *Personality and Individual Differences* 26(3) (1999), 511–30; Boele De Raad, Dick P.H. Barelds, Boris Mlačić, A. Timothy Church, Marcia S. Katigbak, Fritz Ostendorf, Martina Hřebíčková, Lisa Di Blas, and Zsófia Szirmák, 'Only three personality factors are fully replicable across languages: Reply to Ashton and Lee', *Journal of Research in Personality* 44(4) (2010), 442–5; Laetta M. Hough, Frederick L. Oswald, and Jisoo Ock, 'Beyond the Big Five', *Annual Review of Organizational Psychology and Organizational Behavior* 21(1) (2015), 183–209; Amber Gayle Thalmayer, Gerard Saucier, and Annemarie Eigenhuis, 'Comparative Validity of Brief to Medium-Length Big Five and Big Six Personality Questionnaires', *Psychological Assessment* 23(4) (2011), 995–1009.

8. Paul Ekman, 'Are There Basic Emotions?', *Psychological Review* 99(3) (1992), 550–53; Paul Ekman, Wallace V. Friesen, and Phoebe K. Ellsworth, *Emotion in the human face: Guidelines for research and an integration of findings* (Pergamon Press, 1972); Paul Ekman and Wallace V. Friesen, 'A new pan-cultural expression of emotion', *Motivation and Emotion* 10 (1986), 159–68.

9. Andrew Ortony and Terence J. Turner, 'What's basic about basic emotions?', *Psychological Review* 97 (1990), 315–31.

10. Barry Kort, Rob Reilly, and Rosalind W. Picard, 'An affective model of interplay between emotions and learning: reengineering educational

pedagogy-building a learning companion', *Proceedings IEEE International Conference on Advanced Learning Technologies* (Madison, WI, USA, 2001), 43–6; Richard S. Lazarus and Bernice N. Lazarus, *Passion and Reason: Making Sense of Our Emotions* (Oxford University Press, 1994).

11. Paul Ekman, 'Basic Emotions', in Tim Dalgleish and Mick Power (eds.), *Handbook of Cognition and Emotion* (John Wiley & Sons, 1999), 45–60.

12. Alan S. Cowen and Dacher Keltner, 'Self-report captures 27 distinct categories of emotion bridged by continuous gradients', *Proceedings of the National Academy of Sciences* 114(38) (2017); Andrew Ortony, Gerald L. Clore, and Allan Collins, *The Cognitive Structure of Emotions* (Cambridge University Press, 1988); Jaak Panksepp and Lucy Biven, *The Archaeology of Mind: Neuroevolutionary Origins of Human Emotion* (New York: W. W. Norton & Co., 2012); James A. Russell, 'Culture and the Categorization of Emotions', *Psychological Bulletin* 110(3) (1991), 426–50; Tiffany Watt Smith, *The Book of Human Emotions: An Encyclopedia of Feeling from Anger to Wanderlust* (Wellcome Collection, 2016).

13. Phillip Shaver, Judith Schwartz, Donald Kirson, and Cary O'Connor, 'Emotion knowledge: Further exploration of a prototype approach', *Journal of Personality and Social Psychology* 52(6) (1987), 1061–86; W. Gerrod Parrott, *Emotions in Social Psychology* (Psychology Press, 2001).

14. Carroll Ellis Izard, *The Face of Emotion* (Appleton–Century–Crofts, 1971); Robert Plutchik, *The Emotions* (University Press of America, 1991).

15. Robert Plutchik, 'A general psychoevolutionary theory of emotion', in Robert Plutchik and Henry Kellerman (eds.), *Emotion: Theory, research, and experience: Vol. 1. Theories of emotion* (Academic Press, 1980), 3–33; Robert Plutchik, 'The Nature of Emotions', *American Scientist* 89(4) (2001), 344–50; James A. Russell, 'Affective space is bipolar', *Journal of Personality and Social Psychology* 37(3) (1979), 345–56.

16. Warren D. TenHouten, *A General Theory of Emotions and Social Life* (Taylor & Francis, 2006).

17. Erik Cambria, Andrew G. Livingstone, and Amir Hussain, 'The hourglass of emotions', in Anna Esposito, Antonietta M. Esposito, Alessandro Vinciarelli, Rüdiger Hoffmann, and Vincent C. Müller (eds.), *Cognitive Behavioral Systems (Lecture Notes in Computer Science), vol. 7403* (Springer, 2012), 144–57.

18. Andrew Ortony, 'Are All "Basic Emotions" Emotions? A Problem for the (Basic) Emotions Construct', *Perspectives in Psychological Science* 17(1) (2022), 41–61.

19. Yosephine Susanto, Andrew G. Livingstone, Bee Chin Ng, and Erik Cambria, 'The Hourglass Model Revisited', *IEEE Intelligent Systems* 35(5) (2020), 96–102.

20. For a broad selection, see Jeromy Anglim, Gavin Morse, Patrick D. Dunlop, Amirali Minbashian, and Andrew Marty, 'Predicting trait emotional

intelligence from HEXACO personality: Domains, facets, and the general factor of personality', *Journal of Personality* 88(2) (2020), 324–38; Mujeeba Ashraf and Aisha Sitwat, 'Personality dimensions, positive emotions and coping strategies in the caregivers of people living with HIV in Lahore, Pakistan', *International Journal of Nursing Practice* 22(4) (2016), 364–74; Urszula Barańczuk, 'The five factor model of personality and emotion regulation', *Personality and Individual Differences* 139 (2019), 217–27; Michael Barthelmäs and Johannes Keller, 'Adult emotional crying: Relations to personality traits and subjective well-being', *Personality and Individual Differences* 177 (2021), 110790; Robert M. Buckingham, Margaret A. Charles, and Helen C. Beh, 'Extraversion and neuroticism, partially independent dimensions?', *Personality and Individual Differences* 31(5) (2001), 769–77; Violeta Cardenal, Victoria Cerezo, Joaquina Martínez, Margarita Ortiz-Tallo, and José Blanca, 'Personality, emotions and coping styles: Predictive value for the evolution of cancer patients', *Spanish Journal of Psychology* 15(2) (2012), 756–67; Marijn A. Distel, Timothy J. Trull, Gonneke Willemsen, Jacqueline M. Vink, Catherine A. Derom, Michael Lynskey, Nicholas G. Martin, and Dorret I. Boomsma, 'The five-factor model of personality and borderline personality disorder', *Biol Psychiatry* 66(12) (2009), 1131–8; Randy J. Larsen and Timothy Ketelaar, 'Personality and susceptibility to positive and negative emotional states', *Journal of Personality and Social Psychology* 61(1) (1991), 132–40; Julia A. Penley and Joe Tomaka, 'Associations among the Big Five, emotional responses, and coping with acute stress', *Personality and Individual Differences* 32(7) (2002), 1215–28; Michelle N. Shiota, Dacher Keltner, and Oliver P. John, 'Positive emotion dispositions differentially associated with Big Five personality and attachment style', *Journal of Positive Psychology* 1(2) (2006), 61–71; Hae-Kyung Sohn and Timothy Jeonglyeol Lee, 'Relationship between HEXACO personality factors and emotional labour of service providers in the tourism industry', *Tourism Management* 33(1) (2012), 116–25; Jatin G. Vaidya, Elizabeth K. Gray, Jeffrey R. Haig, Daniel K. Mroczek, and David Watson, 'Differential stability and individual growth trajectories of Big Five and affective traits during young adulthood', *Journal of Personality* 76(2) (2008), 267–304; David Watson and Kristin Naragon-Gainey, 'Personality, Emotions, and the Emotional Disorders', *Clinical Psychological Science* 2(4) (2014), 422–42; Kay Wilson and Eleonora Gullone, 'The relationship between personality and affect over the lifespan', *Personality and Individual Differences* 27(6) (1999), 1141–56.

21. Angus Campbell, Philip E. Converse, Warren E. Miller, and Donald E. Stokes, *The American Voter* (John Wiley, 1960); Philip E. Converse, 'The Nature of Belief Systems in Mass Publics', in David E. Apter (ed.), *Ideology and Discontent* (Free Press, 1964); James S. Fishkin, 1995, *The Voice of the*

People: Public Opinion and Democracy (Yale University Press, 1995); James S. Fishkin, When the People Speak: Deliberative Democracy and Public Consultation (Oxford University Press, 2009); Valdemar O. Key, Public Opinion and American Democracy (Knopf, 1967 [1961]); Marshall McLuhan, Understanding Media (Routledge, 2001 [1964]); Claus Mueller, The Politics of Communication (Oxford University Press, 1973); Slavko Splichal (ed.), Public Opinion & Democracy: Vox Populi – Vox Dei? (Hampton Press, Inc., 2001).

22. Leonard Berkowitz (ed.), Advances in Social Psychology (Academic Press, 1978); Hans-Georg Gadamer, Truth and Method, Joel Weinsheimer and Donald G. Marshall (tr.) (Bloomsbury, 2013 [1975]); William J. McGuire, 'The nature of attitudes and attitude change', in Gardner Lindzey and Elliot Aronson (eds.), The handbook of social psychology, vol.2 (Addison-Wesley, 1969); Vincent Price, 'Social identification and public opinion: Effects of communicating group conflict', Public Opinion Quarterly 53(2) (1989), 197–224; Athanassios Raftopoulos, Cognition and Perception (Oxford University Press, 2007); Richard D. Wright and Lawrence M. Ward, Orienting of Attention (Oxford University Press, 2008); John R. Zaller, The Nature and Origins of Mass Opinion (Cambridge University Press, 1992).

23. Jürgen Habermas, The Theory of Communicative Action, vol.2: Lifeworld and System: A Critique of Functionalist Reason, Thomas McCarthy (tr.) (Beacon Press, 1989 [1985]); Elisabeth Noelle-Neumann, 'Public opinion and the classical tradition', Public Opinion Quarterly 43(1) (1979), 143–56; Elisabeth Noelle-Neumann, The spiral of silence: Public opinion – our social skin (University of Chicago Press, 1984).

24. Bernard Berelson and Gary A. Steiner, Human behavior: An inventory of scientific findings (Harcourt, Brace & World, 1964); Harwood L. Childs, Public Opinion: Nature, Formation, and Role (D. van Nostrand, 1965); Leonard W. Doob, Public opinion and propaganda (Holt, Rinehart & Winston, 1948); Vincent Price, Public Opinion (Sage, 1992); G.D. Wiebe, 'Some implications of separating opinions from attitudes', Public Opinion Quarterly 17(3) (1953), 328–52.

25. For a broad selection, see Adam J. Berinsky (ed.), New Directions in Public Opinion (Routledge, 2012); Gianvittorio Caprara, Michele Vecchione, and Shalom H. Schwartz, 'Mediational Role of Values in Linking Personality Traits to Political Orientation', Asian Journal of Social Psychology 12(1) (2009), 82–94; Dana R. Carney, John T. Jost, Samuel D. Gosling, and Jeff Potter, 'The Secret Lives of Liberals and Conservatives: Personality Profiles, Interaction Styles, and the Things They Leave Behind', Political Psychology 29(6) (2008), 807–40; Bryce J. Dietrich, Scott Lasley, Jeffery J. Mondak, Megan L. Remmel, and Joel Turner, 'Personality and Legislative Politics: The Big Five Trait Dimensions among U.S. State Legislators', Political

Psychology 33(2) (2012), 195–210; Moshe Eizenman, Lawrence H. Yu, Larry Grupp, Erez Eizenman, Mark Ellenbogen, Michael Gemar, and Robert D. Levitan, 'A naturalistic visual scanning approach to assess selective attention in major depressive disorder', *Psychiatry Research* 118 (2003), 117–28; Alan S. Gerber, Gregory A. Huber, David Doherty, and Conor M. Dowling, 'Personality Traits and the Consumption of Political Information', *American Politics Research* 39(1) (2010), 32–84; Kai Kaspar and Peter König, 'Emotions and personality-traits as high-level factors in visual attention: a review', *Frontiers in Human Neuroscience* (2012); Paulo N. Lopes, Peter Salovey, and Rebecca Straus, 'Emotional intelligence, personality, and the perceived quality of social relationships', *Personality and Individual Differences* 35(3) (2003), 641–58; Jeffery J. Mondak, *Personality and the Foundations of Political Behavior* (Cambridge University Press, 2010); Jeffery J. Mondak and Karen D. Halperin, 'A Framework for the Study of Personality and Political Behavior', *British Journal of Political Science* 38(2) (2008), 335–62; Rosemary Pacini and Seymour Epstein, 'The relation of rational and experiential information processing styles to personality, basic beliefs, and the ratio-bias phenomenon', *Journal of Personality and Social Psychology* 76(6) (1999), 972–87; Rainer Riemann, Claudia Grubich, Susanne Hempel, Susanne Mergl, and Manfred Richter, 'Personality and Attitudes towards Current Political Topics', *Personality and Individual Differences* 15(3) (1993), 313–21; Lawrence J. Walker, 'The perceived personality of moral exemplars', *Journal of Moral Education* 28(2) (1999), 145–62; Lawrence J. Walker and Karl H. Hennig, 'Differing conceptions of moral exemplarity', *Journal of Personality and Social Psychology* 86(4) (2004), 629–47; Kun Zhao, Eamonn Ferguson, and Luke D. Smillie, 'Prosocial personality traits differentially predict egalitarianism, generosity, and reciprocity in economic games', *Frontiers in Psychology* 7 (2016).

26. Robert Abelson, Donald Kinder, Mark Peters, and Susan Fiske, 'Affective and Semantic Components in Political Personal Perception', *Journal of Personality and Social Psychology* 42(4) (1982), 619–30; Dan G. Blazer, *The Age of Melancholy: 'Major Depression' and its Social Origin* (Routledge, 2005); Ted Brader, *Campaigning for Hearts and Minds: How emotional appeals in political ads work* (University of Chicago Press, 2006); Pamela J. Conover and Stanley Feldman, 'Emotional Reactions to the Economy: I'm mad as hell and I'm not going to take it anymore', *American Journal of Political Science* 30(1) (1986), 30–78; Linda Isbell and Victor C. Ottati, 'The Emotional Voter', in Victor C. Ottati, R. Scott Tindale, John Edwards, Fred B. Bryant, Linda Heath, Daniel C. O'Donnell, Yolanda Suarez-Balcazar, and Emil J. Posavac (eds.), *The Social Psychology of Politics* (Kluwer, 2002), 55–74; Donald Kinder, 'Reason and Emotion in American Political Life', in Roger Schank and Ellen Langer (eds.), *Beliefs, Reasoning, and Decision Making* (Lawrence

Erlbaum, 1994); Rinaldo Kühne, Christian Schemer, Jörg Matthes, and Werner Wirth, 'Affective Priming in Political Campaigns: How Campaign-Induced Emotions Prime Political Opinions', *International Journal of Public Opinion Research* 23(4) (2011), 485–507; George E. Marcus, Michael MacKuen, and W. Russell Neuman, 'Parsimony and Complexity: Developing and Testing Theories of Affective Intelligence', *Political Psychology* 32(2) (2011), 323–36; George E. Marcus, W. Russell Neuman, and Michael MacKuen, *Affective Intelligence and Political Judgment* (University of Chicago Press, 2000); George E. Marcus, John Sullivan, Elizabeth Theiss-Morse, and Daniel Stevens, 'The Emotional Foundation of Political Cognition', *Political Psychology* 26(6) (2005), 949–63; Wendy M. Rahn, 'Affect as Information: The Role of Public Mood in Political Reasoning', in Arthur Lupia, Mathew McCubbins, and Samuel Popkin (eds.), *Elements of Reason* (Cambridge University Press, 2000), 135–50; Wendy M. Rahn, Brian Kroeger, and Cynthia M. Kite, 1996, 'A Framework for the Study of Public Mood', *Political Psychology* 17(1) (1996), 29–58; Deborah A. Small and Jennifer S. Lerner, 'Emotional Policy: Personal Sadness and Anger Shape Judgments About a Welfare Case', *Political Psychology* 29(1) (2008), 149–68; Baldwin M. Way and Roger D. Masters, 'Political Attitudes: Interactions of Cognition and Affect', *Motivation and Emotion* 20(3) (1996), 205–36.
27. Friedrich Engels, *Anti-Dühring*, in Marx and Engels, *Collected Works, vol.25: Engels 1873–83* (Lawrence & Wishart, 1987); Walter Lippmann, *Public Opinion* (Wilder Publications, Inc, 2010 [1922]); Slavko Splichal, *Public Opinion: Developments and Controversies in the Twentieth Century* (Rowman & Littlefield, 1999).
28. Maxwell R. Bennett and Peter M.S. Hacker, *Philosophical Foundations of Neuroscience* (Blackwell, 2003); William A. Brant, *Mental Imagery and Creativity: Cognition, Observation and Realization* (Akademikerverlag, 2013); Richard Hodder-Williams, *Public Opinion Polls and British Politics* (Routledge, 1970); Robert E. Lane and David O. Sears, *Public Opinion* (Prentice Hall, 1964); Gladys Engel Lang and Kurt Lang, *The Battle for Public Opinion: The President, the Press, and the Polls during Watergate* (Columbia University Press, 1983).
29. Jesús Mosterín, *Lo mejor posible: Racionalidad y acción humana* (Alianza Editorial, 2008); Samuel Popkin, *The Reasoning Voter* (University of Chicago Press, 1991).
30. John Dewey, *The Public and its Problems* (The Pennsylvania State Press, 2012 [1927]); John R. Parkinson, *Democracy and Public Space: The Physical Sites of Democratic Performance* (Oxford University Press, 2012); Karl R. Popper, *The Myth of the Framework: In Defence of Science and Rationality* (Routledge, 1994).

31. For a selection of the wide-ranging debates on this topic, see James Bohman (ed.), *Deliberative Democracy: Essays on Reason and Politics* (MIT Press, 1998); Joel Cooper, *Cognitive dissonance: Fifty years of a classic theory* (Sage, 2007); Anthony Downs, *An Economic Theory of Democracy* (Prentice-Hall, 1997 [1957]); Leon Festinger, *A Theory of Cognitive Dissonance* (Stanford University Press, 1957); James S. Fishkin, *The Voice of the People: Public Opinion and Democracy* (Yale University Press, 1995); Gerd Gigerenzer and Reinhard Selten, *Bounded Rationality* (MIT Press, 2002); Amy Gutmann and Dennis Thompson, *Why Deliberative Democracy?* (Princeton University Press, 2004); Eddie Harmon-Jones and Judson Mills (eds.), *Cognitive Dissonance: Progress on a Pivotal Theory in Social Psychology* (American Psychological Association, 1999); Daniel Kahneman, 'Maps of bounded rationality: Psychology for behavioral economics', *The American Economic Review* 93(5) (2003), 1449–75; Ken Manktelow, *Reasoning and Thinking* (Psychology Press, 2000); Michael A. Neblo, *Deliberative Democracy between Theory and Practice* (Cambridge University Press, 2015); Karine Nyborg, 'I Don't Want to Hear About It: Rational Ignorance among Duty-Oriented Consumers', *Journal of Economic Behavior and Organization* 79(3) (2011), 263–74; Shawn W. Rosenberg, 'Citizen competence and the psychology of deliberation', in Stephen Elstub and Peter McLaverty (eds.), *Deliberative Democracy: Issues and Cases* (Edinburgh University Press, 2014), 98–117; Ariel Rubinstein, *Modeling bounded rationality* (MIT Press, 1997); Herbert A. Simon, *Administrative Behavior: A Study of Decision-Making Processes in Administrative Organization* (Macmillan, 1947); Herbert A. Simon, 'A behavioural model of rational choice', *Quarterly Journal of Economics* 59(1) (1955), 99–118; Herbert A. Simon, 'Rational Choice and the Structure of the Environment', *Psychological Review* 63(2) (1956), 129–38; Herbert A. Simon, *Models of Man: Social and Rational: Mathematical Essays on Rational Human Behavior in a Social Setting* (Wiley, 1957); Jürg Steiner, *The Foundations of Deliberative Democracy* (Cambridge University Press, 2012); Carol Tavris and Elliot Aronson, *Mistakes were made (but not by me): Why we justify foolish beliefs, bad decisions, and hurtful acts* (Harcourt, 2007); Clem Tisdell, *Bounded Rationality and Economic Evolution: A Contribution to Decision Making, Economics, and Management* (Brookfield, 1996).
32. Jürgen Habermas, 'Reconciliation Through the Public Use of Reason: Remarks on John Rawls's Political Liberalism', *The Journal of Philosophy* 92(3) (1995), 109–31; John Rawls, *Political Liberalism* (Columbia University Press, 1996); W.M. Sibley, 'The Rational Versus the Reasonable', *The Philosophical Review* 62(4) (1953), 554–60.
33. Gerd Gigerenzer, 'On narrow norms and vague heuristics: A reply to Kahneman and Tversky', *Psychological Review* 103(3) (1996), 592–6; Gerd Gigerenzer, Peter M. Todd, and the ABC Research Group, *Simple Heuristics*

That Make Us Smart (Oxford University Press, 1999); Thomas Gilovich, Dale Griffin, and Daniel Kahneman (eds.), *Heuristics and Biases: The Psychology of Intuitive Judgment* (Cambridge University Press, 2002), 49–81; Daniel Kahneman, *Thinking, fast and slow* (Farrar, Straus and Giroux, 2011); Daniel Kahneman, Paul Slovic, and Amos Tversky (eds.), *Judgment under uncertainty: Heuristics and biases* (Cambridge University Press, 1982); Herbert A. Simon, *Models of Thought*, 2 vols., (Yale University Press, 1979); John Sweller, 'Cognitive load during problem solving: Effects on learning', *Cognitive Science* 12(2) (1988), 257–85; Amos Tversky and Daniel Kahneman, 'Judgments Under Uncertainty: Heuristics and Biases', *Science* 185(4157) (1974), 1124–31.

34. For a sense of the scale of the work being conducted on heuristics, see Dan Ariely and Ziv Carmon, 'The Sum Reflects only Some of its Parts: A Critical Overview of Research about Summary Assessment of Experiences', in George Loewenstein, Daniel Read, and Roy Baumeister, *Time & Decision: Economic & Psychological Perspectives on Inter-temporal Choice* (Russell Sage Foundation, 2003), 323–50; Jonathan Baron, *Thinking and deciding* (Cambridge University Press, 2008); Andrea Ceschi, Arianna Costantini, Riccardo Sartori, Joshua Weller, and Annamaria Di Fabio, 'Dimensions of decision-making', *Personality and Individual Differences* 146 (2019), 188–200; Victor DeMiguel, Lorenzo Garlappi, and Raman Uppal, '1/N', *EFA 2006 Zurich Meetings* (2006); Jennifer M. Fletcher, Anthony D.G. Marks, and Donald W. Hine, 'Working memory capacity and cognitive styles in decision-making', *Personality and Individual Differences* 50(7) (2011), 1136–41; Ralph Hertwig, Stefan M. Herzog, Lael J. Schooler, and Torsten Reimer, 'Fluency heuristic: A model of how the mind exploits a by-product of information retrieval', *Journal of Experimental Psychology: Learning, Memory, and Cognition* 34(5) (2008), 1191–1206; E. Tory Higgins and G. King, 'Accessibility of social constructs: Information-processing consequences of individual and contextual variation', in N. Cantor and J.F. Kihlstrom (eds.), *Personality, Cognition, and Social Interaction* (Erlbaum, 1981), 69–121; Derek J. Koehler and Nigel Harvey, *Blackwell Handbook of Judgment and Decision-making* (Blackwell, 2004); Justin Kruger, Derrick Wirtz, Leaf van Boven, and T. William Altermatt, 'The effort heuristic', *Journal of Experimental Social Psychology* 40(1) (2004), 91–8; Ziva Kunda, *Social Cognition: Making Sense of People* (MIT Press, 1999); Michael Lynn, 'Scarcity effects on desirability: Mediated by assumed expensiveness?', *Journal of Economic Psychology* 10(2) (1989), 257–74; Michael Lynn, 'The Psychology of Unavailability: Explaining Scarcity and Cost Effects on Value', *Basic and Applied Social Psychology* 13(1) (1992), 3–7; Talya Miron-Shatz, 'Evaluating multiepisode events: Boundary conditions for the peak-end rule', *Emotion* 9(2) (2009), 206–13; Benoît Monin, 'The Warm Glow Heuristic: When Liking Leads

to Familiarity', *Journal of Personality and Social Psychology* 85(6) (2003), 1035–48; Thorsten Pachur, Ralph Hertwig, and Jörg R. Rieskamp, 'Intuitive judgments of social statistics: How exhaustive does sampling need to be?', *Journal of Experimental Social Psychology* 49(6) (2013), 1059–77; Daniel Read and George Loewenstein, 'Diversification Bias: Explaining the Discrepancy in Variety Seeking between Combined and Separated Choices', *Journal of Experimental Psychology: Applied* 1(1) (1995), 34–49; Itamar Simonson, 'The Effect of Purchase Quantity and Timing on Variety-Seeking Behaviour', *Journal of Marketing Research* 27(2) (1990), 150–62; Amos Tversky and Daniel Kahneman, 'Availability: A Heuristic for Judging Frequency and Probability', *Cognitive Psychology* 5(2) (1973), 207–32; Robert Wyer and Thomas Srull, *Memory and Cognition in their Social Context* (Erlbaum, 1989); Henry Zukier, 'The dilution effect: The role of the correlation and the dispersion of predictor variables in the use of nondiagnostic information', *Journal of Personality and Social Psychology* 43(6) (1982), 1163–74.

35. Maurice Allais, 'Le comportement de l'homme rationnel devant le risque: critique des postulats et axioms de l'école Américaine', *Econometrica* 21(4) (1953), 503–46; Daniel Ellsberg, 'Risk, Ambiguity, and the Savage Axioms', *Quarterly Journal of Economics* 75(4) (1961), 643–69; Daniel G. Goldstein and Gert Gigerenzer, 'Models of ecological rationality: the recognition heuristic', *Psychological Review* 109(1) (2002), 75–90; David Hardman, *Judgment and decision making: psychological perspectives* (Wiley-Blackwell, 2009); Scott Plous, *The Psychology of Judgment and Decision Making* (McGraw-Hill, 1993); Rüdiger F. Pohl (ed.), *Cognitive Illusions: A Handbook on Fallacies and Biases in Thinking, Judgement, and Memory* (Psychology Press, 2004); Shoshana Shiloh, Efrat Salton, and Dana Sharabi, 'Individual differences in rational and intuitive thinking styles as predictors of heuristic responses and framing effects', *Personality and Individual Differences* 32(3) (2002), 415–29; Anuj K. Shah and Daniel M. Oppenheimer, 'Heuristics made easy: An effort-reduction framework', *Psychological Bulletin* 134(2) (2008), 207–22; Stuart Sutherland, *Irrationality: The enemy within* (Pinter & Martin Ltd, 2013 [1992]).

36. For a relatively exhaustive cross-section of this literature, see Nuran Bayram and Mine Aydemir, 'Decision-making styles and personality traits', *Proceedings of the International Conference on Multiple Academic Disciplines, Vietnam – VM714* (2017); Vivek M. Belhekar, 'Cognitive and non-cognitive determinants of heuristics of judgment and decision-making', *Journal of the Indian Academy of Applied Psychology* 43(1) (2017), 75–84; Shawn Blau, J. Ryan Fuller, and Thomas P. Vaccaro, 'Rational-emotive disputing and the five-factor model: Personality dimensions of the Ellis Emotional Efficiency Inventory', *Journal of Rational-Emotive and Cognitive-Behavior Therapy* 24(2) (2006), 87–100; Andrea Caputo, 'Relevant information, personality traits and anchoring effect', *International Journal of Management and Decision*

Making 13(1) (2013); Daniel Freeman, Nicole Evans, and Rachel Lister, 'Gut feelings, deliberative thought, and paranoid ideation: A study of experiential and rational reasoning', *Psychiatry Research* 197(1–2) (2012), 119–22; Adrian Furnham and Hua Chu Boo, 'A literature review of the anchoring effect', *Journal of Socio-Economics* 40(1) (2011), 35–42; Adrian Furnham, John Crump, and Viren Swarmi, 'Abstract Reasoning and Big Five Personality Correlates of Creativity in a British Occupational Sample', *Imagination, Cognition and Personality* 28(4) (2009), 361–70; Vinod Goel and Oshin Vartanian, 'Negative emotions can attenuate the influence of beliefs on logical reasoning', *Cognition and Emotion* 25(1) (2011), 121–31; Katherine Hamilton, Shin-I Shih, and Susan Mohammed, 'The Development and Validation of the Rational and Intuitive Decisions Styles Scale', *Journal of Personality Assessment* 98(5) (2016), 523–35; Benjamin E. Hilbig, 'Individual differences in fast-and-frugal decision making', *Journal of Research in Personality* 42 (2008), 1641–5; Dirk Ifenthaler, 'Effects of experimentally induced emotions on model-based reasoning', *Learning and Individual Differences* 43 (2015), 191–8; Amanda Jarrell, Jason M. Harley, Susanne Lajoie, and Laura Naismith, 'Success, failure, and emotions: examining the relationship between performance feedback and emotions in diagnostic reasoning', *Educational Technology Research and Development* 65 (2017), 1263–84; Biljana Jokić and Danka Purić, 'Relating rational and experiential thinking styles with trait emotional intelligence in broader personality space', *Europe's Journal of Psychology* 15(1) (2019), 140–58; Nadine Jung, Christina Wranke, Kai Hamburger, and Markus Knauff, 'How emotions affect logical reasoning', *Frontiers in Psychology* (2014); Randy J. Larsen and Timothy Ketelaar, 'Extraversion, neuroticism and susceptibility to positive and negative mood induction procedures', *Personality and Individual Differences* 10(12) (1989), 1221–8; Anthony D.G. Marks, Donald W. Hine, Rebecca L. Blore, and Wendy J. Phillips, 'Assessing individual differences in adolescents' preference for rational and experiential cognition', *Personality and Individual Differences* 44(1) (2008), 42–52; K.V. Petrides, Ria Pita, and Flora Kokkinaki, 'The location of trait emotional intelligence in personality factor space', *British Journal of Psychology* 98(2) (2007), 273–89; Muhammad Naveed Riaz, Muhammad Akram Riaz, and Naila Batool, 'Personality types as predictors of decision making styles', *Journal of Behavioural Sciences* 22(2) (2012), 99–114; Donald H. Saklofske, Elizabeth J. Austin, and Paul S. Minski, 'Factor structure and validity of a trait emotional intelligence measure', *Personality and Individual Differences* 34(4) (2003), 707–21; Stephanie M. Samar, Kate E. Walton, and Wilson McDermut, 'Personality traits predict irrational beliefs', *Journal of Rational-Emotive and Cognitive-Behavior Therapy* 31 (2013), 231–42; Parvin Rafienia, Parviz Azadfallah, Ali Fathi-Ashtiani, and Kazem Rasoulzadeh-Tabatabeiei, 'The role of extraversion, neuroticism and positive and negative mood in emotional information processing', *Personality and Individual Differences* 44(2) (2008), 392–402; Heidi R. Riggio and Ronald E. Riggio, 'Emotional Expressiveness, Extraversion, and Neuroticism: A Meta-Analysis', *Journal of Nonverbal Behavior* 26(4) (2002), 195–218; Norbert Schwarz and Gerald L. Clore, 'Mood, misattribution, and judgments of well-being: Informative and directive functions of affective states', *Journal of Personality and Social Psychology* 45(3) (1983), 513–23; Kathleen W. Smith, Oshin Vartanian, and Vinod Goel, 'Dissociable neural systems underwrite logical reasoning in the context of induced emotions with positive and negative valence', *Frontiers in Human Neuroscience* (2014); Lazar Stankov, 'Low correlations between intelligence and Big Five personality traits', *Journal of Intelligence* 6(2) (2018), 26; Predrag Teovanović, Goran Knežević, and Lazar Stankov, 'Individual differences in cognitive biases: Evidence against one-factor theory of rationality', *Intelligence* 50 (2015), 75–86; Jari Tuuva, Petri Näätänen, Arto Ryynänen, Pertti Keskivaara, and Liisa Keltikangas-Järvinen, 'Extraversion, neuroticism and emotional reactivity', *International Journal of Psychophysiology* 25(1) (1997); Cilia Witteman, John van den Bercken, Laurence Claes, and Antonio Godoy, 'Assessing rational and intuitive thinking styles', *European Journal of Psychological Assessment* 25(1) (2009).

37. Mathias Allemand and Christoph Flückiger, 'Changing personality traits: Some considerations from psychotherapy process-outcome research for intervention efforts on intentional personality change', *Journal of Psychotherapy Integration* 27(4) (2017), 476–94; Thomas J. Bouchard and Matthew McGue, 'Genetic and Environmental Influences on Human Psychological Differences', *Journal of Neurobiology* 54(1) (2003), 4–45; Matt McGue, Steven Bacon, and David T. Lykken, 'Personality stability and change in early adulthood: A behavioral genetic analysis', *Developmental Psychology* 29(1) (1993), 96–109; Jule Specht, Boris Egloff, and Stefan C. Schmukle, 'Stability and Change of Personality Across the Life Course: The Impact of Age and Major Life Events on Mean-Level and Rank-Order Stability of the Big Five', *Journal of Personality and Social Psychology* 101(4) (2011), 862–82.

38. For classic theoretical and applied statements on this, see Émile Durkheim, *The Division of Labour in Society*, Steven Lukes (ed.) (Free Press, 2014 [1893]); International Labor Office, *International Standard Classification of Occupations: ISCO-88* (ILO, 1990 [1968]); Talcott Parsons, *The Structure of Social Action*, 2 vols. (Free Press, 1967 [1937]); Max Weber, *Economy and Society: An Outline of Interpretive Sociology*, Guenther Roth and Claus Wittich (eds.) (University of California Press, 1978 [1922]).

39. Indra Abeysekera, 'Intellectual capital practices of firms and the commodification of labour', *Accounting, Auditing and Accountability Journal* 21(1) (2008), 36–48; Birgitta Bergvall-Kåreborn and Debra Howcroft, 'Amazon Mechanical Turk

and the commodification of labour', *New Technology, Work and Employment* 29(3) (2014), 213–23; Koray Çalışkan and Michel Callon, 'Economization, part 1: Shifting attention from the economy towards processes of economization', *Economy and Society* 38(3) (2009), 369–398; Koray Çalışkan and Michel Callon, 'Economization, part 2: A research programme for the study of markets', *Economy and Society* 39(1) (2010), 1–32; Louis Putterman, 'Commodification of labor follows commodification of the firm: On a theorem of the new institutional economics', *Annals of Public and Cooperative Economics* 60(2) (2007), 161–79; Barry Smart, 'An economic turn', *Journal of Classical Sociology* 3(1) (2003), 47–66.

40. Göran Therborn, *The Ideology of Power and the Power of Ideology* (Verso, 1980); Slavoj Žižek, *The Parallax View* (MIT Press, 2006).
41. Roland Barthes, *Mythologies* (Seuil, 1957); Raymond Boudon, *The Analysis of Ideology* (Polity, 1989 [1986]); bell hooks, *Ain't I a Woman? Black Women and Feminism* (South End Press, 1981); Teun A. van Dijk, *Ideology: A Multidisciplinary Approach* (London: Sage, 1998).
42. Michel Foucault, 'The subject and power', in H.L. Dreyfus and P. Rabinow (eds.), *Michel Foucault: Beyond Hermeneutics and Structuralism* (Harvester, 1982), 208–26; Julia Kristeva, *Desire in Language: A Semiotic Approach to Literature and Art* (Columbia University Press, 1980).
43. Judith Butler, 'Performative Acts and Gender Constitution: An Essay in Phenomenology and Feminist Theory', *Theatre Journal* 40(4) (1988), 519–31; Judith Butler, *Gender Trouble: Feminism and the Subversion of Identity* (Routledge, 1990); Silvan S. Tomkins, 'Script Theory', in Joel Arnoff, A.I. Rabin, and Robert A. Zucker (eds.), *The Emergence of Personality* (Springer, 1987), 147–216.
44. Anthony Giddens, *The Constitution of Society: Outline of the Theory of Structuration* (Polity, 1984); Nicos Poulantzas, *Political Power and Social Classes* (NLB and Sheed and Ward, 1975 [1968]); William H. Sewell, 'A Theory of Structure: Duality, Agency, and Transformation', *American Journal of Sociology* 98(1) (1992), 1–29; John B. Thompson, *Studies in the Theory of Ideology* (Polity, 1984).
45. Gregory Bateson, *A Sacred Unity: Further Steps to an Ecology of Mind* (HarperCollins, 1991); Jean Baudrillard, *Simulacra and Simulation* (Semiotext(e), 1983); Niklas Luhmann, *Social Systems*, John Bednarz and Dirk Baecker (tr.) (Stanford University Press, 1995 [1984]); Niklas Luhmann, *Theory of Society*, 2 vols. (Stanford University Press, 2012–13 [1997]); Talcott Parsons, *The Social System* (Routledge, 1951).
46. Pierre Bourdieu, *The Logic of Practice*, R. Nice (tr.) (Cambridge University Press, 1990); Norbert Elias, *The Civilizing Process: Sociogenetic and Psychogenetic Investigations* (Blackwell, 2000 [1939]); Marcel Mauss, *Sociologie et anthropologie* (Presses universitaires de France, 1936).

47. Louis Althusser, *On the Reproduction of Capitalism: Ideology and Ideological State Apparatuses* (Verso, 2014 [1970]); Pierre Bourdieu, *Outline of a Theory of Practice*, Richard Nice (tr.) (Cambridge University Press, 1977 [1972]); Michel Pêcheux, *Analyse automatique du discours* (Dunod, 1969); Michel Pêcheux, 'The Mechanism of Ideological (Mis)recognition', in Slavoj Žižek (ed.), *Mapping Ideology* (Verso, 1994), 141–51.

48. Sara Ahmed, *The Cultural Politics of Emotion* (Edinburgh University Press, 2004); Jack Barbalet, *Emotion, Social Theory, and Social Structure: A Macrosociological Approach* (Cambridge University Press, 1998); Michael Freeden, *The Political Theory of Political Thinking: The Anatomy of a Practice* (Oxford University Press, 2015); Carol Gilligan, *In a Different Voice: Psychological Theory and Women's Development* (Harvard University Press, 1982); Arlie Russell Hochschild, *The Managed Heart: Commercialization of Human Feeling* (University of California Press, 1983); Martha Nussbaum, *Hiding from Humanity: Disgust, Shame, and the Law* (Princeton University Press, 2004); Marius S. Ostrowski, *Ideology* (Polity, 2022); William Reddy, *The Navigation of Feeling: A Framework for the History of Emotions* (Cambridge University Press, 2001).

49. Louis Althusser, *Philosophy of the Encounter: Later Writings, 1978–87* (Verso, 2006 [1993–4]); Judith Butler, *The Psychic Life of Power: Theories in Subjection* (Stanford University Press, 1997); Joannah Caborn, 'On the Methodology of Dispositive Analysis', *Critical Approaches to Discourse Analysis Across Disciplines* 1(1) (2007), 115–23; Michel Foucault, *Discipline and Punish: The Birth of the Prison* (Pantheon, 1977 [1975]); Michel Foucault, *Power/Knowledge: Selected Interviews and Other Writings, 1972–77*, Colin Gordon (ed.) (Penguin, 1980); Martin Heidegger, *Being and Time*, John Macquarrie and Edward Robinson (trs.) (Blackwell, 1962 [1927]); Siegfried Jäger, 'Discourse and knowledge: Theoretical and methodological aspects of a critical discourse and dispositive analysis', in Ruth Wodak and Michael Meyer (eds.), *Methods of Critical Discourse Analysis* (Sage, 2009), 32–62.

50. Jeffrey Jensen Arnett, 'Broad and narrow socialization: The family in the context of a cultural theory', *Journal of Marriage and Family* 57(3) (1995), 617–28; Robert B. Denhart and Philip W. Jeffress, 'Social learning and economic behavior: The process of economic socialization', *American Journal of Economics and Sociology* 30(2) (1971), 113–25; Eleanor E. Maccoby and John A. Martin, 'Socialization in the context of the family: Parent–child interaction', in Paul H. Mussen and E. Mavis Hetherington (eds.), *Handbook of Child Psychology, Vol. 4: Socialization, Personality, and Social Development* (John Wiley & Sons, 1983), 1–101; Dietrich Rueschemeyer, Evelyne Huber Stephens, and John D. Stephens, *Capitalist Development and Democracy* (University of Chicago Press, 1992); Erik Olin Wright (ed.), *Approaches to Class Analysis* (Cambridge University Press, 2005).

51. Alain Badiou, *Being and Event* (Continuum, 2005 [1988]); Michael Billig, *Ideology and Opinions: Studies in Rhetorical Psychology* (Sage, 1991); Mark Fisher, *The Weird and the Eerie* (Repeater Books, 2017); Stuart Hall, *Encoding and Decoding in the Television Discourse* (Centre for Contemporary Cultural Studies, 1973); Stuart Hall, 'Encoding/Decoding', in Stuart Hall, Dorothy Hobson, Andrew Lowe, and Paul Willis (eds.), *Culture, Media, Language: Working Papers in Cultural Studies, 1972–79* (Hutchinson, 1980), 128–38; Anne Phillips, 'What's wrong with Essentialism?', *Distinktion: Journal of Social Theory* 11(1) (2010), 47–60.
52. Homi K. Bhabha, *The Location of Culture* (Routledge, 1994); Marius S. Ostrowski, 'Ideology and the individual', *Journal of Political Ideologies* 29(1) (2024), 1–25.

Index

A
Agonisers
   becoming an 91–5
   creating chances 98–101
   concern for others 101–3
   description of 5, 88–90
   and emotions 90
   hypervigilance of 95–6
   importance of talking for 96–8
   and information 91
   morality in thinking 106–8
   multitasking for 104–6
   and personality 90
   and predispositions 91
   and reasoning 91
Alchemist, The (Coelho) 162

B
Babel (Kuang) 184
Bell Jar, The (Plath) 75

Black Swan (film) 185
Breakfast at Tiffany's (Capote) 167

C
Candide (Voltaire) 33
Catcher in the Rye (Salinger) 99
Chicago (film) 61
Cool Cats
   becoming a 134–7
   benevolent neutrality 141–4
   description of 5, 131–3
   and emotions 132–3
   impulse control 141–4
   and information 132–4
   inquisitiveness of 145–8
   and personality 132–3
   and predispositions 132–4
   and reasoning 133–4
   sense of self 138–41
   social presence of 148–50
   staying in control 150–2

D

Dangerous Liaisons (Laclos) 213
Death of a Salesman (Miller) 97
Devil Wears Prada, The (film) 208–9

E

elements of thinking
    emotions in 7, 9, 14
    information in 7, 9–11, 15
    personality in 7–9, 14
    predispositions in 7, 9–11, 15
    reasoning in 7, 11, 15
    and thinker-types 11–14
    as thinking tools 16–18
emotions
    and Agonisers 90
    and Cool Cats 133
    in elements of thinking 7, 9, 14
    and Gloomsters 69
    and Happy Campers 27
    and Hotheads 111
    and Jokesters 48
    and Keen Beans 155
    and Quibblers 197
    and Revellers 219
    science and philosophy of 248–50
    and Worrywarts 175

F

Falstaff, Sir John 56

G

Game of Thrones (TV series) 120
Girl with the Dragon Tattoo, The (Larsson) 212

Gloomsters
    becoming a 68–72
    description of 5, 66–8
    and emotions 67, 69
    and information 68, 70
    isolation of 73–5
    methodical thinking 85–7
    and personality 67, 69
    and predispositions 68, 70
    and reasoning 68, 70
    at rock-bottom 78–81
    sense of failure 75–8
    survival tactics for 81–5
Grapes of Wrath, The (Steinbeck) 93

H

habitus 258–9
Happy Campers
    adaptability of 35–8
    becoming a 29–31
    community activity 38–40
    confidence of 43–5
    description of 4, 25–7
    and emotions 26–7

INDEX

hope for 41–3
and information 27–8
and personality 26–7
and predispositions 27–8
projecting satisfaction to others 32–5
and reasoning 27–8
heuristics 254–6
HEXACO model 247–8
His Dark Materials (Pullman) 169
Hotheads
becoming a 112–15
and conflict 125–8
description of 5, 109–11
and emotions 110–11
fixated thinking 120–3
and information 111–12
losing control 118–20
motivations 123–5
and personality 110–11
and predispositions 111–2
and reasoning 111–2
resolute strength 128–30
uses/abuses of anger 116–18
House on Mango Street, The (Cisneros) 105
hybridity 260

I
Iliad, The (Homer) 115
information

and Agonisers 91
and Cool Cats 134
in elements of thinking 7, 9–11, 15
and Gloomsters 70
and Happy Campers 28
and Hotheads 112
and Jokesters 49
and Keen Beans 156
and Quibblers 198
and Revellers 220
science and philosophy of 251–3
and Worrywarts 176
Inside Out (film) 34–5

J
Jokesters
becoming a 50–2
charm of 60–1
checks on sense of humour 55–7
combative goal-setting 62–3
contrarian aspects of 64–5
description of 5, 46–8
and emotions 47–8
and information 48–9
levels of thinking 57–60
and personality 47–8
and predispositions 48–9
and reasoning 48–9

sense of humour as
protection 53–5

K
Keen Beans
becoming a 156–9
description of 5, 153–5
and emotions 154–5
and information 155–6
interacting with others
168–70
intensity of 170–2
overdoing things 160–2
and personality 154–5
and predispositions 155–6
and reasoning 155–6
self-assured enthusiasm
162–5
wide-ranging focus 165–8

L
Lady Chatterley's Lover
(Lawrence) 144
Little Women (Alcott) 159
Lord of the Rings (Tolkien)
83

M
Man for All Seasons, A (Bolt)
140–1
mental outlooks 7, 12–14, 18,
22, 250, 253–5

mental pictures 7, 12, 15, 22,
250, 253–5
Minnesota Multiphasic
Personality Inventory
(MMPI) 247

N
No. 1 Ladies' Detective Agency,
The (Smith) 138

O
OCEAN model 247–8
On the Waterfront (film) 78
One Hundred Years of Solitude
(Márquez) 93

P
personality
and Agonisers 90
and Cool Cats 133
in elements of thinking 8–9,
14
and Gloomsters 69
and Happy Campers 27
and Hotheads 111
and Jokesters 48
and Keen Beans 155
and Quibblers 197
and Revellers 219
science and philosophy of
246–8
and Worrywarts 175

philosophy of thinking 246–56
Piranesi (Clarke) 164
predispositions
   and Agonisers 91
   and Cool Cats 134
   in elements of thinking 7,
     9–11, 15
   and Gloomsters 70
   and Happy Campers 28
   and Hotheads 112
   and Jokesters 49
   and Keen Beans 156
   and Quibblers 198
   and Revellers 220
   science and philosophy of
     251–3
   and Worrywarts 176

Q
Quibblers
   authenticity and aversion
     208–12
   becoming a 199–202
   critical judgement 212–14
   description of 5, 195–7
   emotional attack/defence
     205–8
   and emotions 196–7
   and information 197–8
   and personality 196–7
   and predispositions 197–8
   as purists 214–16

   and reasoning 197–8
   and withdrawal 202–5

R
reasoning
   and Agonisers 91
   and Cool Cats 134
   in elements of thinking 7, 15
   and Gloomsters 70
   and Happy Campers 28
   and Hotheads 112
   and Jokesters 49
   and Keen Beans 156
   and Quibblers 198
   and Revellers 220
   science and philosophy of
     253–6
   and Worrywarts 176
Revellers
   becoming a 221–4
   description of 6, 217–19
   and emotions 218–19
   forms of attraction 227–9
   getting transfixed 236–8
   inconstancy of 230–2
   and information 219–20
   meeting desires 224–7
   and personality 218–19
   and predispositions 219–20
   and reasoning 219–20
   as social butterflies 233–6

S
Scarlet Letter, The (Hawthorne) 72
science of thinking 246–56
society
  role in thinking 16–22, 256–60
  social action 257
  social occupations 19, 257–8
  socialisation 18–20, 259
Star Wars (movie series) 143

T
thinker-types
  and elements of thinking 6–15
  on an excursion 239–40
  as tendencies 16–22
thinking
  changing thinking 20–2, 241–2, 261–2
  and heuristics 254–6
  philosophy and science of 246–56
  societal role in 256–60
  a user's guide 22–4
To Kill a Mockingbird (Lee) 105

W
Wicked (musical) 100–1
Winnie-the-Pooh (Milne) 182
Worrywarts
  becoming a 177–9
  description of 5, 173–5
  and emotions 174–5
  expecting problems 183–6
  and information 175–6
  isolation of 180–3
  making plans 190–2
  overthinking 186–90
  and personality 174–5
  and predispositions 175–6
  and reasoning 175–6
  reticence of 192–4

RAISING READERS
Books Build Bright Futures

Dear Reader,

We'd love your attention for one more page to tell you about the crisis in children's reading, and what we can all do.

Studies have shown that reading for fun is the **single biggest predictor of a child's future life chances** – more than family circumstance, parents' educational background or income. It improves academic results, mental health, wealth, communication skills, ambition and happiness.[1]

The number of children reading for fun is in rapid decline. Young people have a lot of competition for their time. In 2024, 1 in 10 children and young people in the UK aged 5 to 18 did not own a single book at home.[2]

Hachette works extensively with schools, libraries and literacy charities, but here are some ways we can all raise more readers:

- Reading to children for just 10 minutes a day makes a difference
- Don't give up if children aren't regular readers – there will be books for them!
- Visit bookshops and libraries to get recommendations
- Encourage them to listen to audiobooks
- Support school libraries
- Give books as gifts

There's a lot more information about how to encourage children to read on our website: **www.RaisingReaders.co.uk**

Thank you for reading.

---

[1] OECD, '21st-Century Readers: Developing Literacy Skills in a Digital World', 2021, https://www.oecd.org/en/publications/21st-century-readers_a83d84cb-en.html

[2] National Literacy Trust, 'Book Ownership in 2024', November 2024, https://literacytrust.org.uk/research-services/research-reports/book-ownership-in-2024